Haun

Also by Merlin Coverley

London Writing
Psychogeography
Occult London
Utopia
The Art of Wandering
South

Hauntology

MERLIN COVERLEY

OLDCASTLE BOOKS

First published in 2020 by
Oldcastle Books Ltd,
Harpenden, UK

www.oldcastlebooks.com

Editor: Nick Rennison

A CIP catalogue record for this book is available from the British Library

ISBNs
978-0-85730-419-3 (print)
978-0-85730-421-6 (ebook)

4 6 8 10 9 7 5

Typeset in 12.6 on 14.4pt Perpetua
by Avocet Typeset, Bideford, Devon, EX39 2BP
Printed and bound by Clays Ltd, Elcograf S.p.A

CONTENTS

Introduction

The ghosts are swarming at the moment. Hauntology has caught on. It's a zeitgeist. Mark Fisher (2006)[1]

Hauntology may be a thing of the past, but this of course means that it will always be with us. Mark Pilkington (2012)[2]

Ghosts and spectres, the eerie and the occult. Why is contemporary culture so preoccupied by the supernatural, so captivated by the revenants of an earlier age, so haunted? The answer to this question is to be found through an examination of what one critic has described recently as 'perhaps the most important, political-philosophical concept we have right now': hauntology.[3] This is a term that was first coined in the early 1990s by the French philosopher, Jacques Derrida, in his discussion of the enduring legacy of Marxism. Since then, however, hauntology has evolved and entered the cultural mainstream, becoming a shorthand for the ways in which the past returns to haunt the present. Today its use is widespread, its effects visible across a broad spectrum of academic and popular culture, from film and television to music, the visual arts and literature, as well as informing our understanding of the political currents that have shaped our recent history. Despite its growing familiarity, however, hauntology remains a term whose origins and antecedents are unclear, and whose meaning is stubbornly obscure.

'I believe that ghosts are a part of the future', claimed Jacques Derrida in 1983.[4] This statement was a prophetic one, for ghosts were to become an integral part both of Derrida's future and our own, thanks in large part to the publication of his *Specters of Marx* in 1993. The title of Derrida's book, which I shall be discussing in detail in a later chapter, recalls the opening line of *The Communist Manifesto* of 1848 by Marx and Engels: 'There is a spectre haunting Europe, the spectre of Communism'. Marx's famous proclamation marks the moment at which a spectre was invoked that has been haunting Europe and the wider world ever since, lending retrospective validation to the paradox at the heart of hauntology, in which certain futures have the potential to haunt us even before they have come to pass. As a result, it is 1848, that year of revolutionary near-misses, which marks the beginning of my own account of hauntology and its precursors. It is in Derrida's maddeningly opaque book that we find the textual origin of hauntology, or rather *l'hantologie*, a pun on hauntology and ontology that loses much in translation, through which Derrida expresses his belief that being and haunting are interwoven concepts, the ghostly coming to invade every aspect of our lives, from the political and the technological to the cultural and the literary: to be is to be haunted. Derrida's resuscitation of Marxism was a response to those on the political right in the early 1990s, such as Francis Fukuyama, who had proclaimed the final victory of western liberalism and with it the end of history. Derrida used hauntology, his science of ghosts, to demonstrate that far from this being the case, the spectre of Marx, like all ghosts which have yet to be laid to rest, would return, repeatedly, disrupting the present and continuing to remind us of another possible future. In fact, so influential was Derrida's account that the figure of the spectre was soon to escape the confines of his text, triggering a 'spectral turn' in the academic study of the ghost. A subject which had hitherto been largely dismissed as unworthy of serious critical attention now returned with a vengeance, as ghosts, spectres, revenants and all manner of occult entities came to haunt seemingly every aspect of our culture. As we shall see, ours is by no means the first historical period to be preoccupied by the ghosts of its past, but in the western world, at least, the 1990s was the beginning of such a moment, one in which hauntology, accompanied by the uncanny, the eerie and the weird, first came to public prominence.

If it was the 1990s which witnessed the emergence of hauntology in its first incarnation, it was to gain what Mark Fisher called its 'second (un)life' in the middle of the following decade.[5] The name of Mark Fisher is one that will recur throughout this account, for if Derrida is the father of hauntology then it is Fisher who played the greatest role in bringing this concept within the purview of popular culture. In correspondence with his friend, the music journalist Simon Reynolds, in 2005 Fisher began to refer to hauntology on his blog, *k-punk*, as a means of describing this spectral resurgence, and in particular his belief that the first decade of the twenty-first century was experiencing what he described as the 'failure of the future', as cultural time decelerated and went into reverse, overwhelmed by a nostalgia for the pop-cultural artefacts of our recent past.[6] From these beginnings, hauntology soon emerged as a means of highlighting this cultural, and increasingly political, impasse, a failure of social imagination that left us seemingly unable to envisage any other society than our own.

No sooner had it re-emerged, however, than some critics began to distance themselves from the term, fearing that hauntology was in danger of attracting an unwelcome degree of mainstream recognition, and with it the misuse and oversimplification that often accompanies such overexposure.[7] But since his untimely death in 2017, Mark Fisher's work has reached a new audience, thus ensuring hauntology's most recent and prolonged return to fashion. Once again, the term has evolved, outgrowing its earlier manifestation as a musical micro-genre and recasting itself in a more overtly political role. By placing the present in conjunction with the recent past, hauntology highlights the shortcomings of the former, identifying the political failings of the present by returning to those moments when a different path might have been taken, turning points whose promise remains unfulfilled and which continue to offer us hope for the future. For Fisher, one such moment was that of the early 1970s, as the revolutionary spirit of the counterculture began to subside and the neoliberal world we inhabit today first started to emerge. At the end of his life Fisher was working on a project that he hoped would recuperate the lost potential of this era and in doing so provide a means of challenging what he saw as the deadening ubiquity of life under late-capitalism.

In both Derrida's and Fisher's conceptions of hauntology, the crucial element is that of time. For Derrida, the return and repetition of the past in the present is manifested through the figure of the revenant, that which returns each time as if it were the first, unchanging and insistent, demanding a reckoning for a message that went unheard or was ignored. For Fisher, as we shall see, there are two opposing temporal currents intrinsic to hauntology: the *no longer* and the *not yet*.[8] The former haunts the present from the past, an event, idea or entity whose moment is past but which continues to make its presence felt. The latter haunts the present from the future, through the unfulfilled promise of that which never came to pass but which may yet do so. In both instances, their impact is felt now, in the present, either through repetition or anticipation. The very idea of the ghost as that which comes from the past to manifest itself in the present and yet which belongs to neither, simultaneously both absent and present, challenges our belief in the unbroken progression of linear time. Hauntology foregrounds such temporal disjuncture or 'dyschronia', questioning whether we truly experience time in so straightforward a manner as the linear model suggests. Instead, both Derrida and Fisher see history as one characterised by repetition and disruption, as the past recurrently irrupts into the present, forcing us to reconsider events and ideas we might have regarded as safely consigned to the past. Fisher goes further, arguing that since the closing decades of the twentieth century, cultural time has faltered, dragged to a standstill by the ever-growing weight of our recorded past; not so much the end of history as an excess of history, beneath which we struggle to move forward.[9]

One way in which the repetitions and discontinuities of history are manifested is through the emergence of new technologies which allow us to record and replay the past. This is a process whose uncanny effects began to be felt in the nineteenth century as new forms of media such as telegraphy, photography and later cinema allowed us to capture and control time, bringing the past back to life and allowing us to revisit it at our leisure. As we shall see, it was innovations in Victorian stagecraft which first allowed the ghost to take on a seemingly corporeal form, enabling audiences to visualise what contemporary expressions of supernatural belief such as Spiritualism could only hint at. The evolution of such ghostly media is one which forms a backdrop to many of the precursors of hauntology, from the role of television and early computer technology in the residual haunting of TC Lethbridge and Nigel Kneale, to the haunting obsolescence of Space Age technology depicted in the work of JG Ballard. In recent years, an increasing preoccupation with analogue technology has become a staple element of hauntology, as we contrast the imperfections of earlier recording techniques with the timeless anonymity of the digital. Of course, this strand of what Fisher has labelled the 'technological uncanny' reached its zenith with the emergence of internet technology.[10] It was in cyberspace that the ever-growing archive of the recorded past first became instantaneously accessible, releasing a seemingly endless deluge of recorded time from which it seemed no aspect of the past, however trivial, was able to escape. According to Fisher, it was directly as a result of this technological revolution in the early years of the twenty-first century that hauntology re-emerged, as a cultural and political response to the atemporality of a present in which the past no longer dies.

In the face of what may appear a growing obsession with excavating and examining the cultural detritus of our recent past, hauntology is often viewed as little more than a new form of nostalgia. In her history of the subject, which I will examine in a later chapter, Svetlana Boym charts the evolution of nostalgia in all its forms, as it moved from a longing for one's homeland to an urge to return to an earlier era, often that of the reassuring rhythms of one's childhood. This transmutation in the subject of one's nostalgia from place to time, has culminated in the epidemic which has engulfed us in recent years, as increasingly we turn away from the present in favour of the styles and ideas of an earlier age. Manifesting itself principally through music but displaying its effects across a myriad of forms, nostalgia has morphed into 'retromania', Simon Reynolds's term for this obsessive grip the recent past now holds over us. Such an analysis is not new to hauntology, however, being a central component of Fredric Jameson's celebrated formulation of postmodernity in the 1980s. What hauntology has identified in subsequent decades is, then, less a change in content than in degree, as the formal nostalgia that Jameson first described has since grown to an overwhelming extent, expanding to fill our cultural horizons and effectively denying a foothold to the new. As a result, Fisher claims, nostalgia has now become so ubiquitous as to be taken for granted, effectively losing its meaning as it no longer has anything against which it might be measured. In such circumstances hauntology may be regarded as post-nostalgic, describing a world in which the present can no longer be experienced as anything other than a sum of its pasts. And yet, as the concluding chapter of this book explores, in an era as obsessed with recycling its past as hauntology suggests, it seems there is one particular past towards which we are unerringly drawn. From the folk horror revival, to the fictions of Alan Garner and Susan Cooper, from *The Stone Tape* to *Scarfolk*, it appears that there is only one decade, both culturally and politically, that hauntology wishes us to revisit: the 1970s. If, however, this is an era that hauntology appears to hold in preference to all others, it is less the result of what that society achieved than the promise it failed to deliver. The early 1970s are now seen as exemplary of the unfulfilled potential hauntology wishes to revive. This is not a nostalgia for the past but one directed towards the lost futures it encapsulates.

In his recent book on the work of Mark Fisher, the author Matt Colquhoun employs a splendid neologism, one of which Derrida himself would surely have been proud: 'Blobjective'. Colquhoun uses this term to describe the way in which capitalism absorbs all it comes into contact with, bringing otherwise disparate elements within its orbit: 'The goal, for Mark', he writes, 'was to stay one step ahead of capitalism's consolidatory forces and its "blobjective" nature. Alternatives were of no use if they could be immediately folded back into the system they were attempting to escape from.'[11] In as far as its appropriation of cultural forms appears as rapacious as that of capitalism itself, it seems to me that this is a term equally applicable to hauntology, in which all that comes within its reach is likewise rendered hauntological. As a result, everything from Marx and Engels's *Manifesto* to *The Wicker Man*, the works of Arthur Machen to those of WG Sebald, have since been drawn within its borders. In both its academic format and even through its repurposed popular incarnation, discussions of hauntology often encourage an overly narrow understanding of the term, alongside a lament at what are considered the pernicious effects of mainstream recognition. It seems to me, however, that it has been precisely through such recognition, as its carefully policed boundaries are at first threatened and then overrun, that terms such as hauntology, rather like its intellectual cousin, psychogeography, come into their own, mutating in new and unexpected ways, broadening their conceptual depth and range of reference, and bringing ideas and figures into conjunction that might otherwise have never been brought together. In this respect, rather than persisting in a misguided and ultimately futile attempt at maintaining conceptual purity, we should instead welcome the results of hauntology's rampant blobjectivity as it hoovers up an eclectic and ever-growing mixture of canonical and pop-cultural elements.

As readers of this book will soon discover, this is a principle I have employed in marshalling the wide range of material which either anticipates, encapsulates or reiterates the formal characteristics of temporal disjunction, the technological uncanny and a nostalgia for lost futures common to hauntology. At first glance it will be clear that in doing so I have largely privileged the literary and the theoretical over the audio and the visual, a choice wholly at odds with hauntology's latter-day origins in the music of a small group of artists on the Ghost Box label and elsewhere. Thankfully, however, this decision has been rendered largely academic by two books published in 2011: Simon Reynolds's astonishing *Retromania*, in which he painstakingly details the emergence of hauntology in the music of the early twenty-first century; and Rob Young's equally encyclopaedic *Electric Eden* in which hauntological music is seen as the most recent manifestation of the English folk tradition. But just as music, through the very manner of its recording and dissemination appears to foreground many of the ghostly characteristics attributed to hauntology, so too may the literary be regarded as a similarly spectral form, its 'unheard voices and unspoken perspectives' communicated to us from beyond the confines of the printed page.[12]

In line with hauntology's desire to unearth those points in time at which lost futures may be reanimated, I have chosen three such moments with which to begin the chapters of this book, each of them heralding an era during which our conception of time was to undergo a profound reappraisal: 1848, 1921 and 1989. Thus my opening chapter begins in the Victorian London of Marx and Dickens, a city haunted not only by the spirit of revolutionary change taking hold across Europe but by an array of ghostly phenomena closer to home, as the façade of secular rationalism was threatened by the emergence of Spiritualism and other supernatural beliefs. Such beliefs were articulated not merely through the stories of Dickens and his contemporaries but found their visible manifestation on the stage through such pioneering theatrical devices as Pepper's Ghost, innovations which were soon to be reflected in the similarly uncanny transformation of urban life itself. But such changes were to be overshadowed by an equally revolutionary recalibration of time, as the theories of Darwin and others vastly extended the Victorians' sense of the prehistorical past, opening up the dizzying expanse of deep time. In the closing decades of the century, the fears and anxieties such changes had provoked were reworked in the tales of writers such as Vernon Lee and Arthur Machen whose fictional explorations of the cyclical nature of the mythic past and the atavistic return of our evolutionary forbears undermined the idea of history as one of unbroken progression. In the final years of the nineteenth century, the nascent discipline of psychoanalysis would seek to explain such anxieties; in his celebrated essay on the uncanny, Freud explored a phenomenon which is still perplexing us a century later. It is, however, MR James, the final figure of my opening chapter, whose work most clearly embodies the temporal disruptions and uncanny repetitions that have since been recognised as the hallmarks of hauntology.

The subject matter of this book is almost entirely English, for as one critic notes, hauntology is a peculiarly English phenomenon, bound up with the haunting and haunted landscapes of the English countryside and the ambivalent response they continue to evoke.[13] Nowhere is this more clearly demonstrated than in the work of Alfred Watkins, with which I begin my second chapter. It was in Herefordshire in 1921 that Watkins experienced the epiphany that was to result in his theory of ley lines, a temporal and topographical reordering of the English landscape that was to inaugurate an esoteric tradition that continues to this day. The 1920s were a time of great temporal experimentation, as an array of writers and mystics sought to establish a new theory of time with which to replace the model dismantled by Einstein and others a generation before. Chief amongst them was the now all but forgotten JW Dunne, whose theory of serial time was both impossibly abstruse and hugely influential. Drawing upon his own experience of precognitive dreams, Dunne was led to conclude that past, present and future could be accessed by us all, allowing us to revisit the events of our lives in any order we wish. The paranormal consequences of such a theory were to be outlined by Dunne's successor, TC Lethbridge, who employed a similar temporal model in his theory of residual haunting, in which he proposed that materials such as stone could record and store moments of heightened emotional intensity through time, which might then later be replayed. It was this theory which was to form the basis of perhaps the most resonant of all hauntological texts: Nigel Kneale's television play, *The Stone Tape*. Kneale's contribution to hauntology will be explored alongside that of another figure whose works have been memorably translated to the screen, Alan Garner. Garner's idiosyncratic account of what he calls 'inner time', a perpetual present experienced through myth and the rituals of primitive religion, informs both *The Owl Service* and *Red Shift*, two novels whose characters are compelled to re-enact events from a time alien to them. Britain's mythic past re-emerges once again in the novels of Susan Cooper, as the familiar landscapes of the present become the backdrop to an elemental struggle for the control of time. Finally, the myths of the past give way to those of the near future in the work of JG Ballard, an author whose preoccupation with temporal paradox is displayed in an array of fictional futures in which time decays, regresses or ceases altogether.

My final chapter begins in 1989, some months before the fall of the Berlin Wall, as Francis Fukuyama announced the final victory of Western liberalism and with it the end of history. It was in response to Fukuyama's provocative thesis, that Jacques Derrida published *Specters of Marx* in 1993, arguing that we had been too hasty to consign Marxism to its grave and predicting that we would continue to be haunted by his ideas. Quoting *Hamlet*, Derrida's epigraph reads 'The time is out of joint', a striking encapsulation of the meaning of his newly minted neologism, hauntology, and one which would subsequently prove considerably easier to understand.

Derrida's concept swiftly developed a life of its own. The past, as he had suggested, refused to remain quarantined from the present and instead returned in unsettling and disruptive ways. In *The Rings of Saturn*, his melancholy recollection of a ramble through the East Anglian countryside, the author, WG Sebald, seems positively overwhelmed by the ghosts of the past, which at times threaten to negate his memory and undermine his health. Both here and in my discussion of his final novel, *Austerlitz*, the boundary between past and present, between memory and history, appears decidedly porous, Sebald's own recollections often indistinguishable from those whose stories he uncovers. Perhaps Sebald's narrator, one might speculate, is suffering from a malady similar to the nostalgic illnesses Svetlana Boym describes in her book *The Future of Nostalgia*. I will be drawing upon Boym's work in my account of the epidemic of nostalgia that appears to have taken hold in recent times.

Nostalgia gives way to retromania in Simon Reynolds's account before I turn to Laura Grace Ford's refreshingly hard-edged series of drifts through the streets of 1990s London, an uncommon example of hauntology in action and one in which the decaying urban landscapes she reveals seem startlingly at odds with the predominantly rural settings to be found elsewhere in this book. Coming in her wake, my discussion of the work of Mark Fisher brings us full circle, his invocation of Marx and the leftist social projects of the post-war years reaffirming the spirit of political engagement from which hauntology first emerged. Fisher's work concludes with an unexpectedly hopeful vision of a future revitalised by the spirit of the 1970s, the decade to which I return in my final chapter.

The linear chronology which I have observed throughout finally arcs back as it approaches the present to re-emerge in the early years of the 1970s, an era celebrated today through the folk horror revival, the most recent cultural expression of hauntology.

In his collection of essays, *Ghosts of My Life,* Mark Fisher acknowledges the different ways in which hauntology is now employed: 'There is the specific sense', he explains, 'in which it has been applied to music culture, and a more general sense, where it refers to persistences, repetitions, prefigurations. There are also more or less benign versions of hauntology.'[14] As Fisher's comments suggest, hauntology ought not to be regarded as monolithic but rather as a plural manifestation of the many different ways in which our culture and our politics are shaped by the revisions and repetitions of the past. Over recent decades, hauntology has itself been the subject of such revisions, as fluctuations in intellectual fashion result in a cycle of acclamation and dismissal, a process suggestive of the similarly episodic manner in which the past may return to haunt the present. Indeed, it appears that hauntology's changing fortunes may be symptomatic of its subject, as if this concept has come finally to mirror the very condition it seeks to describe. Could it be that we are now haunted by hauntology itself?[15] The following account will seek to establish the role of hauntology in our present, outlining the future it may help to enable, as well as exploring the many versions of its past.

Notes

1 Mark Fisher, 'Hauntology Now', *k-punk*, 17 January 2006 at http://k-punk.abstractdynamics.org/archives/007230.html

2 Mark Pilkington, 'Hauntologists mine the past for music's future', *boingboing*, 12 October 2012 at https://boingboing.net/2012/10/12/hauntologists-mine-the-past-fo.html

3 Tom Whyman, 'The Ghosts of our Lives', *New Statesman*, 31 July 2019.

4 Jacques Derrida in *Ghost Dance*, dir. Ken McMullen, Channel Four Television, 1983.

5 Mark Fisher, 'What is Hauntology?', *Film Quarterly*, Vol. 66, 1 (Fall 2012), 16-24, p. 16.

6 Fisher, 'What is Hauntology?', p. 16.

7 In 2011, James Bridle warned: 'Hauntology, already old, is about six months away from becoming the title of a column in a Sunday supplement magazine; of going the way of psychogeography.' See James Bridle, 'Hauntological Futures', *booktwo.org*, 20 March 2011 at https://booktwo.org/notebook/hauntological-futures/

8 Fisher, 'What is Hauntology?', p. 19.

9 Mark Pilkington sounds a more hopeful note, suggesting that 'rather than an all-consuming black hole, the vast weight of the past will slingshot us into a new, weird, and always-haunted future.' See Pilkington, 'Hauntologists mine the past for music's future'.

10 'Hauntology is not just some lazy, hazy term for the ethereal', Fisher writes, 'hauntology isn't about hoky atmospherics or "spookiness" but a *technological uncanny.*' See Mark Fisher, 'Phonograph Blues', *k-punk*, 19 October 2006 at http://k-punk.abstractdynamics.org/archives/008535.html

[11] Matt Colquhoun, *Egress: On Mourning, Melancholy and Mark Fisher*, London; Repeater Books, 2020, p. 88.

[12] See Katy Shaw, *Hauntology: The Presence of the Past in Twenty-First Century English Literature*, London: Palgrave Macmillan, 2018, pp. 15-19.

[13] See Shaw, p. 2.

[14] Mark Fisher, 'The Slow Cancellation of the Future' in *Ghosts of My Life: Writings on Depression, Hauntology and Lost Futures*, Winchester: Zero Books, 2014, 2-29, p. 28.

[15] Andrew Gallix writes: 'hauntology is not just a symptom of the times, it is itself haunted by a nostalgia for all our lost futures.' See Andrew Gallix, 'Hauntology: A not-so-new critical manifestation. The new vogue in literary theory is shot through with earlier ideas', *The Guardian*, 17 June 2011.

Part I: Hauntings

A spectre is haunting Europe – the spectre of Communism.
Karl Marx and Friedrich Engels, *The Communist Manifesto* (1848)[1]

The dread word, GHOST, recalls me.
Charles Dickens, *The Haunted Man and the Ghost's Bargain* (1848)[2]

London, 1848

'The year 1848 is turning out well', proclaimed Engels in February of that year, as he gleefully reported the outbreak of revolution on the streets of Paris: 'Our age, the age of democracy, is breaking. The flames of the Tuileries and the Palais Royal are the dawn of the proletariat. Everywhere the rule of the bourgeoisie will now come crashing down, or be dashed to pieces.'[3] A few weeks earlier, a 23-page pamphlet, written in German, had been published anonymously by the German Workers' Educational Society at Bishopsgate in London. Its impact was negligible, at least at first, but the spectre revealed by Marx in his *Communist Manifesto* had now been released, or rather the hobgoblin, as Helen Macfarlane's first English translation of 1850 was to proclaim: 'A frightful hobgoblin stalks throughout Europe. We are haunted by a ghost, the ghost of Communism.'[4]

Thankfully for Marx, and also for Jacques Derrida, who was to be spared the indignity of writing a book entitled *Hobgoblins of Marx*, Macfarlane's translation was soon superseded. The timing of the publication of Marx's *Manifesto* may have been fortunate but the radical sentiments it espoused could do little to bolster the impact of the uprisings of 1848 which failed to take root and were remembered subsequently for having promised rather more than they delivered. Despite revolutionary outbreaks in France, Germany, and across Europe, Britain's liberal government was largely a passive spectator to events, and aside from the activities of the Chartists, who staged a mass meeting on Kennington Common in April 1848, there was little sense of imminent revolt. Then, as now, it seems, Britain cast a largely sceptical eye upon the behaviour of its European cousins, and continued with business as usual. Shortly after the publication of his *Manifesto*, Marx's peripatetic existence continued with his expulsion from Belgium, soon followed by his deportation from France; with his options now dwindling he finally arrived in London in August 1849.

The author of *The Future of Nostalgia*, Svetlana Boym, has written: 'Outbreaks of nostalgia often follow revolutions.' Through such examples as the French Revolution of 1789 to the more recent 'velvet' revolutions in Eastern Europe, Boym notes how such events 'were accompanied by political and cultural manifestations of longing', often for the stability which preceded such periods of upheaval. But what of failed revolutions? Here, claims Boym, the nostalgia one feels is redirected towards 'unrealized dreams of the past and visions of the future that became obsolete. The history of nostalgia might allow us to look back at modern history as a search not only for newness and technological progress, but also for unrealized possibilities, unpredictable turns and crossroads.'[5]

This surely is the nostalgia that would have afflicted Marx during his long London exile until his death in 1883, certainly not a longing for the apparent solidity of a pre-revolutionary past but rather a mourning for what might have been, for precisely that sense of an unrealised future which has since been identified as the hallmark of hauntology. For Marx never lived to see the widespread acceptance of the beliefs he espoused in his *Manifesto* and while revolutionary unrest continued to erupt sporadically throughout Europe during the nineteenth century, it was the events of 1848, the year zero of hauntological thought, which marked the turning point that never came to pass.[6]

The environment that Marx and those of his fellow revolutionaries who had fled Europe for the UK would have encountered in London would have been quite alien to them. The prevailing sense of nostalgia in Victorian London was directed not towards a revolutionary past (or future) but instead harked back to the utopian medievalism of 'Merrie England', a mythical reimagining of a long-distant past which, while repeatedly recreated, had never actually existed. Alongside this sense of the national past as a sort of never-ending Arthurian pageant, Victorian England was also subject to a powerful and newly emergent sense of the supernatural. In this respect, quite apart from its revolutionary history, the year 1848 is also significant, if largely unremembered, for quite different reasons.

On 31 March 1848, as public unrest continued across

Germany and Austria, the Fox family in the small town of Hydesville, near Rochester in upstate New York, were experiencing domestic unrest of their own, as their home had become plagued by unexplained rappings. On this particular evening, however, these were so vigorous that the family called in their neighbours to witness the event. Sensing that these mysterious noises must have an otherworldly origin, an impromptu séance was soon underway, as the family and their neighbours began a tentative exchange of questions and answers with their supernatural visitor. He revealed himself to be the spirit of a peddler who claimed to have been murdered in their house. As rumours of the 'Rochester Rappings' grew more widespread, similar outbreaks began to occur across New York and what was soon to become known as the Spiritualist movement had begun. Years later, in 1888, Margaret, the youngest of the three daughters of the Fox family, acknowledged that she and her sisters had engineered a hoax (she later recanted her confession) but by then it was far too late. Spiritualism, in essence the belief that the spirits of the dead exist and can communicate with the living, had been embraced by the public both in the US and Europe, and 31 March 1848 remains the founding date of the movement. At first glance, these events would appear to have little in common with political upheaval in Europe, and yet as European socialists fled to the US after the failings of the 1848 uprising, many of them found a home with like-minded radical and reformist thinkers, and it was in such an environment that Spiritualism first flourished; prominent spiritualists were later to include such socialist thinkers as Robert Owen and Alfred Russel Wallace.

Spiritualism didn't reach London until 1852, with the arrival from the USA of the medium, Maria B Hayden, but the city that Marx had made his home was to prove extremely fertile ground for supernatural beliefs of every kind, from mesmerism and Spiritualism to Theosophy and psychical research. Despite the widely-held perception of the Victorian era as one of predominantly secular thought, the reality was somewhat less rational:

> The Victorians were haunted by the supernatural. [...] Disembodied voices over the telephone, the superhuman speed of the railway, near instantaneous communication through telegraph wires: the collapsing of time and distance achieved by modern technologies that were transforming daily life was often felt to be uncanny. The mysterious powers of electricity, the baffling feats of mesmerists and apparently real communications from the dead elicited by Spiritualist mediums made the world seem as if it were full of invisible, occult forces. [...] The supernatural was both fearful and terrible and ardently desired; it was a spooky sense that there was more to the world than the everyday, and an intimation that reality might be transfigured by something above and beyond.[7]

As we shall see, the London of this period was a melting pot of radical ideas which were to become embedded within the wider culture of the day, from revolutionary politics to the challenge to scientific and religious orthodoxy presented by Darwin. And just as 1848 may now be identified as the hauntological year zero, so too can London be pronounced its ground zero, the city of Marx and his *Manifesto*, and one home to spectres of its own.

Dickens, the Haunted Man

If 1848 was a significant year for Marx and Engels, as well as for the Fox family in New York, the same might also be said for Charles Dickens (1812-70). In February, Dickens reviewed Catherine Crowe's bestselling compendium of 'true' ghost stories, *The Night Side of Nature; or, Ghosts and Ghost Seers* (1848) for *The Examiner*. Crowe's casebook of anecdotes and stories was dismissed by Dickens on the grounds that rather than being metaphysical in origin, the spectres that Crowe 'revealed' had in fact a physiological basis and were merely the symptoms of a diseased imagination. Ghosts, claimed Dickens:

> Always elude us. Doubtful and scant of proof at first, doubtful and scant of proof still, all mankind's experience of *them* is, that their alleged appearances have been, in all ages, marvellous, exceptional, and resting on imperfect grounds of proof; that in vast numbers of cases they are known to be delusions superintended by a well-understood, and by no means uncommon disease.[8]

Despite his reputation as one of the foremost practitioners of the ghost story and a writer whose entire body of work is infused with references to the ghostly and the supernatural, Dickens remained an ardent sceptic of the kinds of unexplained occurrences that fascinated Crowe and her audience. Dickens was a collector of ghostly ephemera and yet the roots of his obsession lay in his desire to find common sense or rational explanations for extraordinary events and to challenge what he saw as the fraudulent attempts of mediums to dupe a gullible public. In the Victorian London of the mid-nineteenth century there was an insatiable demand for all things supernatural (a demand that Dickens's own works played a significant role in fuelling) and it was in response to this unbridled demand that the Ghost Club, one of the first paranormal research organisations, was founded in 1862. Originating in a group of Cambridge academics in the 1850s, the Ghost Club was dissolved following Dickens's death in 1870, although in later incarnations it was to attract such figures as WB Yeats and Sir Arthur Conan Doyle, and it continues to this day.[9] As an early member, Dickens and his fellow enthusiasts set out to debunk the spurious claims of mediums, spiritualists and their sympathisers. Yet such attempts were not always as straightforwardly scientific as they claimed, and Dickens himself was not immune to the often contradictory attitude towards the supernatural displayed by his Victorian contemporaries. He was, for example, a believer in the therapeutic benefits of mesmerism, and despite his misgivings was a regular attendee of séances. It is in his fiction, however, that Dickens demonstrates an attitude towards the occult frequently at odds with his publicly voiced scepticism, an ambivalence most famously articulated in *A Christmas Carol* (1843), in which Scrooge and the ghost of Jacob Marley act out a dialogue between their creator and his public:

> 'You don't believe in me,' observed the ghost.
> 'I don't,' said Scrooge.
> 'What evidence would you have of my reality beyond that of your senses?'

'I don't know,' said Scrooge.

'Why do you doubt your senses?'

'Because,' said Scrooge, 'a little thing affects them. A slight disorder of the stomach makes them cheats. You may be an undigested bit of beef, a blot of mustard, a crumb of cheese, a fragment of an underdone potato. There's more of gravy than of grave about you, whatever you are!'[10]

A Christmas Carol was the first of Dickens's celebrated 'Christmas Books' and his ghosts of Christmas Past, Present and Yet to Come foreground the theme of temporal dislocation, between what is and ought to be, what was and what might have been. Here, as in so much of Dickens's fiction, it is greed and the corrupting power of money which stunts spiritual (and physical) progression, leading characters such as Scrooge to live their lives in a manner contrary to their true selves.

'Marley was dead, to begin with.'[11] From the opening line we are forewarned of what lies ahead, of the ghost as revenant, that which is compelled to come back, in violation of the natural passage of time. But of all the ghosts that he is to encounter, it is the ghost of Christmas Yet to Come that Scrooge fears the most, for despite offering him the possibility of redemption, it shows him the fearful consequences of the life he has chosen: '"Ghost of the Future!" he exclaimed, "I fear you more than any spectre I have seen. But as I know your purpose is to do me good, and as I hope to live to be another man from what I was, I am prepared to bear you company, and do it with a thankful heart. Will you not speak to me?"'[12] These ghosts may appear essentially benign, indeed positively angelic in offering Scrooge the chance to reclaim his better nature, but there is another more malevolent haunting at work in Dickens's tale, an equally invisible but insidious and all-embracing spectral underworld of relationships, exchanges and circulation: the capitalist system itself. The links between the spectral and the economic are manifest throughout Dickens's work, for as one critic explains, at a time in which paper, in the form of promissory notes, could be redeemed for gold, increasingly paper money became perceived as a ghostly entity in contrast with 'real' money, a spectral quality that lends itself to the entire system of invisible transactions on which capital depends.[13] It is only by presenting the possibility of counteracting the spell cast by this malevolent web of invisible transactions, that Dickens is able to present his readers with an alternative conception of their future (and their present), a utopian vision with which to challenge the prevailing ideology of his day.

So endlessly has Dickens's most famous story since been retold and reimagined that the characters themselves have escaped the confines of the text to haunt the public imagination. In this respect, *A Christmas Carol* takes its place alongside those other canonical texts which inhabit a kind of virtual afterlife somewhere between fiction and reality. The story has itself become a revenant, and one which returns punctually each Christmas. As a result, Scrooge and Marley, Tiny Tim and Bob Cratchit, have come to resemble the ghosts whose story they share, in as far as they now haunt our own culture, condemned to enjoy (or endure) a perpetual Christmas, a Christmas that for us it seems can no longer be truly experienced or understood without reference to their ghostly presence. Yet despite the seeming ubiquity of Dickensian haunting in popular culture, his supernatural tales with their barely disguised moral message have not inspired universal affection. The writer China Miéville, for example, has argued that rather than reflecting the (ghostly) spirit of the age, Dickens's ghosts are enfeebled and already outdated remnants of the past, describing them as 'apotheoses of the instructional ghosts of the preceding century – out of time, rearguard in their sentimentality. Themselves haunted by the future. They are not so much convincing, morally, as performatively flourished. These are not modern ghosts, but the last, already-dead walking dead of a dead epoch, bobbed about on sticks.'[14] In describing Dickens's ghosts as 'instructional', however, Miéville is merely acknowledging the moral conservatism of all traditional ghost stories in which ghosts perform a social function in upholding the societal and moral norms of the day. For while hauntings and hauntology itself may since have acquired a political radicalism born of association with Marx and sustained through popular culture, it should be remembered that ghosts themselves are more traditionally associated with the retribution of past wrongs, and the unexpiated guilt of sins for which they (or we) are yet to atone. Ghosts, as Philip Ball reminds us, are 'the invisible police, all-seeing agents that patrol norms and boundaries. In this respect traditional ghosts are not emissaries of chaos, but are on the contrary social conservatives.'[15]

In Dickens's work, ghosts and hauntings abound. In stories such as 'The Signal-Man', written for the Christmas edition of the magazine *All the Year Round* in 1866 (and the subject of Lawrence Gordon Clark's memorable television adaptation in 1976), Dickens relived his traumatic experience of the Staplehurst train crash the previous year. The tale is of a lonely signalman haunted by a spectre whose every appearance forewarns him of an accident he is powerless to prevent, including that which will result in his own death. Dickens uses the emerging technology of the Victorian telegraph network as the medium with which to transmit his ghostly communications. In this respect, as Adam Scovell has suggested, 'The Signal-Man' may be read as a pioneering example of the hauntological interaction between pre-digital, analogue technology and the supernatural.[16] *Bleak House* (1853) is a similarly, if less explicitly, haunted work, whose twofold narration interweaves past and present in a manner which appears to subject the living to the same temporal imperatives that govern their ghostly counterparts; one in which the supply of ghosts is constantly replenished through Dickens's habit of introducing characters only to have them die almost immediately (Jenny's baby), not long afterwards (Jo) or to be dead at the point of discovery (Nemo). In *Great Expectations* (1861), we find what is surely the foremost example of literary dyschronia, as time slows to a standstill within the confines of Satis House, an atemporal zone in which Miss Havisham exists in a perpetual present, the clocks forever frozen at 8.40 am as she relives the moment at which she first learns that she is not to be married. On visiting Satis House and meeting its spectral inhabitant, Pip experiences a profound sense of dislocation: 'So unchanging was the dull old house, the yellow light in the darkened room, the faded spectre in the chair by the dressing-table glass, that I felt as if the stopping of the clocks had stopped Time in that mysterious place, and, while I and everything else outside it grew older, it stood still.'[17]

'As a term,' Steven Connor writes, '"haunting" has an

almost disappointingly innocuous past.'[18] From the sixteenth century onwards, he informs us, the term was used to describe those persons possessed by spirits but gradually it became assigned less to people than to the places they inhabited. By the time at which Dickens was writing, the word 'haunt' was most commonly used simply to describe a location which one frequented. As the nineteenth century progressed, however, the spaces such a 'haunt' might evoke moved away from the natural world to a more urban and domestic setting, the family home. Within such a setting, the home and its inhabitants could become identified with one another as place and person became increasingly interchangeable. Who then was the haunter and who the haunted became less easy to discern. It is this sense of an almost claustrophobic proximity between the ghost and their subject that lies at the heart of Dickens's fifth and final Christmas book, *The Haunted Man and the Ghost's Bargain*, which was published in December 1848, a coincidence of dates that recurs throughout this book, returning us repeatedly to the year of Marx's *Manifesto*.

With its preoccupation with temporal continuity and the power of memory to shape the personality, Dickens's novella shares many of the concerns of its more celebrated predecessor, *A Christmas Carol*, and yet *The Haunted Man* is a much darker and less sentimental work. Its protagonist is haunted in a manner even more unsettling than that experienced by Scrooge, for the ghost encountered here is that of his own ghostly double. Like Scrooge, the embittered chemist Redlaw is similarly tormented by his past, memories of hurt and injustice denying him the ability to take any pleasure in the present. One evening, however, he is subject to a ghostly visitation, an all-too-familiar embodiment of his desire to extinguish the past:

> As the gloom and shadow thickened behind him, in that place where it had been gathering so darkly, it took, by slow degrees, – or out of it there came, by some unreal, unsubstantial process – not to be traced by any human sense, – an awful likeness of himself.
>
> Ghastly and cold, colourless in its leaden face and hands, but with his features, and his bright eyes, and his grizzled hair, and dressed in the gloomy shadow of his dress, it came into his terrible appearance of existence, motionless, without a sound. As *he* leaned his arm upon the elbow of his chair, ruminating before the fire, *it* leaned upon the chair-back, close above him, with its appalling copy of his face looking where his face looked, and bearing the expression his face bore.
>
> This, then, was the Something that had passed and gone already. This was the dread companion of the haunted man![19]

Thanks to his phantom doppelgänger, Redlaw is offered the chance to be rid of his memories, an apparent blessing that comes at a cost – he will thenceforth pass on his gift of forgetfulness to everyone with whom he comes into contact. Haunting soon becomes a contagion as Redlaw moves through the city, spreading his curse of forgetfulness as he passes. Of course, the message that Redlaw finally learns is that in memory lies compassion. Good and evil, joy and suffering, are inextricably linked and, in extinguishing his memories, Redlaw denies himself and those he encounters the ability to experience either. Redlaw is haunted by loss – he grieves for the deaths of his beloved sister and the woman he hoped to marry, who was seduced by his best friend – and in this respect he mirrors his creator. At the time of writing, Dickens was mourning the death of his own sister Fanny, who died in September 1848. These are the memories that Redlaw (and Dickens) struggle to contain: 'I saw them, in the fire, but now,' he murmured. 'They come back to me in the music, in the wind, in the dead stillness of the night, in the revolving years.'[20] Loss is the major theme of Dickens's tale – of love, family, of memory itself – but the traces that such absence leave behind persist and can never be fully eradicated. 'I have the power to cancel remembrance', claims Redlaw's spectral double, 'to leave but very faint, confused traces of them, that will die out soon'.[21] But Dickens's tale emphasises the persistence of memory, for regardless of the spectre's claim to the contrary, traces do remain and we can never fully escape our past as Redlaw believes: 'The past is past,' said the Chemist. 'It dies like the brutes. Who talks to me of its traces in my life? He raves or lies!'[22] Yet Redlaw is mistaken and he is unable to fully efface his deepest sense of self. In the end, it is only music which has the power to recall Redlaw to himself, for on hearing a familiar strain of Christmas song 'some dumb stir within him made him capable, again, of being moved by what was hidden, afar off, in the music.'[23] As hauntology in its current manifestation would attest, music has a unique and restorative power to evoke the past, to reach emotional depths and to provoke memory in a manner seemingly denied to other media.

Both *A Christmas Carol* and *The Haunted Man* explore a mourning for failed potentialities, alongside a recognition of the spectral nature of memory itself: 'in the likenesses of forms and faces from the past, from the grave, from the deep, deep gulf, where the things that might have been, and never were, are always wandering.'[24] But the lost futures that Dickens's describes here and throughout his work are those which a Victorian readership would have recognised rather more literally than the nostalgic recall of our recent past evoked by hauntology today. In an era of high infant mortality, this mourning for unrealised futures is directed not towards the cultural or political landscape of mid-Victorian Britain but rather at an absent population exemplified by figures such as Paul Dombey, Little Nell and (in another future) Tiny Tim. *The Haunted Man* may have been the product of that fateful year, 1848, haunted both by spectres of communism and Christmases yet to come, but Dickens's novella was to have an unexpected afterlife of its own, a ghostly presence beyond the pages of his book.

Pepper's Ghost

'The best ghosts have always been theatrical ghosts', claims Jim Steinmeyer in *Hiding the Elephant*, his history of the golden age of stage magic.[25] 'Real ghosts', he adds, the kind most commonly sighted in stately homes, appear to function independently of the world around them and do little to support our belief in them: 'They don't make sense. When photographed, they are hardly there. When questioned, they have nothing to say. Mediums are necessary to interpret for them, and they generally do a bad job.'[26] Onstage, however, ghosts have an important function to fulfil:

> They're characters that inject meaning into a story by haunting it; they can presage a disaster or mysteriously direct a plot. Often they have a lot to say. Shakespeare was an expert at writing for ghosts. Hamlet's deceased father drifted across the stage, uttered eighty-four lines in blank verse, and efficiently initiated a great and tragic story [...] In various stage plays throughout the nineteenth century, a ghost's entrance would be announced with a rumble of tympani. The gaslights were dimmed with dark blue glass. An actor draped in white gauze might be greeted with open-mouthed stares or screams by other characters. The audience knew he was a ghost because for centuries the tricks and machinery of the stage had made it all clear. [...] Victorian audiences found the ghosts in their favourite melodramas provided emphatic sensations, supernatural thrills, and cliff-hanging action. Considered to be on the borderline with reality, the spirits could be cloying and sentimental or irrational and terrifying.[27]

By the mid-eighteenth century, the theatrical ghost, particularly in as far as Shakespeare's plays were concerned, had largely vanished from the stage. A literal depiction by an actor had come to be seen as increasingly vulgar, for rather than any physical manifestation it was only the responses of the actors themselves which were considered necessary to indicate to the audience the arrival of a ghostly presence.[28] By the mid-nineteenth century, however, the fashion for an embodied ghost had returned and Victorian audiences were well aware of all the array of tricks and stage machinery that were required for their entertainment. But the very nature of the theatrical ghost was about to be transformed into something materially (or immaterially) different.

In 1858, a civil engineer, author and part-time inventor named Henry Dircks (1806-73) presented a small model of his latest invention to a meeting of the British Association for the Advancement of Science in Leeds. The Dircksian Phantasmagoria was, he believed, a device that would revolutionise the science of stage mechanics, by using a trapdoor and a hidden sheet of glass, placed between the audience and the stage, to project a figure through the glass to appear on stage alongside the actors. Dircks, however, was unable to convince either the scientific community or the theatre owners of the merits of his idea and it aroused little interest. It was only in the autumn of 1862 when he met 'Professor' John Henry Pepper (1821-1900) at the Royal Polytechnic Institution on Regent Street in London that he was finally able to attract the attention of someone able to understand the potential of his invention. When Pepper saw the small transparent figures generated within Dircks's model he sensed immediately the possibilities it afforded. Dircks received £500 for his idea, and despite his request that his name should be attached to his invention the Dircksian Phantasmagoria was soon consigned to history, and what would from that point onward be regarded as 'Pepper's Ghost' was born. On Christmas Eve, 1862, on stage at the Polytechnic, the invention was presented to the public for the first time. To enhance the dramatic experience, the apparatus was used to illustrate a scene from a suitably ghostly short story: Dickens's *The Haunted Man*. Henry Dircks provides the following account of what contemporary audiences would have experienced:

> A student is seen sitting at a table spread over with books, papers and instruments. After a while he rises and walks about the chamber. In this there is nothing remarkable. But the audience is perplexed by a different circumstance: they see a man rising from his seat and see him walking about, but they also see that he still sits immovably in his chair – so that evidently there are two persons instead of one, for, although alike in dress, stature, and person, their actions are different. They cross and recross; they alternately take the same seat; while one reads, the other is perhaps walking; and yet they appear very sullen and sulky, for they take no notice of each other, until one, after pushing down a pile of books, passes off by walking through the furniture and walls.[29]

Dickens and his friend Mark Lemon had first dramatised *The Haunted Man* for the Adelphi Theatre in 1848 and the production had opened on 20 December, the day following the publication of the book. But Dickens had been keen to stress the allegorical nature of the spectre, insisting that rather than having the ghost appear, it should instead be represented simply by a darkening of the stage; showing the Phantom, he said, would 'involve an absurdity in reference to the prevailing idea of the book'.[30] Lemon's production was a success and the play was revived the following year but these performances would have done little to prepare the public for the 1863 revival which was, thanks to Pepper's Ghost, an astonishing success. In May of 1863 the Prince and Princess of Wales visited the Polytechnic and were given a demonstration, and soon after the ballad writers of the day had immortalised the illusion:

At Music Halls, Theatres too,
This 'Patent Ghost' they show,
The Goblin novelty to view,
Some thousands nightly go;
For such a sight they gladly pay,
In order just to boast,
To all their 'country cousins' – they –
Have seen a perfect Ghost.[31]

Although, as one critic notes, perhaps the most telling indication of the wider cultural impact of Pepper's Ghost, in London at least, can be found in the fact that cabmen soon adopted the name to describe those customers in the habit of vanishing without paying their fare.[32] From a twenty-first century perspective, the cultural impact of Pepper's Ghost may now seem difficult to comprehend. How could an optical illusion essentially involving little more than a sheet of glass and carefully arranged lighting create such a response? The answer lies largely in the context of supernatural belief in the 1860s, in which competing 'ghostly media' such as Spirit Photography offered a similarly uncanny sense of insubstantial figures floating on air.[33] More relevant still was the widespread belief in Spiritualism at this time, which would have meant that many of the audience at the Polytechnic shows would have been those seeking to communicate with the spirits of dead family and friends. In this respect the function of the illusionist and the spiritualist were considered largely the same: to produce ghosts.[34]

Yet the manner in which Pepper's Ghost was presented was precisely to counter such beliefs. The shows at the Polytechnic were conducted not as supernatural events but rather as a well-rehearsed blend of entertainment and science, in which a brief drama such as *The Haunted Man* was accompanied by a lecture on optics and illusion, designed principally to free its audience from 'the folly of ghost beliefs and supposed spiritualist manifestations.'[35] If, however, the intention was truly to alert the public to the fraudulence of supernatural belief, then the results were perhaps not as Pepper would have expected. For despite, or perhaps because of, the inordinate success of the illusion, its audience proved reluctant to discard their spiritualist beliefs, and the medium that Pepper had introduced proved just as likely to confirm the audience in its supernatural beliefs as it was to undermine them. Pepper's illusion produced better and more convincing ghosts than anything its audience might have hoped for and in the process it fostered a belief in Spiritualism and the supernatural by 'helping people to picture the ghosts they desired to see.'[36] The question of exactly what an audience thought they were seeing is crucial to understanding the lasting influence of this illusion. For Pepper's Ghost demonstrated the way in which the manipulation of an image projected upon a stage can trick both the eye and mind of the beholder, ensuring that an audience which was alert to the customary techniques by which it would be willingly deceived was still unable to apprehend the nature of what they were experiencing. In demonstrating the technical manipulation of a projected image, and through the undeniable impact of its result, Pepper's Ghost acts as an important precursor to the history of the early cinema, and the illusion is said to have inspired the Lumière brothers to choose the Polytechnic for the first English exhibition of their cinematograph in 1896.

Given the public's response to the illusion, however, Pepper's Ghost failed to have the revolutionary impact on the portrayal of the theatrical ghost that one might have expected. There were strong practical and economic reasons why its use was confined only to tableaux and the dramatisations of short stories: the production of the sheet of glass was costly and its use restricted the sound and movement of the actors; it required a theatre with a stage sufficiently large to employ it; and the actor hidden beneath the stage who was to provide the ghostly reflection could usually endure the sweltering conditions for little more than a short period. For these reasons most theatres continued to rely upon the more traditional methods of lights and trap-doors to conjure their ghostly illusions and Pepper's Ghost was relegated to the fairs and circuses that toured the country in the last decades of the nineteenth century.[37] By the mid-1890s, the illusion was in decline, and just as it had superseded the magic lantern and stereoscopic ghosts of the 1850s, so too was it forced to give way to the rise of the English cinema.

As the role of Pepper's Ghost was declining in late Victorian London, however, the large panes of glass to which it owed its success were becoming more widespread. During the late nineteenth century the manufacture of such glass panes, free from imperfections, became technically viable for the first time, and with the emergence of commercial display culture, so such reflective surfaces moved from being a luxury item to become mass-produced commodities.[38] Soon store windows were adorning city streets, as the reflective surfaces that had been at the heart of the Pepper's Ghost illusion moved from their concealed position within the theatre to a more prominent position at the heart of the modern city:

Instead of being restricted to multiplying the image of the king and his courtiers, store windows and mirrors greeted passersby on busy streets, endowing them with optical doubles, mixing passing crowds with their visual phantoms. Optical devices designed entirely as entertainment, such as the stereoscope and kaleidoscope that Brewster produced, joined scientific optical devices that had emerged in the seventeenth century and spawned a new realm of visual amusements ranging from the theatre to the parlor to the nursery. As the Renaissance phantasms faded from history, their optically manufactured doppelgangers appeared multiplied in a new daily environment of transparency and reflection.[39]

Furthermore, as Tom Gunning explains, once the use of glass windows was incorporated into modern transportation systems, so such transparent surfaces began to move for the first time. Soon travellers on the bus and train became accustomed to seeing their reflections in the windows, while passers-by navigated a new urban environment 'that mingled real and virtual images, visions transmitted or reflected by glass.' As one visitor to St Petersburg in 1899 declared: 'The quality of multiple reflections that the modern city provides us with has turned it into the natural medium of haunting.'[40] Seen in this light, Pepper's Ghost may be regarded as having had an influence well beyond the confines of Victorian stagecraft. Its illusion came to encapsulate (and reflect) the ghostly and increasingly illusory nature of the modern city itself, as the city dweller came to be haunted by reflections of himself and others on every side. In tandem with Dickens's *The Haunted Man*, Pepper's Ghost created an entirely new form of visual experience, one in which the separation of memory and identity could be visualised for the first time. Dickens's tale and the illusion which brought it to life ought then to be regarded as a single ghostly entity, a multi-media conjunction of text and image, science and the supernatural, and one which provides us with an exemplary hauntological precursor to future innovations in film and visual technology.

Mythic Time: Vernon Lee

'Those pedants say that the dead are dead, the past is past. For them, yes; but why for me? [. . .] Why should there not be ghosts to such as can see them?' So writes the author Vernon Lee in her short story, 'Amour Dure' (1890).[41] Lee, the pen-name of Violet Paget (1856-1935), may at first glance appear an unlikely inclusion in a survey such as this, and yet her pioneering gothic tales, in which history is experienced as a kind of haunting, demonstrate many of the temporal traits which have since come to be associated with hauntology. Educated in Germany and Italy, Violet Paget adopted the masculine *nom de plume* 'Vernon Lee' at the age of 19 because, in her own words, she was 'sure that no one reads a woman's writing on art, history or aesthetics with anything but unmitigated contempt'.[42] Her first work of scholarship, *Studies of the Eighteenth Century in Italy* (1880), was published at the age of 24 and brought her great acclaim; over the next 50 years she was to produce 43 major works of fiction, history, philosophy and aesthetics. Yet by the time of her death in 1935 these works were largely neglected. It is only since the 1980s and the revival of overlooked feminist voices from the late nineteenth century, that her supernatural tales have been rediscovered and her reputation as a pioneering modernist restored.

An acknowledged disciple of the art critic, Walter Pater (1839-94), Lee was particularly influenced by his essay 'Pico della Mirandola' (1871) in which Pater translates from Heinrich Heine's 'The Gods in Exile' (1853). Heine's essay imagines the deposed pagan deities returning to medieval Christian society where they are forced to disguise themselves or to undertake humble employment, an idea of the return of the mythical pagan past into later Christian history which was to have a powerful impact upon late Victorian society. Heine (1797-1856) believed that the exuberance of the Greek myths had been superseded by an ascetic Christian tradition which rendered these pagan deities as little more than malignant spirits. But what if these gods remained amongst us still, albeit in rather reduced circumstances? With Apollo now a lowly shepherd in Austria and Mars an Italian peasant and soldier, Heine depicts these dethroned deities as little more than a band of melancholy and malevolent wanderers:

> I am speaking here of that metamorphosis into demons which the Greek and Roman gods underwent when Christianity achieved supreme control of the world. The superstition of the people ascribed to those gods a real but cursed existence, coinciding entirely in this respect with the teaching of the Church. The latter by no means declared the ancient gods to be myths, inventions of falsehood and error, as did the philosophers, but held them to be evil spirits, who, through the victory of Christ, had been hurled from the summit of their power, and now dragged along

> their miserable existences in the obscurity of dismantled temples or in enchanted groves, and by their diabolic arts, through lust and beauty, particularly through dancing and singing, lured to apostasy unsteadfast Christians who had lost their way in the forest [...] then these unfortunate heathen divinities were again compelled to take to flight, seeking safety under the most varied disguises and in the most retired hiding-places. Many of these poor refugees, deprived of shelter and ambrosia, were now forced to work at some plebeian trade in order to earn a livelihood.[43]

The gods have become revenants forced to return from mythic time to historical time by the loss of belief in the pagan religion that sustains them. Seen out of their true temporal context they become in Christian terms no longer godly but demonic, a ghostly trace of a pagan prehistoric past that never went away. In her essay 'Dionysus in the Euganean Hills' (1921), Lee describes the exile of the gods in supernatural terms, as 'a kind of *haunting*; the gods [...] partaking of the nature of ghosts even more than all gods do, *revenants* as they are from other ages.'[44] Here, Lee's appropriation of Heine's motif is both an extension of her preoccupation with Hellenic culture and an expression of her understanding of history as governed by the ghostly return of the past.

First published in her most celebrated collection of supernatural tales, *Hauntings* (1890), 'Dionea' is the story in which Lee draws most explicitly on Heine's work. Through a fragmentary exchange of letters, Lee describes the rebirth of Venus (Aphrodite) in late nineteenth-century Italy and the malignant consequences of her return. Dionea, a young girl of mysterious origins, is cast ashore after a storm and placed in a local convent. Needless to say, she soon reveals herself to be ill-suited to her new environment, and quickly alienates her companions. As she grows older, her beauty and her behaviour begin to have an increasingly unsettling effect, particularly on the men with whom she comes into contact, and this malign influence soon proves fatal for those who follow in her wake. Dionea is a strangely ambivalent figure who seems detached from and wholly unconcerned by the evil influence she exerts, a character both out of place and out of time, whose very existence is at odds with modern Christian society. Early in the narrative, lest her readers might have overlooked Heine's influence, one of the narrators, a scholar of pagan mythology, reveals himself to be 'enthralled by a tragic history, the history of the fall of the Pagan Gods', asking 'Have you ever read of their wanderings and disguises, in my friend Heine's little book?'[45] Soon Dionea's otherworldly nature begins to exert itself upon her environment as her true identity becomes apparent:

> Certain it is that the Pagan divinities lasted much longer than we suspect, sometimes in their own nakedness, sometimes in the stolen garb of the Madonna or the saints. Who knows whether they do not exist to this day? And, indeed, is it possible they should not? For the awfulness of the deep woods, with their filtered green light, the creak of the swaying, solitary reeds, exists, and is Pan; and the blue, starry May night exists, the sough of the waves, the warm wind carrying the sweetness of the lemon-blossoms, the bitterness of the myrtle on our rocks, the distant chaunt

> of the boys cleaning out their nets, of the girls sickling the grass under the olives, Amor-amor-amor, and all this is the great goddess Venus.[46]

As the story ends, Dionea disappears, having overseen the ritualistic death of the sculptor who was creating her statue, returning from historical time to the realm of myth: 'Some say they have seen her, on stormy nights, wandering among the cliffs [...] a Greek boat, with eyes painted on the prow, going full sail to sea, the men singing as she went. And against the mast, a robe of purple and gold about her, and a myrtle-wreath on her head, leaned Dionea, singing words in an unknown tongue, the white pigeons circling around her.'[47] 'Dionea' reveals the clash between two different and incompatible forms of temporality and the cultures through which they are sustained; on the one hand, the cyclical time of mythology and the eternal return of the pagan gods, and on the other the linear historical time of a Christian society on the cusp of secular modernity. Both here and throughout her work, Lee explores the impact of the mythic past as it returns momentarily to destabilise the present, with chaotic and unpredictable results.[48]

In her preface to *Hauntings*, Lee outlines her belief that the supernatural is a peculiar kind of history, a past that refuses to remain dormant and which exists in tandem with the present:

> That is the thing – the Past, the more or less remote Past, of which the prose is clean obliterated by distance – that is the place to get our ghosts from. Indeed, we live ourselves, we educated folk of modern times, on the borderland of the

> Past, in houses looking down on its troubadours' orchards and Greek folks' pillared courtyards; and a legion of ghosts, very vague and changeful, are perpetually to and fro, fetching and carrying for us between it and the Present.[49]

The past that Lee evokes is not the recent past that preoccupies hauntology, but rather the distant past of mythological time. And yet, paradoxically, despite its apparent distance from the present, this past continues to exist alongside us, just beneath the surface, and can be accessed by those attuned to its presence. 'They exist, these ghosts', Lee writes, 'only in our minds [...] They are things of the imagination, born there, bred there, sprung from the strange confused heaps, half-rubbish, half-treasure, which lie in our fancy, heaps of half-faded recollections, of fragmentary vivid impressions, litter of multi-coloured tatters'.[50] Lee's ghosts reside both in the distant past and within our heads, triggered by half-forgotten memories of time and place. Lee was dismissive of psychical research which she saw as antithetical to the imagination, arguing instead that there are 'no genuine ghosts in the scientific sense [...] no hauntings such as could be contributed by the Society for Psychical Research [...] no spectres that can be caught in definite places and made to dictate judicial evidence.' 'My ghosts', she claims, 'are what you call spurious ghosts (according to me the only genuine ones), of whom I can affirm only one thing, that they haunted certain brains, and have haunted, among others, my own and my friends.'[51]

These ghosts may reside in our memories and imagination rather than in physical reality but their presence is no less keenly felt as a result. Indeed, in her essay 'Faustus and Helena:

Notes on the Supernatural in Art' (1880) Lee argues that it is precisely because the ghostly is experienced through feeling and suggestion rather than reason that it maintains its power to evoke the past, providing us with a residual substitute for the primitive religions of antiquity:

> We none of us believe in ghosts as logical possibilities, but we most of us conceive them as imaginative possibilities; we can still feel the ghostly, and thence it is that a ghost is the only thing which can in any respect replace for us the divinities of old, and enable us to understand, if only for a minute, the imaginative power which they possessed, and of which they were despoiled not only by logic, but by art. By ghost we do not mean the vulgar apparition which is seen or heard in told or written tales; we mean the ghost which slowly rises up in our mind, the haunter not of corridors and staircases, but of our fancies. Just as the gods of primitive religions were the undulating, bright heat which made mid-day solitary and solemn as midnight [...] so the ghost, their only modern equivalent, is the damp, the darkness, the silence, the solitude [...] Each and all of these things, and a hundred others besides, according to our nature, is a ghost, a vague feeling we can scarcely describe, a something pleasing and terrible which invades our whole consciousness, and which, confusedly embodied, we half dread to see behind us, we know not in what shape, if we look around. [...] And the more complete the artistic work, the less remains of the ghost. Why do those stories affect us most in which the ghost is heard but not seen? [...] Why, as soon as a figure is seen, is the charm half-lost? [...] Do

not these embodied ghosts owe what little effect they still possess to their surroundings, and are not the surroundings the real ghost?[52]

Lee suggests that the ghostly resides in the apprehension of our immediate environment, in our sense of place or *genius loci*, and in asserting that the supernatural may be found in the ephemeral and impressionistic rather than in the logical and experiential she is proposing an aesthetic theory at odds with those aspects of the gothic which sought to present the ghostly in a more clearly embodied manner. This outlook is apparent throughout her fiction, both in *Hauntings* and elsewhere, in which the ghostly is always rendered as insubstantial and associative. It is her insistence that the very conception of the supernatural resides within the mythic time of pagan antiquity that foreshadows later studies of primitive religions as well as furthering our understanding of the temporal antecedents to hauntology.

It was the historian of religion, Mircea Eliade (1907-86) who famously distinguished between the sacred and the profane, and the two opposing forms of temporality through which they are expressed. Sacred time describes the point at which myths entered our world to give it meaning, the fabled time of 'beginnings', while profane or historical time is chronological and linear, and is the setting for the ordinary (non-religious) duration of time. According to Eliade, sacred or mythological time is cyclical by nature and allows for the reiteration of mythical events through ritual, in which the protagonists are transfigured, stepping outside of chronological time and returning to re-enact these primordial myths, not as spectators but as participants, experiencing the event as if for the first time. These myths therefore describe those moments when the sacred or supernatural breaks through into the world, the point at which the mythical and the historical intersect:

> For religious man time too, like space, is neither homogeneous nor continuous. On the one hand there are the intervals of sacred time, the time of festivals (by far the greater part of which are periodical); on the other there is profane time, ordinary temporal duration, in which acts without religious meaning have their setting. Between these two kinds of time there is, of course, solution of continuity; but by means of rites religious man can pass without danger from ordinary temporal duration to sacred time.
>
> One essential difference between these two qualities of time strikes us immediately: by its very nature sacred time is reversible in the sense that, properly speaking, it is a primordial mythical time made present. Every religious festival, any liturgical time, represents the reactualization of a sacred event that took place in the mythical past, 'in the beginning'. Religious participation in a festival implies emerging from ordinary temporal duration and reintegration of the mythical time reactualized by the festival itself. Hence sacred time is indefinitely recoverable, indefinitely repeatable. [....] The sacred time periodically reactualized in pre-Christian religions (especially in the archaic religions) is a mythical time, that is, a primordial time, not to be found in the historical past, an original time, in the sense that it came into existence all at once, that it was not preceded by another time, because no time

could exist before the appearance of the reality narrated in the myth.[53]

For the religious man of primitive or archaic society, Eliade explains, the eternal repetition of mythical time gives human existence its meaning. This cycle of eternal recurrence as time returns periodically through the observance of sacred ritual is experienced positively as significant and celebratory. This only remains the case, however, as long as the beliefs which underpin such rituals are maintained. In their absence, life is stripped of its meaning and cyclical time becomes hollow, mechanised and terrifying, an oppressive and endlessly repetitive cycle of meaningless time:

> For religious man of the primitive and archaic societies, the eternal repetition of paradigmatic gestures and the eternal recovery of the same mythical time of origin, sanctified by the gods, in no sense implies a pessimistic vision of life. [...] The perspective changes completely when the sense of the religiousness of the cosmos becomes lost. This is what occurs when, in certain more highly evolved societies, the intellectual élites progressively detach themselves from the patterns of the traditional religion. The periodical sanctification of cosmic time then proves useless and without meaning. The gods are no longer accessible through the cosmic rhythms. The religious meaning of the repetition of paradigmatic gestures is forgotten. But repetition emptied of its religious content necessarily leads to a pessimistic vision of existence. When it is no longer a vehicle for reintegrating a primordial situation, and hence

> for recovering the mysterious presence of the gods, that is, when it is desacralized, cyclic time becomes terrifying; it is seen as a circle forever turning on itself, repeating itself to infinity.[54]

This, Eliade tells us, is what happened in India, where the religious and philosophical elites despaired at the prospect of 'cyclic time repeating itself *ad infinitum*.'[55] Indeed, as the West appears to move inexorably towards a post-Christian society, so has our own sense of the duration of time become similarly divorced from the repetition of religious ritual that once lent it meaning. It is precisely such a sense of temporal disjunction, the belief that the linear flow of historical time has been disrupted or curtailed, which is characteristic of hauntology. In this context both Eliade's distinction between sacred and profane time, as well as Lee's depiction of history as a form of haunting, demonstrate similar and allied concerns with the ways in which the present may be undermined or haunted by a mythic past which falls outside our schema of temporal duration.

As we have seen, in 'Dionea' Lee outlines precisely such a scenario in her depiction of the impact of mythic return upon historical time, and this is a theme she returns to throughout her work. Elsewhere in *Hauntings*, for example, it is 'A Wicked Voice' (1890) which seems most directly relevant to our discussion of hauntology, for which it provides a clear precursor. Here, once again, Lee depicts the past as a trap, as her narrator is exposed to the horror of cyclical time. Set in a Venice floating 'in the stagnant lagoon of the past', the story has as its central character Magnus, a composer who is attempting to complete his opera; but following the disparaging comments he makes about a portrait of the eighteenth-century castrato, Zaffirino, he soon finds himself haunted by his voice.[56] Zaffirino, we learn, was once said to possess a voice of such unearthly beauty that women found it irresistible, and anyone exposed to its sound three times in succession would be struck dead. Magnus is soon bewitched by this ghostly, and potentially fatal, earworm which he comes both to despise and to long for in equal measure, recognising an agonising dependence upon a music he detests and which eventually drowns out his own musical inspiration. Unlike the castrato's earlier victims, however, Magnus survives, but only with the realisation that he must forever remain in thrall to Zaffirino, whose music has now displaced the possibility of him ever creating his own:

> Recovery? But have I recovered? I walk, and eat and drink and talk; I can even sleep. I live the life of other living creatures. But I am wasted by a strange and deadly disease. I can never lay hold of my own inspiration. My head is filled with music which is certainly by me, since I have never heard it before, but which still is not my own, which I despise and abhor: little, tripping flourishes and languishing phrases, and long-drawn, echoing cadences.[57]

The idea of a voice of such power that it can enchant the listener instinctively recalls us to the mythic past and the similarly destructive song of the Sirens; for Lee's depiction of music as both a haunted and haunting medium is particularly powerful in conveying the endless repetitions of myth. 'A

Wicked Voice', with its unwilling listener forced into a dependency upon a past he cannot escape, clearly foreshadows contemporary discussions around sonic hauntology, but it is another of Lee's tales that most memorably encapsulates the circularity of mythic time.[58]

'Amour Dure' (1890), also published in *Hauntings*, is again written in a rather fragmentary form, this time through the pages of its narrator's journal. The story describes the experiences of a Polish historian named Spiridion Trepka, who is conducting archival research in Umbria in 1885. As we shall see, the figure of the obsessive historian who becomes haunted by the subject of his research is something of a staple in the stories of MR James, and in this respect Lee's story acts as a template for much of James's work. In this instance, Trepka becomes infatuated by the portrait of a medieval noblewoman named Medea da Carpi, whose lovers, suitors and husbands all suffered mysterious deaths, seemingly at Medea's bidding, before she herself was finally put to death. As he learns more of her past, so Trepka's obsession grows, and gradually Medea's story begins to bleed into the present, his journal revealing glimpses of Medea in the street and in church. The past is being relived in the present with Trepka fulfilling the role of Medea's latest victim in a cyclical re-enactment of infatuation and vengeance. As the story reaches its conclusion, Trepka appears resigned to his fate, trapped within a historical cycle he is powerless to resist: 'And I, for what am I waiting? I don't know; all seems as a dream; everything vague and unsubstantial about me, as if time had ceased, nothing could happen, my own desires and hopes were all dead, myself absorbed into I know not what passive dreamland. Do I long for to-night? Do

I dread it? Will to-night ever come? Do I feel anything, does anything exist all around me?'[59]

Trépka has stepped out of historical time into mythic time, the still point where 'time had ceased', becoming a passive spectator to his own impending death, for despite the warnings he receives from the ghosts of Medea's earlier victims, the story unfolds inevitably towards his murder.[60] Lee's tale is a curious retelling of the myth of Medea, in which the past is repeatedly and violently restaged in the present. In the *Medea* of Euripides, Medea, deserted by Jason, takes her revenge by killing both his daughter and her own two sons by him. It is this vengeful figure which haunts Lee's tale, and through whom this cycle of violent retribution is enacted. Lee's concern here is for the mythic time of eternal recurrence, the primordial time outside of time which continues to repeat itself in the present, and which is symbolised by the inscription sealed on Medea's letter to Trepka, 'AMOUR DURE – DURE AMOUR', 'Love that lasts, cruel love.' This punning use of 'Dure' and the circularity of the inscription itself only re-emphasises the cyclical nature of mythic time, in which Trepka assumes a sacrificial role within the unending cycle of Medea's retribution.[61]

If Lee's peculiar sense of the past was coloured by her fondness for an assortment of pagan gods, classical myths and Renaissance artists, so too was she equally alert to the preoccupations of her late Victorian contemporaries. In her depiction of the uncanny effects of temporal disjunction, she not only foreshadows our own disquiet at the ways in which the present is subject to the distortions and repetitions of the past, but also highlights the widespread sense of temporal anxiety that underpinned her own age. We may well believe ourselves to be uniquely haunted by the revenants of our recent past, but there have been few historical periods subject to as profound a shift in the perception of time as the latter half of the nineteenth century, an era in which the remnants of the mythic past exhumed by Lee were overshadowed by the newly discovered realms of deep time.

Deep Time: Arthur Machen

Discussions of the work of Arthur Machen (1863-1947) are commonly prefaced with a reference to his unjust and prolonged obscurity; yet in recent years his works have enjoyed a welcome revival of interest. The reasons behind this new-found popularity are twofold: firstly, as a consequence of his role as an exemplary practitioner of weird fiction, a sub-genre which has garnered significant critical attention since the publication of ST Joshi's *The Weird Tale* in 1990, and which has since been explored in the work of, amongst others, China Miéville and Mark Fisher; and secondly through the identification of Machen's work as a significant precursor to psychogeography.[62] As his prominent position within the tradition of psychogeography would suggest, Machen is a figure who is regarded principally as a writer of place, both of his native Wales and his adopted home, London. Throughout his work, but particularly in his three volumes of autobiography, his recollections of these two locations take precedence over his discussion of both family and career.[63] Yet, not only is Machen a writer of place, he is also a writer of time, both of his own and also that of 'deep time', the vertigo-inducing expanse of the prehistoric past which forms the backdrop to so many of his early, and best-known stories. It is here, in his descriptions of those moments in which the ancient may unexpectedly intrude upon the present, in ways both malignant and benign, that Machen's work intersects with the contemporary concerns of hauntology.

In his discussion of the history of Gothic literature, Roger Luckhurst suggests a pattern of ebb and flow, in which he identifies three distinct waves in which the Gothic comes momentarily to the forefront of the popular imagination before once again retreating.[64] The first wave was inaugurated by the publication of Horace Walpole's *The Castle of Otranto: A Gothic Story* in 1764 and was followed by works such as Mary Shelley's *Frankenstein* (1818) before concluding with Charles Maturin's *Melmoth the Wanderer* (1820); the second wave struck in the late Victorian period with a cluster of the most famous works of the genre: Robert Louis Stevenson's *Strange Case of Dr Jekyll and Mr Hyde* (1886), Oscar Wilde's *The Picture of Dorian Gray* (1891), HG Wells' *The Island of Dr Moreau* (1896), and Bram Stoker's *Dracula* (1897) and continued into the early twentieth century before subsiding; the third wave, less clearly agreed upon, is marked by the 'horror boom' of the 1970s. 'For about 250 years', Luckhurst writes, 'this lowly, hybrid, barely controlled, vaguely embarrassing literature has not just survived but insisted on coming back repeatedly.'[65]

Characterised in this way, of course, the Gothic as a form comes strangely to resemble its content, a revenant form of fiction that refuses to be laid to rest, a hauntological, perhaps *the* hauntological literary genre, and one which, it would appear, is never far from the surface. But once these periods of ascendancy have been identified, the question then remains as to the cause of such periodic irruptions at these particular historical moments. The popularity of the Gothic in the 1790s has since been equated with the violent upheavals of the French Revolution, but what happened in the late Victorian era to provoke its re-emergence? Any explanation is less dependent upon a single historical event than it is upon the intellectual currents of the day, but what seems clear is that this period is one in which established distinctions between life and death, the material and the spiritual, the self and the other, the historical and the atemporal, were challenged by radical new ideas which threatened to erode or efface the boundaries between such categories.[66]

The publication of Charles Darwin's *The Origin of Species* in 1859 was the major intellectual challenge to the certainties of the Victorian worldview with its assault upon both the hitherto unquestioned division between the human and the animal, and the accepted timescale of biblical creation. Darwin's theory of evolution was, however, a one-way street, a progressive journey towards human perfectibility. But what if man were capable not only of evolution towards an enlightened future, but its opposite, a regression to some primordial state of bestial ignorance? By the late nineteenth-century, Darwin's successors had begun to pose such uncomfortable questions to a horrified public. The theory of degeneration, the belief in an evolutionary ladder which man might slip down as well as climb, originated in observations of regressions in the life cycle of sea squirts described by Edwin Ray Lankester in his *Degeneration: A Chapter in Darwinism* (1880).[67]

Foreshadowing the distinctly aquatic, or tentacular, nature of many of our subsequent literary encounters with the horrors of human reversion, Lankester's account of the downward spiral of evolutionary regression was soon extended to account for 'the animalism of the criminal classes, female hysterics and the insane, the hereditary taint that caused sons or daughters to regress, or even the decline of races, nations, and empires.'[68] The identification of degeneration as the evolutionary explanation for societal ills was given further impetus by the publication of Max Nordau's *Degeneration* in 1892 which played upon the middle-class public's fears of racial and biological pollution with great success. It was this widespread perception of a future haunted by the biological imperatives of an unwanted past that formed the backdrop to the emergence of the late Victorian gothic and to Machen's fledgling career as a writer. Machen's first published text, 'Eleusinia' (1881), a long poem he wrote at the age of 17, depicts the rites of Demeter's worship, reflecting an interest in the pre-Christian mythic time of the pagan gods which was expressed so vividly in the work of Vernon Lee; and it is this anachronistic conflict between an allegedly secular present and a pagan, pre-Celtic past which is the hallmark of Machen's most celebrated tale, 'The Great God Pan' (1890).

Machen's story begins in the haunted landscape of his Welsh homeland, in the ancient woodland of Gwent, as a doctor performs an experimental brain procedure on a young girl: 'a slight lesion in the grey matter, that is all; a trifling rearrangement of certain cells, a microscopical alteration that would escape the attention of ninety-nine brain specialists out of a hundred.'[69] The clinical language used by Dr Raymond to describe this operation masks its true purpose, however, which is a rather less than scientific attempt to rent the veil between present and past, between the material and immaterial: 'You see me standing here beside you, and hear my voice', Dr Raymond announces, 'but I tell you that all these things – yes, from that star that has just shone out in the sky to the solid ground beneath our feet – I say that all these are but dreams and shadows: the shadows that hide the real world from our eyes. There *is* a real world, but it is beyond this glamour and vision [...] beyond them all as beyond a veil [...] and the ancients knew what lifting the veil means. They called it seeing the god Pan.'[70] Needless to say, this experiment doesn't go quite as planned, and the patient, reduced to a grinning idiot by the horror of what she has seen dies nine months later having given birth to a child as a result of her demonic union with Pan. It is her daughter, Helen Vaughan, who, under various guises, haunts this story, leaving death and despair in her wake along with repeated inferences to unmentionable and unspeakable acts. The story ends with the extraordinary manner of her death as her body undergoes what appears to be a process of grotesquely accelerated degeneration: 'The blackened face, the hideous form upon the bed, changing and melting before your eyes from woman to man, from man to beast, and from beast to worse than beast'.[71]

There may seem little in Machen's tale, to the modern reader at least, to justify the overexcited critical reception it received, with *The Westminster Gazette* describing it as 'an incoherent nightmare of sex.'[72] Yet in its depiction, or rather presumption, of transgressive sex, alongside the startling dénouement of bodily dissolution, 'The Great God Pan' manages to play successfully upon many of the late Victorian era's fears over degeneration – corporal, moral, and spiritual

– in scenes to which Machen was to return repeatedly. For in this tale, as in many of those which were to follow, the present and all it represents – civilisation, progress, science, morality – is challenged by a distant past that refuses to remain dormant but instead threatens to return and overturn everything that the Victorians held dear. History is threatened by an ahistorical past, while the future is haunted by the ever-present possibility of a reversion to an earlier state. Time is clearly out of joint and not behaving as the Victorian public might have expected, in a linear fashion towards a preordained future; forward and upward, not backward and downward. Yet the theorists of evolutionary degeneration were not the only figures to upset the Victorian's sense of temporal equanimity, for the nineteenth century was to witness a revolution in the very conceptualisation of time itself.[73]

Until as late as the mid-nineteenth century the age of the Earth was a question less speculative than one might have presumed. There was a broad religious and scientific consensus that the world was 'no more than fifty or sixty centuries old', a span large enough to encapsulate 'the unfolding of the whole of known human history and therefore for the natural world, the stage on which it had been played out'.[74] In short, human history was coterminous with the history of the planet itself, leaving no need for the concept of prehistory. In fact, in the mid-seventeenth century the historian and archbishop, James Ussher, had calculated the precise date of the Creation to 4004 BC, a figure which was to remain remarkably durable over the next two centuries. One cannot then overestimate the profound shock which was to result from the 'time revolution' of the 1860s, as the Victorian world suddenly awoke to the idea that human history was a barely significant span of historical time preceded by an unimaginably vast expanse of unrecorded time. Thanks to Darwin's theory of natural selection, millions of years were now required to provide a timeframe for human evolution.[75] Archaeologists began to stratify human history into the Stone, Bronze and Iron Ages, while the publication of John Lubbock's *Prehistoric Times* (1865) introduced a further distinction between the Palaeolithic and the Neolithic, the Old and New Stone Age. Faced by the immensity of this newly revealed past, historians responded by using the concept of prehistory (the five-million year span between the emergence of the first humans and the beginning of recorded or written history some 6,000 years ago) as a 'buffer zone' with which to protect human history from the 'abysses of deep temporality'.[76]

Soon the newly emerging disciplines of ethnography and anthropology were attempting to fill this blank space with speculative outlines of our rediscovered ancestors. But the evolutionary model suggested that human development was an uneven process and that not all cultures might have progressed at the same rate. Alongside the belief in atavism, the possibility that human evolution might revert to a more primitive form, or that an earlier biological modification might reappear, it was now suggested that cultures or entire races might be classified according to the degree of cultural, intellectual and physical development they displayed.[77] In this light, the present could be haunted by the past in the form of a living race or individual in whom the past was embodied. For just as persons, events or objects might be subject to a chronological inconsistency that rendered them anachronisms, so too it seemed, to the Victorians at least, entire cultures or races might become misplaced in time, evolutionary anachronisms whose development had stalled or regressed within the aeons of this newly discovered past. It is through his recognition of intellectual currents such as these and the terrifying sense of an atemporal void that underpins them, that Machen's stories gain their enduring power. For the temporal juxtapositions he employs throughout his work act as a reminder to his readers, then as now, of the fragility of our historical categorisations and the futility of our attempts to keep 'deep history' at bay.[78]

The intrusion of the prehistorical past into the present is a recurrent theme of Machen's fiction but nowhere is he more explicit in his expression of these ideas than in 'The Novel of the Black Seal', first published as part of the series of interlinked tales that form *The Three Impostors* (1895). Here, the ethnologist, Professor Gregg, having come into the possession of a black seal containing the seemingly indecipherable markings of what he believes to be an ancient troglodytic race, eventually learns of their continued survival in the hills of South Wales. Gregg pursues his quarry only to discover that this malignant species possesses astonishing powers of transmutation, retained from an earlier evolutionary stage. When he fails to return from his final attempt to establish contact, a written record of these events is found:

> While I should be very loath to receive any one specific instance of modern spiritualism as containing even a grain of the genuine, yet I was not wholly prepared to deny that human flesh may now and then, once perhaps in ten million cases, be the veil of powers which seem magical to us – powers which, so far from proceeding from the

> heights and leading men thither, are in reality survivals from the depths of being. The amoeba and the snail have powers which we do not possess; and I thought it possible that the theory of reversion might explain many things which seem wholly inexplicable. Thus stood my position; I saw good reason to believe that much of the tradition, a vast deal of the earliest and uncorrupted tradition of the so-called fairies, represented solid fact, and I thought that the purely supernatural element in these traditions was to be accounted for on the hypothesis that a race which had fallen out of the grand march of evolution might have retained, as a survival, certain powers which would be to us wholly miraculous. [...] What if the obscure and horrible race of the hills still survived, still remained haunting wild places and barren hills, and now and then repeating the evil of the Gothic legend, unchanged and unchangeable as the Turanian Shelta, or the Basques of Spain?[79]

Two years later, Machen was to return to what he called his 'Little People' mythology in 'The Red Hand' (1897), in which the existence of an evolutionary survival from the ancient past once again threatens to upset the scientific and cultural certainties of late Victorian London:

> Who can limit the age of survival? The troglodyte and the lake-dweller, perhaps representatives of yet darker races, may very probably be lurking in our midst, rubbing shoulders with frock-coated and finely-draped humanity, ravening like wolves at heart and boiling with the foul passions of the swamp and the black cave. Now and then

> as I walk in Holborn or Fleet Street I see a face which I pronounce abhorred, and yet I could not give a reason for the thrill of loathing that stirs within me. [...] There are sacraments of evil as well as of good about us, and we live and move to my belief in an unknown world, a place where there are caves and shadows and dwellers in twilight. It is possible that man may sometimes return on the track of evolution, and it is my belief that an awful lore is not yet dead.[80]

It may be difficult for today's reader to see beyond the anxieties of race and class thinly concealed within the 'science' of ethnology employed in these tales, and yet the belief that previous cultures may have been left behind and that evolution operates at a different pace at different times was not then regarded as a work of fiction. Indeed, the anthropological theory of euhemerism, widely accepted at this time, suggested that the contemporary belief in 'little people' was in fact based upon the prehistoric existence of such a race. For just as the fossilised remains of the dinosaurs might provide retrospective validation for the belief in mythological dragons, so the euhemerist hypothesis of Victorian anthropologists such as David MacRitchie posited that 'a race of smaller-than-average people' had colonised Western Europe prior to the incursion of taller, Aryan or Celtic, tribes: 'Hounded out by the taller, more powerful Celts, these "Turanians" hid under the hills, appearing only at night, dancing by moonlight for exercise, and occasionally stealing food, and sometimes even women or babies, from their oppressors.'[81] Such a theory appeared to provide a scientific basis to the surprisingly widely-held belief in fairies at this time, and throughout the late nineteenth century accounts were published which suggested that such people still survived in inaccessible areas of Morocco, the Pyrenees and Switzerland.[82] Indeed, writing in 1898, Machen himself appears to subscribe to this view:

> Of recent years abundant proof has been given that a short, non-Aryan race once dwelt beneath ground, in hillocks, throughout Europe, their raths have been explored, and the weird old tales of green hills all lighted up at night have received confirmation. Much in the old legends may be explained by a reference to this primitive race. The stories of changelings, and captive women, become clear on the supposition that the "fairies" occasionally raided the houses of the invaders.[83]

In this light, in which the existence of the 'little people' is no longer presented as the subject of supernatural belief but rather as a matter of historical fact, the Victorian idea of atavistic degeneration becomes less a fear of a recurrent past than of a past that has always been with us. For such evolutionary 'survivals' no longer predate modernity as throwbacks to the deep history of a pre-human past but exist alongside the present, hidden, enduring and evolving, no longer a revenant race that comes back to haunt the present, but one that never went away. Machen's fiction once again calls into question the linearity of historical time, suggesting an alternative past located not prior to the present but adjacent to it, not the pre-historical but the ab-historical, an unrecognised realm that lies within our own and upon which it may intrude.[84]

Machen's work is preoccupied with borders and the consequences that arise when they are crossed, boundaries between reality and illusion, the material and immaterial, between life and death itself. But the boundaries that are most frequently challenged in his work are temporal, those between the present and the historical past, and the deep time that precedes them, whose return or revelation disrupts the certainties of the day. As we shall see in later chapters, it is precisely this interpenetration of past and present which is characteristic of hauntology, and it is to be found in the works of later writers such as Alan Garner, Susan Cooper and Nigel Kneale. Nowhere, however, has this theme been so singularly developed as in Machen's tales from the late nineteenth century. Perhaps one further reason behind Machen's welcome return to recognition in recent years lies precisely in his concern with the immeasurable depths of geologic time. For today we are all becoming increasingly accustomed to thinking in terms of deep time, or at least in categorising the present in increasingly geologic terms as we attempt to account for the consequences of humanity's effect on our environment. The proposed epochal classification of the Anthropocene is in this respect both an acknowledgement that the divergent scales of human and geologic time have momentarily intersected as well as an opportunity to recalibrate our own sense of the past in line with Machen's more expansive vision.

Freud and the Uncanny

Before hauntology there was the uncanny. In any discussion of hauntology and its antecedents, mention of Freud's essay, 'The

Uncanny' (1919) is inevitable, unavoidable. It is a work which continues to haunt academic discourse, a ghostly contagion that knows no borders, 'disordering any field supposedly extraneous to it.'[85] 'The world is uncanny', wrote Nicholas Royle in his study of the subject in 2003, concluding that everything it touched upon was brought within its remit, from machines and feelings, to concepts and beliefs, even Freud's essay itself: 'More than perhaps any other work by Freud, 'The Uncanny' itself seems uncanny in the sense that it keeps on doing different things not only to the reader but also, somehow, *to itself*.'[86]

Of course, the uncanny has a history of its own, one which predates Freud's examination of the concept, but in as far as it has been considered the subject of critical and philosophical reflection in its own right, its origins lie alongside those of hauntology, in the mid-nineteenth century, at the point from which this book embarks: 'Everything in Marx that speaks of a spectre that is haunting Europe, everything that has to do with notions of alienation, revolution and repetition, comes down to a thinking of the uncanny [...] It is not by chance that Derrida in 1993 thought to subtitle his long-awaited book on Marxism "Marx – *das Unheimliche*".'[87] Marx's fondness for the supernatural metaphor is well-documented and his works abound with reference to the spectral and the ghostly, to vampires and phantoms; while Derrida's indecision regarding the eventual title of his book simply affirms the degree to which the origins of hauntology are bound up with the works of both Marx and Freud.[88]

Just as the uncanny remains a notoriously slippery concept, eluding definition and allowing each new reader to find something different within the pages of Freud's essay, so too its relationship to time itself is similarly unmoored, floating free from the date of its publication in 1919, a period with which strangely it now seems to have little in common, and subsequently proving as resistant to temporal constraints as it has to any other form of categorisation. Within the chronology of my account, Freud's essay acts as a postscript to the extravagantly haunted years of the late nineteenth and early twentieth centuries, but in fact Freud's essay was largely overlooked at the time of its composition and for much of the time since has been allocated only a marginal position within the Freudian canon. Like the Gothic however, with which it shares a distinct family resemblance, the uncanny is also a revenant that refuses to lie dormant or to remain marginalised, and it has since returned with an impact immeasurably greater than that which greeted its introduction. It is only since the 1970s, when the uncanny re-emerged, firstly in France in the work of Lacan, Derrida and others, and then later in English and American literary theory, that Freud's essay has been widely disseminated, with the resulting claim that in fact the Freudian uncanny should be rightly regarded as a late-twentieth century theoretical concept.[89] In her book, *The Unconcept: The Freudian Uncanny in Late-Twentieth-Century Theory*, Anneleen Masschelein explores the history of the uncanny and its resurgence in recent decades, describing its heyday in the closing decades of the twentieth century, and identifying the 1990s as 'the phase of canonization and dissemination.'[90] Since then, however, the uncanny has retreated from its high-water mark and been subsumed within the wider continuum of haunting and spectrality that its re-emergence helped to instigate. An enduring characteristic of the uncanny, however, has been its ability to adopt new forms, a malleability that has allowed it to outlive fluctuations in intellectual fashion, a characteristic demonstrated by its appropriation of (or colonisation by) hauntology which has allowed the uncanny to sustain itself in recent years.[91]

Mark Fisher, a writer who returns repeatedly to Freud in his discussions of both hauntology and wider contemporary culture, has questioned whether Freud's insights still have the power to shock (or haunt) us given their almost total integration within mainstream culture: 'Cod Freudianism has long been metabolised by an advertising-entertainment culture which is now ubiquitous, as psychoanalysis gives way to a psychotherapeutic self-help that is diffused through mass media.'[92] Yet if this is true of Freudianism, cannot the same be said of the uncanny itself, whose recent overexposure has resulted in a similar fate at the hands of an academic-critical culture which is equally deadening in its effect.[93] In this sense, the uncanny may also be instructive as a case history, revealing how academic scrutiny can at first illuminate a subject before gradually mining the seam to its extinction, or at least to the point at which no one can bring themselves to discuss it any further. Freud's essay is nowadays not so much unfashionable as exhausted, and what was everywhere in the 1990s is now nowhere to be found. Superseded by the concept of hauntology, into whose spectral domain the uncanny has now largely been absorbed, the term has lost its currency to such an extent that one is forced to ask, is the uncanny still uncanny?

Freud begins his essay with a detailed semantic investigation of the *unheimlich*, the 'uncanny', 'eerie', 'unhomely', acknowledging that the term 'is not always used in a clearly definable sense, and so it commonly merges with what arouses fear in general.'[94] The task he sets himself is to identify just what it is about the uncanny that allows us to distinguish the word from that which is merely frightening, but also from that which is 'familiar' or 'homely', the *heimlich*. Looking at Freud's essay today, in the light of the endless scrutiny these terms have since been subjected to, it remains easy to forget that we are reading a translation from the German, and yet translation and the difficulty in rendering a precise English translation of the *unheimlich* is central to the exploration of these terms and the subtle shades of meaning they encapsulate. Thus it is the rather more awkward 'unhomely' which is in fact the English term etymologically closest to the German *unheimlich*, and which best captures that homely or familiar element that is encased within its uncanny opposite (or double). It is not the distance between the homely and unhomely, the *heimlich* and *unheimlich*, that Freud wants to emphasise, but rather their closeness, even their interchangeability; for as one critic notes 'the familiar and secure is always haunted by the strange and unfamiliar, while the unfamiliar often has a troubling familiarity about it':[95]

> among the various shades of meaning that are recorded for the word heimlich there is one in which it merges with its formal antonym, unheimlich, so that what is called heimlich becomes unheimlich. [...] This reminds us that this word heimlich is not unambiguous, but belongs to two sets of ideas, which are not mutually contradictory, but very different from each other – the one relating to what is familiar and comfortable, the other to what is concealed

> and kept hidden. [...] the term 'uncanny' (unheimlich) applies to everything that was intended to remain secret, hidden away, and has come into the open.[96]

Freud's essay famously fails to pin down a fixed definition of the uncanny, either in semantic terms, or through his attempts to elucidate examples of uncanny experiences, for the uncanny contains its own double within it, forever undermining its meaning and preserving its ambiguity. In this respect, the uncanny has much in common with the idea of haunting, for to 'haunt' is a similarly ambiguous term, one which, like the *unheimlich*, denotes the domestic familiarity of the habitual and the homely, alongside its more uncanny connotations.[97]

The second part of Freud's essay is largely given over to a close reading of ETA Hoffmann's celebrated uncanny tale 'The Sand-Man' (1816) whose protagonist, Nathanael, is haunted by his childhood terror of this legendary figure, which is said to steal the eyes of children. Both here and in Freud's discussion of Hoffmann's novel *The Devil's Elixirs* (1815) we encounter an array of images and ideas that have since become recognised as uncanny tropes, amongst them animate dolls, the doppelgänger, the experience of *déjà vu* and other forms of ghostly repetition. Indeed, doubling and repetition appear at the heart of Freud's sense of the uncanny, originating, he claims, in a more primitive phase of our mental development.[98] 'The double', he writes, 'has become an object of terror, just as the gods became demons after the collapse of their cult – a theme that Heine treats in 'Die Götter im Exil' ['The Gods in Exile'].'[99] Invoking the return to the mythic past which informed the tales of Vernon Lee, here Freud interprets the uncanny as a residual trace of an earlier developmental stage that we have failed to surmount. In a similar fashion the repetitive impulse is also understood as a manifestation of infantile or arrested development: 'In the unconscious mind we can recognize the dominance of a *compulsion to repeat*, which proceeds from instinctual impulses. [...] it is still clearly manifest in the impulses of small children and dominates part of the course taken by the psychoanalysis of victims of neurosis. The foregoing discussions have all prepared us for the fact that anything that can remind us of this inner compulsion to repeat is perceived as uncanny.'[100]

In his description of the ways in which the residual traces of primitive developmental phases may later be experienced as uncanny, Freud not only recalls Lee's sense of a present haunted by the mythic past but also Machen's tales of atavistic regression. The key difference, however, is the fact that while these tales were written against the backdrop of the mythic past and of deep time, Freud's anthropological theory is measured through the span of individual human development:

> The analysis of cases of the uncanny has led us back to the old animistic view of the universe, a view characterized by the idea that the world was peopled with human spirits, by the narcissistic overrating of one's own mental processes, by the omnipotence of thoughts and the technique of magic that relied on it, by the attribution of carefully graded magical powers (mana) to alien persons and things, and by all the inventions with which the unbounded narcissism of that period of development sought to defend itself against the unmistakable sanctions of reality. It appears that we

> have all, in the course of our individual development, been through a phase corresponding to the animistic phase in the development of primitive peoples, that this phase did not pass without leaving behind in us residual traces that can still make themselves felt, and that everything we now find 'uncanny' meets the criterion that it is linked with these remnants of animistic mental activity and prompts them to express themselves.[101]

In arguing that the psychological development of the child in modern society recapitulates the evolutionary history of the species, Freud is reworking ideas here that he first proposed in his *Totem and Taboo* (1913) in which the narcissistic animism of childhood is equated with the beliefs of primitive man. Yet if modern man has largely outgrown the childish delusions of his evolutionary forbears, there remains one area in which our primitive fears have remained largely undiminished, and it is here that the uncanny is experienced at its most powerful:

> To many people the acme of the uncanny is represented by anything to do with death, dead bodies, revenants, spirits and ghosts. [...] We might in fact have begun our investigation with this example of the uncanny – perhaps the most potent – but we did not do so because here the uncanny is too much mixed up with the gruesome and partly overlaid by it. Yet in hardly any other sphere has our thinking and feeling changed so little since primitive times or the old been so well preserved, under a thin veneer, as in our relation to death. [...] Since nearly all of us still think no differently from savages on this subject, it is not surprising that the

> primitive fear of the dead is still so potent in us and ready to manifest itself if given any encouragement. [...] Given this unchanging attitude to death, one might ask what has become of repression, which is necessary if the primitive is to return as something uncanny. But it is there too: so-called educated people have officially ceased to believe that the dead can become visible as spirits, such appearances being linked to remote conditions that are seldom realized, and their emotional attitude to the dead, once highly ambiguous and ambivalent, has been toned down, in the higher reaches of mental life, to an unambiguous feeling of piety.[102]

Here, finally, Freud brings himself to mention ghosts and spirits, coupled with the somewhat terse acknowledgement that in dealing with the uncanny one might have expected to find such subjects rather more to the foreground of his essay. In fact, Freud's obvious reluctance to deal with the supernatural is simply a consequence of his awareness of how damaging such a subject is likely to be to his scholarly credentials. In order for his theory to be regarded as sufficiently serious and 'scientific', then it must be clearly disassociated from 'the crude spectre of actual ghosts and the associated animistic worldview.'[103]

In the final part of his essay, Freud attempts to distinguish between uncanny events in life and in fiction, arguing that in the former case the uncanny 'arises either when repressed childhood complexes are revived by some impression, or when primitive beliefs that have been *surmounted* appear to be once again confirmed.'[104] In the case of fiction, however, the uncanny is 'much richer than what we know from experience' for the rules of repression that govern our real lives no longer apply, with the result that '*many things that would be uncanny if they occurred in real life are not uncanny in literature, and that in literature there are many opportunities to achieve uncanny effects that are absent in real life*.'[105] This distinction between life and fiction is an important one, not least because, as many commentators have since observed, Freud's essay appears to display many of the hallmarks of fiction itself, in which Freud alternates between unreliable narrator and protagonist, the hero of a psychoanalytic whodunit seeking to solve the mystery of the uncanny. If this is the case, not everyone has been convinced by his solution to the tale, in which the uncanny is finally unmasked to reveal the castration anxiety it conceals.[106] Yet if Freud's attempts to bring the uncanny within the remit of the psychoanalytic can appear disappointingly reductive, the fact remains that the uncanny has proved remarkably successful in eluding capture, escaping the confines of Freud's essay and coming back subsequently to haunt almost every conceivable form of cultural commentary, from art, photography and literature, to film, music and technology. 'Though written under the sign of the returning past', Hugh Haughton concludes, 'the Freudian uncanny, as both theory and narrative, shows every sign of persisting in new forms into the foreseeable future.'[107]

One such form the uncanny has since assumed is that of hauntology, in which the repetition and doubling to be found at the heart of Freud's concept are replayed through the returns and re-enactments of the historical past. Throughout his work, Freud depicts a future haunted by the unresolved trauma of the past. In *Mourning and Melancholia* (1917), for example, Freud distinguishes between two different responses to loss: on the one hand the conscious, healthy grief of mourning for a loved one; and on the other the unconscious, pathological disorder of melancholia which is confused by the lack of a clear object. Thus in Freudian terms haunting may be understood as the repeated return of the object of one's grief which results from a failure of mourning, a disruption or curtailment of its natural course. In this light, hauntology and psychoanalysis would appear to express a shared recognition that our inability to come to terms with the past and to complete the process of mourning will inevitably result in a failure to lay the ghosts that haunt us, both individually and as a society. In his final work, *Moses and Monotheism*, published shortly before his death in 1939, Freud explores the origins of religion, reinterpreting the biblical story of Moses, and arguing that his murder released an inherited guilt that has been passed down through subsequent generations. Here too, as Mark Fisher outlines, the aims of psychoanalysis and hauntology appear once again to coincide:

> Isn't Freud's thesis – first advanced in *Totem and Taboo* and then repeated, with a difference, in *Moses and Monotheism*, simply this: patriarchy is a hauntology? The father – whether the obscene Alpha Ape Pere-Jouissance of *Totem and Taboo* or the severe, forbidding patriarch of *Moses and Monotheism* – is inherently spectral. In both cases, the Father is murdered by his resentful children who want to re-take Eden and access total enjoyment. Their father's blood on their hands, the children discover, too late, that total enjoyment is not possible. Now stricken by guilt, they find that the dead Father survives – in the mortification of their own flesh,

and in the introjected voice which demands its deadening.[108]

If Fisher's reading of Freud is correct, and patriarchy is indeed a form of hauntology, then it follows by extension that not only are the origins of the family but those of religion and society itself, similarly invested with a 'hauntological dimension'.[109] Hauntology, it would seem, has expanded its remit to bring everything it touches within its ghostly embrace: the individual psyche, haunted by past trauma; the family, governed by the repressive cycle of patriarchy; religion, built upon the repetition and re-enactment of ritual; society, the patriarchal relationship writ large; and history itself, endlessly revisited by the ghosts of all its pasts. Just as once the world was seen as uncanny, so now it appears hauntological.

Archive Fever: MR James

Of all the many writers today associated with hauntology, whose works are routinely name-checked in any discussion of the subject, it is perhaps MR James (1862-1936) who recurs most persistently, his spare and reassuringly formulaic tales of haunted antiquarians and antiquarian hauntings repeatedly invoked in support of a peculiarly English tradition of ghostly imaginings. Writing in 2015, in an article entitled 'The eeriness of the English countryside', Robert Macfarlane states: 'We do not seem able to leave MR James behind. His stories, like the restless dead that haunt them, keep returning to us: re-adapted, reread, freshly frightening for each new era.'[110] The reasons behind James's enduring legacy are twofold, Macfarlane suggests: firstly, his long-acknowledged mastery of the eerie, 'that form of fear that is felt first as unease, then as dread, and which is incited by glimpses and tremors rather than outright attack'; and secondly, his understanding of the uncanny forces – 'part-buried sufferings and contested ownerships' – which underlie the landscape, and the English landscape in particular. 'James's influence, or his example', Macfarlane concludes, 'has rarely been more strongly with us than now. For there is presently apparent, across what might broadly be called landscape culture, a fascination with these Jamesian ideas of unsettlement and displacement. In music, literature, art, film and photography, as well as in new and hybrid forms and media, the English eerie is on the rise.'[111]

MR James is most commonly associated with the coastal landscapes of East Anglia, the setting for several of his best known stories, amongst them 'Oh, Whistle, and I'll Come to You, My Lad' (1904) and 'A Warning to the Curious' (1925), both of which were later the subject of memorable adaptations for television, and it has been through such reworkings of his stories that James's work continues to reach a new audience. It was a series of adaptations directed by Lawrence Gordon Clark as part of *A Ghost Story for Christmas* (1971-77) which were to prove the most influential of these, not only in maintaining James's reputation but in bringing the desolate landscapes of the East Anglian coast to life. Indeed, such has been the success of these and later versions of James's work that his stories are now inseparable from their visual counterparts, the two forever entwined in the popular imagination, with the consequence that many of James's tales have now established an uncanny afterlife of their own. This has resulted in a curious inability to place James's tales within their allotted timescale, one matched by a similar difficulty of categorisation within the tradition of the ghost story itself, of which James's stories are often regarded as foundation texts. For as several commentators have remarked, while the structure of James's fiction is unarguably emblematic of the classic ghost story, the ghosts themselves are altogether different from their disembodied Gothic predecessors:

> In inventing a new type of ghost, he departed considerably from the conventional Gothic traditions; for where the older stock ghosts were pale and stately, and apprehended chiefly through the sense of sight, the average James ghost is lean, dwarfish and hairy – a sluggish, hellish night-abomination midway betwixt beast and man – and usually touched before it is seen.[112]

HP Lovecraft, writing here in 1925, was an enthusiastic admirer of James's tales, to the extent that his own stories often mimic their structure, in which empirical common sense falters and finally crumbles in the face of an encounter with the supernatural. As well as Lovecraft, both China Miéville and Mark Fisher have also questioned the status of James's ghosts, arguing that 'demon' might in fact be a more accurate designation.[113] If the term 'ghost' is too anachronistic a term for James's distinctly tactile creations, then it is similarly misleading to regard James as foremost a writer of landscape, for he is equally at home in a more domestic setting, within the country houses, churches, guesthouses and railway stations in which his stories are so often staged.

There is, however, one setting that is recurrent throughout his fiction, that of the library or archive.

James's ghost stories have tended to be treated quite separately from his academic interests, not least by James himself who dismissed them as little more than idle entertainments; but his own antiquarian and archival pursuits supply the foundations to many of his stories, in which the intellectual curiosity of a lone male archivist or historian leads to horrifying consequences. James's own academic background was predominantly in the fields of palaeography, biblical and apocryphal studies, and much of his life's work was devoted to cataloguing the manuscript collections of the college libraries of Cambridge University. He may be regarded then, with some justification, as a potential victim of 'archive fever', a condition Simon Reynolds has described as 'the occupational ailment of librarians who spend too long in the stacks, a derangement afflicting academics and antiquarians as they test the limits of the human brain to digest information.'[114] Here, Reynolds draws upon Jacques Derrida's *Archive Fever: A Freudian Impression* (1996), a characteristically opaque account of the nature and function of the archive, in which he explores what it means to be '*en mal d'archive*' or 'in need of archives', an obsessive craving comparable to an addiction:

> It is to burn with a passion. It is never to rest, interminably, from searching for the archive right where it slips away. It is to run after the archive, even if there is too much of it [...] It is to have a compulsive, repetitive, and nostalgic desire for the archive, an irrepressible desire to return to the origin, a homesickness, a nostalgia for a return to the most archaic place of absolute commencement. No desire, no passion, no drive, no compulsion, indeed no repetition compulsion,

no "*mal-de*" can arise for a person who is not already, in one way or another, *en mal d'archive*.[115]

At the root of the word 'archive' is the double meaning of both 'commencement' and 'commandment' and, as Reynolds explains, the concept is 'deeply entangled with ideas of origin and order, authenticity and authority.'[116] Derrida identifies something sinister behind this nostalgic compulsion for endless repetition which lies at the heart of the archival impulse, tracing it back to the Freudian death drive, Thanatos, a regressive, primal instinct, more elementary than the pleasure principle, Eros, with which it coexists. Archive fever is then embedded within us, lying dormant but ready to present its symptoms in response to our compulsion to exert control over the past, an ailment clearly at work in James's antiquarian encounters but one increasingly expressive of our own condition, as we are submerged beneath an unprecedented deluge of information:

> 'Archive fever' is a good term for today's delirium of documentation, which extends beyond institutions and professional historians to the Web's explosion of amateur archive creation. There is a feeling of frenzy to all this activity; it's like people are slinging stuff 'up there' – information, images, testimonials – in a mad-dash hurry before some mass shutdown causes all our brains to burn out simultaneously. Nothing is too trivial, too insignificant, to be discarded [...] The result, visible above all on the Internet, is that the archive degenerates into the anarchive: a barely navigable disorder of data-debris and memory-trash. For the archive to maintain any kind of integrity, it

> must sift and reject, consign some memories to oblivion. History must have a dustbin, or History will be a dustbin, a gigantic, sprawling garbage heap.[117]

'The structure of the archive is *spectral*', Derrida writes, 'It is spectral *a priori*: neither present nor absent "in the flesh," neither visible nor invisible, a trace always referring to another whose eyes can never be met'; a ghostly presence, oppressed by the ever-expanding weight of the past, the archive is haunted by that which is missing or excluded.[118]

This spectral presence permeates James's fiction in which texts appear to acquire a malign agency, appearing, disappearing and returning, seemingly at will: in 'Number 13' (1904), for example, an indecipherable vellum document is found beneath the floorboards of a haunted room; 'The Diary of Mr Poynter' (1919) is found to contain a curious insertion within its pages; in 'Casting the Runes' (1911) Karswell's malicious spells are delivered on slips of paper which must be returned to their sender if the curse is to be undone; the removal of 'The Uncommon Prayer-book' (1921) from its rightful setting releases its malignant guardian; the sale of 'Canon Alberic's Scrap-book' (1895) conceals an unholy provenance; and a chance find in the library reveals the secret of 'Mr Humphreys and his Inheritance' (1911). Throughout James's work, texts of various sorts – Bibles, prayer-books, diaries, manuscripts, documents and notes – are used to deliver their invariably maleficent, and often fatal, message. Yet James's tales reveal an ambivalence towards these texts, whose understanding comes at a high cost and which must invariably be both read and destroyed.[119] Nowhere is this ambivalence displayed more clearly, and the archive haunted more feverishly, than in 'The Tractate Middoth' (1911).

James's works abound with the use of scholarly apparatus, those notes, translations and other bibliographical devices designed to add a semblance of authenticity to his tales, but 'The Tractate Middoth' must be one of very few stories to employ library classmarks within its pages. Opening within 'a certain famous library', the story sees the librarian, Mr Garrett, sent in search of an obscure volume: 'Talmud: Tractate Middoth, with the commentary of Nachmanides'. And yet the book resists his attempts to locate it, for someone, something, appears keen that this particular book should not be consulted. Seeking out this volume, Garrett experiences an unpleasant shock, for 'there's something wrong in the atmosphere of the library', 'a sort of unnaturally strong smell of dust' and at its source:

> I tell you, he had a very nasty bald head. It looked to me dry, and it looked dusty, and the streaks of hair across it were much less like hair than cobwebs. [...] He turned round to let me see his face [...] I didn't take in the lower part of his face. I did see the upper part, and it was perfectly dry and the eyes were very deep-sunk; and over them from the eyebrows to the cheek-bone there were cobwebs – thick.[120]

The story offers both an illustration of archive fever as well as a potential cure, for in a pattern familiar to so many of James's stories, our librarian decides upon a short holiday to recover from the shock of his unpleasant encounter, taking a train to Burnstow-on-Sea (Felixstowe) in Suffolk. Needless to say, however, the ghostly presence at the heart of James's story cannot be so easily eluded, and the malignancy which pervades the archive follows in Garrett's wake. On the train to Burnstow, Garrett meets a fellow passenger who, through an uncanny coincidence, reveals to him the story of her own search for a missing book, hidden in which is the will to a lost estate, her only clue being a slip of paper on which five numbers are printed. These Garrett recognises as the classmark of the Tractate Middoth, for this passenger, Mrs Simpson, is the cousin of John Eldred, the patron of the library who first instigated Garrett's search for the book. While the former wishes to locate the will, the latter seeks to destroy it, in accordance with the instructions of their malicious uncle, the clergyman Dr Rant, who died 20 years earlier, bequeathing the book and its puzzle to his heirs. Cutting short his holiday, Garrett returns to the library only to find that Eldred, unwilling to risk an encounter with the book's cobwebbed guardian, has had the book delivered to his home. Garrett follows the book by train hoping to induce Eldred to give it up to him, before pursuing his quarry on foot and finally witnessing his death at the hands of a shadowy form which embraces him just at the moment at which he attempts to tear out the book's fly-leaf, on which the missing will is written. Returning the following day to the site of Eldred's demise, Garrett finds 'a thick black mass of cobwebs, and as he stirred it gingerly with his stick several large spiders ran out of it into the grass.'[121] The story ends with Mrs Simpson inheriting the estate and with Garrett marrying her daughter.

James's tale contains all the familiar elements one is accustomed to finding in his stories: the donnish bachelor and the bookish environment; the haunted object and the ghostly encounter; the train journey and escape to East Anglia; the pursuit and horrifying dénouement. But what is also apparent here, as throughout his work, is a tension between the interior and the exterior, between the domestic and the familiar on the one hand, and a malevolent landscape on the other. Discussing James's work in *The Weird and the Eerie* (2016), Mark Fisher notes the tension between these boundaries: 'For James, the outside is always coded as hostile and demonic. When he read his ghost stories to his Cambridge audience at Christmas, the glimpses of exteriority they offered no doubt brought a thrill to his listeners, but they also came with a firm warning: venture outside this cloistered world at your peril.'[122] Fisher employs this distinction in his analysis of the weird and the eerie, arguing that while both categories are 'fundamentally to do with the outside', the latter 'seldom clings to enclosed and inhabited domestic spaces; we find the eerie more readily in landscapes partially emptied of the human.'[123] But as 'The Tractate Middoth' illustrates, while these landscapes may be imbued with malevolence, they are also the customary retreat of academics and archivists seeking respite from what are often equally haunted interiors. It would appear that the ghosts or demons which populate James's stories have little respect for boundaries, and while the few inhabitants of James's sparsely populated landscapes often appear outnumbered by their ghostly counterparts, so too are his churches, libraries and guesthouses no barrier against the encroachments of the supernatural. In what Adam Scovell has identified as the 'chief meme' of James's stories, 'even when stories remain stubbornly in dusty rooms, libraries and churches; the outside still somehow always seems to find its way in.'[124] And as the library housing the Tractate Middoth demonstrates, the reverse is also true, and what is inside always seems to find its way out.

In addition to this distinction between interior and exterior, Fisher also characterises the weird and the eerie in terms of presence and absence: 'the Weird is constituted by a presence – the presence of *that which does not belong*. [...] The eerie, by contrast, is constituted by a failure of absence or by a failure of presence. The sensation of the eerie occurs when there is something present where there should be nothing, or if there is nothing present when there should be something.'[125] Both categories seem applicable to James's work, in which an array of found objects – a whistle, a crown, binoculars, and myriad texts – carry a powerfully weird charge, but are invariably located within an eerily desolate landscape, characterised by a largely absent population. In 'The Tractate Middoth' these two categories coexist within the library, in which the weirdly demonic presence of Dr Rant is accompanied by an eerie gap in the shelves – a book which ought to be present but is not. The archive itself is something of a challenge to Fisher's distinction, for as Derrida claims, it is by its very nature spectral, neither wholly present nor absent, visible nor invisible, and yet as he also acknowledges, the archive is inevitably haunted by what it excludes. This is certainly true of the Tractate Middoth itself, which is eerily absent throughout, seemingly always one step ahead of its pursuers; but more often in James's work the reverse is true, and libraries and archives are haunted not by what is missing but by what they unexpectedly reveal, a book or manuscript that is present where none was expected, an unexplained addition which has evaded classification and whose discovery heralds an unexpected series of events.[126]

While James's work has been widely considered in terms of the weird and the eerie, it has received far less attention in terms of the third category in this critical triumvirate, the uncanny. In fact James's work has been discussed surprisingly little in Freudian terms, surprising because as even a cursory glance at his work would indicate, one cannot help but feel that Freud would have found ample material here for analysis. Indeed, when one considers the narrowly circumscribed nature of James's Edwardian existence, a life bounded by the twin institutions of Eton and Cambridge, reflected in works populated almost exclusively by similarly donnish figures overwhelmed by forces inexplicable to them, one can only conclude that his fiction has been spared a form of interpretation to which it seems particularly vulnerable. Of course, it has been impossible to overlook the symbolic language of so many of James's stories with their dark wells and cavities, crumpled bedsheets and linen, and above all the *hairiness* of his shockingly tactile creations, seemingly so eager to embrace their victims.[127] But the first writer to risk the outrage of James's loyal readership by exposing his work to a Freudian reading, was one who has since been accorded a major role in the history of hauntology, Nigel Kneale. Kneale's work will be discussed in the following chapter, but it was his brief introduction to the Folio Society edition of James's work in 1973 that risked consternation amongst James's supporters:

> Yet the paradox of James's fiction is that whereas the elaborate documentation was always wholly invented, the

haunting horror may have been the truth – about himself, about his inner world.

In an age when every man is his own psychologist, MR James looks like rich and promising material. Such a story as The Treasure of Abbot Thomas, with its groping down a fetid well and the implications of its climax – but never mind, analysis becomes nonsense here, as irrelevant as smashing a pearl to get at the original particle of grit. [. . .] What went on behind Dr James's scholarly façade is no longer important. All that matters is what his imagination shaped it into and the way he wrote it down.

In his real world his closest companions were a cat and her kittens. In the other '. . . terrible bodies began to break out of the trunk, and it was seen that these were covered with greyish hair . . .' In despising rational explanations he was perhaps paying a kind of respect to himself. There must have been times when it was hard to be Monty James.[128]

Kneale's teasing introduction suggests that James's avoidance of rational solutions to his tales may have been a form of self-defence mechanism protecting him from laying bare his own inner motivations. Kneale acknowledges James's willingness to refashion the landscapes of his own nightmares into a 'wholly alien place' in which inanimate everyday objects 'stir into life beneath one's hand.'[129] And as we shall see, the idea of a recovered object, alien in time and place, returning to disrupt the present, 'the Jamesian object' as one critic has described it, is a hallmark not only of James's and Kneale's work, but one of the most recognisable tropes of hauntology itself.[130]

In 1957, Jacques Tourneur directed *Night of the Demon*,

his adaptation of James's 'Casting the Runes' (1911), thus inaugurating the history of folk horror in England. Folk horror will be the subject of a later chapter, but it is revealing of a movement more commonly associated with the 1960s and 1970s, that it is the Edwardian Monty James who should be regarded as its progenitor. Like hauntology itself, with which it shares a curious symbiosis, folk horror is a constellation of ideas and individuals that has proven similarly resistant to definition and categorisation. In his history of the movement and its recent revival, Adam Scovell names MR James, alongside Robin Hardy, Nigel Kneale and Alan Garner, as one of its key representatives.[131] James sits rather awkwardly amongst this group, a revenant of an earlier age, returning to haunt an era which would no doubt have horrified him, although perhaps not in the manner his inclusion here might suggest. In some ways, however, James's adoption into this movement is curiously apt. Just as his presence here is chronologically disruptive, an anachronism characteristic of his fiction, so too is such temporal dislocation equally representative of the wider strategies of both folk horror and hauntology itself:

> Folk Horror often mimics this idea of looking back, where the past and the present mix and create horror through both anachronisms and uncomfortable tautologies between eras. [...] whereby era and temporality are linked by esoteric, inexplicable events; things that unnerve through a sheer recognisability of darker ages that are beginning to reoccur. Folk Horror, the horror of 'folk', is out of time and within time, with strangers in the landscape who have survived the ravages of modernity.[132]

James's antipathy towards modernity has been well documented and one senses that he felt all future change was to be resisted or ignored.[133] Time comes to a halt in his fiction; it stops within a perpetual present of close, fixed routine mapped out by train timetables and church services, an unalterable past and endlessly replayed present acting as bulwarks against an unwelcome future. Just as the landscapes of the English countryside are depicted as reassuringly impermeable to change, a timeless topography of country houses and comfortable hotels, so too are the institutions of club and college, church and library similarly immutable, symbolic of a world in which the past is catalogued and controlled, the future permanently on hold. Of course, what haunts James's stories is precisely that which eludes control, those remnants of the past which refuse to be domesticated and which return, repeatedly, to disrupt the present.

'For the ghost story a slight haze of distance is desirable. "Thirty years ago", "Not long before the war", are very proper openings.'[134] Written in 1924, these comments reflect James's preference for the late Victorian and Edwardian settings of so many of his stories. On occasion he retreats further into the past but James believed that it was the near and not the distant past that provided the most suitable time-frame for his work: 'It cannot be said too often that the more remote in time the ghost the harder it is to make him effective, always supposing him to be the ghost of a dead person. [...] Roughly speaking, the ghost should be a contemporary of the seer. Such was the elder Hamlet and such Jacob Marley.'[135] His stories articulate a nostalgic longing for the past, but not any past, or indeed anybody's past other than his own. In this regard James shows himself to be faithful not only to the conventions of the ghost story but to the logic of hauntology, of which he must rightly be regarded as a progenitor. For as Dylan Trigg observes, hauntology is bound by precisely the same temporal discipline as James demonstrates in his fiction:

> Exemplary of the logic of hauntology, M.R. James draws together a constellation of different eras in the same figure; namely, the figure of the spectre emerging from the sand on the Suffolk coastline [...] The gesture of imbuing an otherwise placid landscape with the phantoms of antiquity is central to hauntology. Only in the case of hauntology, the past is not a remote one but instead a time that has been compressed, dating back no more than thirty or forty years – that is, largely to the childhood of those who assign their own past as the site of haunting.[136]

Trapped or rather willingly interred within the landscapes of his own endlessly recreated youth, James was able to finesse the rules of his hauntological miniatures, establishing a template for future practitioners of the ghost story.[137] So influential have James's stories since become, however, that his template for the future of the ghost story has effectively curtailed that future, his resistance to change so tightly encoded in his texts that they permit only repetition. Writing in 1977, Julia Briggs bemoaned the state of the contemporary ghost story, arguing that 'it has become a vehicle for nostalgia, a formulaic exercise content merely to recreate a Dickensian or Monty Jamesian atmosphere. It no longer has any capacity for growth or adaptation.'[138] Of course, it is precisely this sense of the reassuringly formulaic that is, for many, the principal attraction of James's stories, their repetitions compelling us to return, repeatedly, to his re-enactments of an unchanging past. Today the ghost story retains the imperative James inaugurated more than a century ago, remaining, in the words of China Miéville, 'overwhelmingly, exclusively hauntological, their figures revenant dead in time out of joint.'[139]

Notes

1 Karl Marx and Friedrich Engels, 'Manifesto of the Communist Party' in *The Communist Manifesto*, ed. by AJP Taylor, Harmondsworth: Penguin, 1967, 77-121, p. 78.

2 Charles Dickens, 'The Haunted Man and the Ghost's Bargain' in *The Christmas Books*, ed. by Ruth Glancy, Oxford: Oxford University Press, 1988, 373-472, p. 373.

3 Friedrich Engels, 'Revolution in Paris', *Deutsche-Brüsseler-Zeitung*, 27 February 1848, at https://marxists.architexturez.net/archive/marx/works/1848/02/27.htm

4 *The Manifesto of the Communist Party* was first translated into English by Helen Macfarlane and was serialised in Julian G Harney's socialist newspaper, *The Red Republican*, between June and November 1850.

5 Svetlana Boym, 'Nostalgia' in *Atlas of Transformation* (2011) at http://monumenttotransformation.org/atlas-of-transformation/html/n/nostalgia/nostalgia-svetlana-boym.html

6 'The turning point at which modern history failed to turn', as the historian GM Trevelyan described the failed uprisings

of 1848. See GM Trevelyan, *British History in the Nineteenth-Century (1782-1901)*, London: Longmans, Green & Co, 1922, p. 292.

[7] Nicola Brown, Carolyn Burdett and Pamela Thurschwell, eds., *The Victorian Supernatural*, Cambridge: Cambridge University Press, 2004, Introduction, 1-19, p. 1.

[8] Charles Dickens, 'Review: '*The Night Side of Nature; or, Ghosts and Ghost Seers* by Catherine Crow', *The Examiner*, 26 February 1848, reprinted in Michael Slater, ed., *Dickens' Journalism: The Amusements of the People and Other Papers: Reports, Essays and Reviews 1834-1851*, Vol. II, London: J.M. Dent, 1996, 80-91, p. 83, and quoted by Andrew Smith in *The Ghost Story, 1840-1920: A Cultural History*, Manchester: Manchester University Press, 2010, Introduction, p. 1.

[9] For a brief history of Dickens's involvement in the Ghost Club, see Peter Hoskin, 'Ghost Club: Yeats's and Dickens's Secret Society of Spirits', *The Paris Review*, 31 October 2017.

[10] Charles Dickens, 'A Christmas Carol' in *The Christmas Books*, ed. by Ruth Glancy, Oxford: Oxford University Press, 1988, 1-90, pp. 18-19.

[11] Dickens, *A Christmas Carol,* p. 5.

[12] Dickens, *A Christmas Carol,* p. 69.

[13] Smith, *The Ghost Story, 1840-1920: A Cultural History*, p. 5.

[14] China Miéville, 'M.R. James and the Quantum Vampire. Weird; Hauntological: Versus and/or and and/or or?', *Weird Fiction Review*, 29 November 2011.

[15] Philip Ball, *Invisible: The Dangerous Allure of the Unseen*, London: The Bodley Head, 2014, p. 59.

[16] See Adam Scovell, 'The Ghost in the Grain: Analogue Hauntings of the 1970s', 22 October 2017 at https://

celluloidwickerman.com/2016/10/22/the-ghost-in-the-grain-folk-horror-revival-the-british-museum-16102016/

17 Charles Dickens, *Great Expectations*, ed. by Margaret Cardwell, Oxford: OUP, 2008, p. 113.

18 Steven Connor, 'Dickens, The Haunting Man (On L-iterature)' (2002) at http://stevenconnor.com/haunting.html

19 Charles Dickens, 'The Haunted Man and the Ghost's Bargain' in *The Christmas Books*, ed. by Ruth Glancy, Oxford: Oxford University Press, 1988, 373-472, pp. 389-90.

20 Dickens, 'The Haunted Man', p. 392.

21 Dickens, 'The Haunted Man', pp. 394-5.

22 Dickens, 'The Haunted Man', p. 421.

23 Dickens, 'The Haunted Man', p. 445.

24 Dickens, 'The Haunted Man', p. 377.

25 Jim Steinmeyer, *Hiding the Elephant: How Magicians Invented the Impossible*, London: Arrow Books, 2005, p. 22.

26 Steinmeyer, p. 22.

27 Steinmeyer, pp. 22-23.

28 Ball, p. 80.

29 Henry Dircks, *The Ghost! As produced in the Spectre Drama, popularly illustrating the marvellous optical illusions obtained by the apparatus called the Dircksian Phantasmagoria*, London: E & FN Spon, 1863, p. 65, quoted by Helen Groth in 'Reading Habits and Magic Lanterns: Dickens and Dr Pepper's Ghost', in *Moving Images: Nineteenth-Century Reading and Screen Practices*, Edinburgh: Edinburgh University Press, 2013, 100-126, pp. 113-114. For an alternative reading of these events see Steinmeyer, pp. 29-30.

30 Ruth Glancy in Charles Dickens, *Christmas Books*, Introduction, p. xxi.

[31] Owen Davies, *The Haunted: A Social History of Ghosts*, Basingstoke: Palgrave Macmillan, 2007, p. 207.

[32] Davies, p. 207.

[33] Tom Gunning, 'To Scan a Ghost: The Ontology of Mediated Vision', in *The Spectralities Reader: Ghosts and Haunting in Contemporary Cultural Theory*, ed. by María del Pilar Blanco and Esther Peeren, London: Bloomsbury, 2013, 207-244, p. 228.

[34] Martin Harries writes: 'In England, in 1863, the year of London's rage for Dircks's machine, it was possible to see a ghost, and sometimes several competing ghosts, any day of the year.' See Martin Harries, *Scare Quotes from Shakespeare: Marx, Keynes, and the Language of Reenchantment*, Stanford CA: Stanford University Press, 2000, pp. 28-9.

[35] Davies, pp. 208-9.

[36] Harries, p. 37.

[37] Davies, p. 238.

[38] Gunning, pp. 228-9.

[39] Gunning, pp. 228-9. In what must surely be the only novel to employ a sheet of glass to such dramatic effect, Christopher Priest's *The Islanders* (2011) appears to pay homage to the Pepper's Ghost illusion. Characterised by the themes of temporal dislocation and the technological uncanny, much of Priest's work has a distinct hauntological flavour. For a discussion of his work in the context of the eerie, see Mark Fisher, *The Weird and the Eerie*, London: Repeater Books, 2016, pp. 65-76.

[40] Gunning, pp. 228-9.

[41] Vernon Lee, 'Amour Dure' in *Supernatural Tales*, ed. by I Cooper Willis, London: Peter Owen, 2004, 86-126, pp. 117-8.

[42] Sondeep Kandola, *Vernon Lee*, Tavistock: Northcote House, 2010, p. 2.

[43] Heinrich Heine, 'The Gods in Exile' in *Prose Miscellanies from Heinrich Heine*, trans. by SL Fleishman, Philadelphia, PA: Lippincott, 1876, 216-244, pp. 216-217.

[44] Vernon Lee, 'Dionysus in the Euganean Hills: W.H. Pater in Memoriam', *Contemporary Review*, 120, September 1921, 346-53. For a modern reworking of Heine's tale which imagines in what form the gods might be employed in twenty-first century society – Poseidon as lifeguard, Apollo as busker – see Alexandra Turney, 'Gods in Exile – a collection of very short stories' at https://unbound.com/books/in-exile/updates/gods-in-exile-a-collection-of-very-short-stories

[45] Vernon Lee, 'Dionea', in *Late Victorian Gothic Tales*, ed. by Roger Luckhurst, Oxford: OUP, 2005, 3-26, p. 8.

[46] Lee, 'Dionea', p. 15.

[47] Lee, 'Dionea', p. 26.

[48] Catherine Maxwell and Patricia Pulham write: 'the mythic return, whether in the form of a person or artefact, can temporarily disturb or irradiate the present with an exotic beauty and power that rouses desire, fear, and a sad awareness of latter-day lacks and deficiencies.' See Vernon Lee, *Hauntings and Other Fantastic Tales*, ed. by Catherine Maxwell and Patricia Pulham, Ontario: Broadview Editions, 2006, Introduction, 9-27, p. 14.

[49] Vernon Lee 'Preface to *Hauntings* (1890)' in *Hauntings*, pp. 37-40.

[50] Lee 'Preface to *Hauntings* (1890)' pp. 37-40.

[51] Lee 'Preface to *Hauntings* (1890)' pp. 37-40.

[52] Vernon Lee, 'Faustus and Helena: Notes on the Supernatural

in Art' (1880) in *Hauntings,* pp. 309-11.

[53] Mircea Eliade, *The Sacred and the Profane: The Nature of Religion*, trans. by Willard R Trask, New York: Harcourt Brace, 1959, pp. 68-72.

[54] Eliade, *The Sacred and the Profane*, p. 107.

[55] Eliade, *The Sacred and the Profane*, p. 109.

[56] Vernon Lee, 'A Wicked Voice' in *Supernatural Tales*, 127-158, p. 137.

[57] Lee, 'A Wicked Voice', p. 158.

[58] For an account of the mythological roots of 'A Wicked Voice' see VH Leslie, 'Lost in Time: The Wicked Voice of Vernon Lee', at https://www.thisishorror.co.uk/columns/bloodlines/voices-work-vernon-lee/

[59] Vernon Lee 'Amour Dure' in *Hauntings,* 41-76, p. 74.

[60] Smith, *The Ghost Story, 1840-1920*, p. 81.

[61] Christa Zorn, *Vernon Lee: Aesthetics, History, and the Victorian Female Intellectual*, Athens, OH: Ohio University Press, 2003, p. 164.

[62] For an account of Machen's role as a precursor to psychogeography, see Merlin Coverley, *Psychogeography*, Harpenden: Oldcastle Books, 2018, and 'The Art of Wandering: Arthur Machen's London Science', in *Walking Inside Out*, ed. by Tina Richardson, London: Rowman and Littlefield, 2015, 103-114.

[63] Aaron Worth, 'Introduction', in Arthur Machen, *The Great God Pan and Other Horror Stories*, Oxford: OUP, 2018, ix-xxx, p. xi.

[64] Roger Luckhurst, 'Introduction', in *Late Victorian Gothic Tales*, Oxford: OUP, 2005, ix-xxxi, p. ix.

[65] Luckhurst, *Late Victorian Gothic Tales* p. ix.

[66] Luckhurst, *Late Victorian Gothic Tales* pp. xii-xii.
[67] Luckhurst, *Late Victorian Gothic Tales* p. xx.
[68] Luckhurst, *Late Victorian Gothic Tales* p. xx.
[69] Arthur Machen, 'The Great God Pan', in *Late Victorian Gothic Tales*, ed. by Roger Luckhurst, 183-233, p. 184.
[70] Machen, 'The Great God Pan', p. 184. 'Pan had an extensive presence in Victorian literature', Roger Luckhurst notes, 'in which his death is seen to mark the passage from a pagan to a Christian World.' (p. 278).
[71] Machen, 'The Great God Pan', p. 232.
[72] Gary Lachman, *The Dedalus Book of the Occult: A Dark Muse*, Sawtry: Dedalus, 2003, p. 191.
[73] See Aaron Worth, 'Arthur Machen and the Horrors of Deep History', *Victorian Literature and Culture*, 40 (1), Cambridge: CUP, 2012, 215-227.
[74] Worth, 'Introduction', in Arthur Machen, *The Great God Pan and Other Horror Stories*, pp. xxii-xxvi.
[75] Worth, 'Introduction', in Arthur Machen, *The Great God Pan and Other Horror Stories*, pp. xxii-xxvi.
[76] Worth, 'Arthur Machen and the Horrors of Deep History', pp. 215-217. Here, Worth writes: 'In the course of the nineteenth century a new conceptual space emerged, itself representing a powerful, collective act of integration, which we call "deep time" (the phrase is of course of recent mintage, but it captures a contemporaneous, and pervasive, conceptual metaphor). Historians were then confronted with a problem: how to integrate the timescale of their own domain, the conceptual space of historical time, with the new chronologies of depth – a prospect fraught, as we have seen, with a number of anxieties.' (pp. 215-7).

[77] For an account of evolutionary atavism, the emergence of the comparative method in anthropology, and the role of both in Machen's work, see Robert Mighall, *A Geography of Victorian Gothic Fiction: Mapping History's Nightmares*, Oxford: OUP, 1999, pp. 130-165.

[78] Aaron Worth writes: 'Machen travesties the very categories that were emerging within Victorian intellectual culture, historiography in particular, to distinguish "civilized" from "savage," "history" from "prehistory" (and both of these from what came before). He articulates, in other words, the "deep history" that the later Victorian era was keen to repress.' Aaron Worth, 'Introduction', Arthur Machen, *The Great God Pan and Other Horror Stories*, pp. xxii-xxvi.

[79] Arthur Machen, 'The Novel of the Black Seal' (1895) in *The White People and Other Weird Stories*, ed. by ST Joshi, London: Penguin, 2011, 29-66, pp. 57-59.

[80] Arthur Machen, 'The Red Hand' (1897) in *The White People and Other Weird Stories*, 83-110, p. 84 & 93.

[81] Emily Fergus, '"A Wilder Reality" Euhemerism and Arthur Machen's "Little People"' in *Faunus: The Decorative Imagination of Arthur Machen*, ed. by James Machin, London: Strange Attractor, 2019, 211-223, pp. 212-215.

[82] Fergus, pp. 212-215.

[83] Arthur Machen, 'Folklore and Legends of the North', *Literature*, 24 September, 1898, p. 272, and quoted by ST Joshi in Arthur Machen, *The White People and Other Weird Stories*, Introduction, p. xiv.

[84] Kimberly Jackson, 'Non-Evolutionary Degeneration in Arthur Machen's Supernatural Tales', *Victorian Literature and Culture*, 41 (1) 2013, Cambridge: Cambridge University Press,

125-135, p. 130.

[85] Nicholas Royle, *The Uncanny*, Manchester: Manchester University Press, 2003, p. 2.

[86] Royle, *The Uncanny*, p. 8.

[87] Royle, *The Uncanny*, pp. 3-4. In his introduction to Freud's essay, Hugh Haughton writes: 'I have found no examples of "uncanny" in this sense prior to the nineteenth century. It gains its spectral aesthetic currency after 1850, during the period in which the modern ghost story developed.' See Hugh Haughton in Sigmund Freud, *The Uncanny*, trans. by David McLintock, London: Penguin, 2003, Introduction, p. lix.

[88] John Fletcher, 'Marx the Uncanny? Ghosts and their Relation to the Mode of Production', *Radical Philosophy*, 75, January/February 1996, 31-37, p. 32.

[89] Anneleen Masschelein, *The Unconcept: The Freudian Uncanny in Late-Twentieth-Century Theory*, Albany, NY: State University of New York Press, 2011, pp. 3-4.

[90] Masschelein, pp. 5-6. See also Martin Jay's essay, 'Force Fields: The Uncanny Nineties', *Salmagundi*, 1995, 20-29.

[91] Dylan Trigg writes: 'Part of the uncanny's appeal is its ability to morph into new forms, infecting the host discipline with a strange horizon of uncertainties. [...] Yet of all the modes of appropriation, it is surely Derrida's concept of "hauntology" that has been the most significant in bearing the mark of the uncanny for ongoing research in the field. [...] In part, this may be because it is a porous concept and has lent itself especially well to our culture, which is defined in large by a glorified relationship with the past, an uneasy relation with the present, and a failure to envision a future different from the present. Hauntology fits neatly into this confused

temporality, blending anxiety and nostalgia in one term.' Dylan Trigg, 'The Return of the Uncanny' *3:AM Magazine*, 13 November 2012, at https://www.3ammagazine.com/3am/the-return-of-the-uncanny/

92 Mark Fisher, 'The Lost Unconscious: Christopher Nolan's *Inception*' (2011), in *Ghosts of My Life: Writings on Depression, Hauntology and Lost Futures,* Winchester: Zero Books, 2014, 208-220, p. 219.

93 Roger Luckhurst writes: 'Gothic criticism, of which there is a vast boiling vat these days, has been rendering down the ectoplasmic energy of "spectrality" into sound bites for 25 years, while critics seem to arrive pre-loaded with cookie-cutter cribs from Freud's "The Uncanny", in which they laboriously explain yet again that the term *unheimlich* means rather more literally the *unhomely* in German, but that the "homely" is housed inside the "unhomely," the outside in the inside, the strange in the familiar.' See Roger Luckhurst, 'Making Sense of "The Weird and the Eerie"', *Los Angeles Review of Books*, 11 March 2017.

94 Sigmund Freud, 'The Uncanny' (1919) in *The Uncanny*, trans. by David McLintock, ed. by Hugh Haughton, London: Penguin, 2003, 123-162, p. 123.

95 Peter Buse and Andrew Stott, 'Introduction: A Future for Haunting' in *Ghosts: Deconstruction, Psychoanalysis, History* ed. by Peter Buse and Andrew Stott, London: Macmillan, 1999, 1-20, p. 9.

96 Freud, 'The Uncanny', p. 132.

97 For a discussion of the semantic relationship between the German 'unheimlich' and the English 'haunt', see Mark Fisher, 'Home is Where the Haunt is: *The Shining*'s

Hauntology' (2006), in *Ghosts of My Life*, 120-127, p. 125.
[98] Freud, 'The Uncanny', p. 143.
[99] Freud, 'The Uncanny', p. 143.
[100] Freud, 'The Uncanny', p. 145.
[101] Freud, 'The Uncanny', p. 147.
[102] Freud, 'The Uncanny', pp. 148-9.
[103] See María del Pilar Blanco and Esther Peeren, 'Introduction: Conceptualizing Spectralities' in *The Spectralities Reader: Ghosts and Haunting in Contemporary Cultural Theory*, ed. by María del Pilar Blanco and Esther Peeren, London; Bloomsbury, 2013, 1-27, pp. 3-5.
[104] Freud, 'The Uncanny', p. 155.
[105] Freud, 'The Uncanny', pp. 155-6.
[106] Mark Fisher writes: 'Freud's ultimate settling of the enigma of the *unheimlich* – his claim that it can be reduced to castration anxiety – is as disappointing as any mediocre genre detective's rote solution to a mystery.' See Mark Fisher, *The Weird and the Eerie*, London: Repeater Books, 2016, p. 9.
[107] Hugh Haughton in Freud, *The Uncanny*, Introduction, p. lv.
[108] Mark Fisher, 'Home is Where the Haunt is: *The Shining*'s Hauntology' (2006), in *Ghosts of My Life*, pp. 123-4.
[109] 'There's a hauntological dimension to many different aspects of culture', Fisher claims, 'in fact, in *Moses and Monotheism*, Freud practically argues that society as such is founded on a hauntological basis (the voice of the dead father).' See Mark Fisher, 'Capitalist Realism: Mark Fisher interviewed by Joe Kennedy', *3:AM Magazine*, 28 July 2010, at https://www.3ammagazine.com/3am/capitalist-realism/
[110] Robert Macfarlane, 'The eeriness of the English countryside', *The Guardian*, 10 April 2015.

[111] Macfarlane, 'The eeriness of the English countryside'.

[112] HP Lovecraft, 'Supernatural Horror in Literature' (1925-7) in *At the Mountains of Madness*, ed. by China Miéville, New York: The Modern Library, 2005, 105-173, p. 169.

[113] See Mark Fisher: 'Some would question whether these dwarven figures [...] could be described as "ghosts" at all; often, it seemed that James was writing *demon* rather than ghost stories'. Mark Fisher, 'Memorex for the Kraken: The Fall's Pulp Modernism', in *K-Punk*, 323-342, pp. 329-330; and China Miéville: 'James is regularly cited as a – or *the* – founder of the "tradition" of English ghost stories. It is commonplace to then wryly point out that James's ghosts are in fact often not ghosts, but inhuman "demons" of one sort or another.' China Miéville, 'M.R. James and the Quantum Vampire. Weird; Hauntological: Versus and/or and and/or or?' *Weird Fiction Review*, 29 November, 2011.

[114] Simon Reynolds, *Retromania: Pop Culture's Addiction to its Own Past*, London: Faber, 2012, pp. 26-7.

[115] Jacques Derrida, *Archive Fever: A Freudian Impression*, trans. by Eric Prenowitz, Chicago, IL: University of Chicago Press, 1996, p. 91, quoted in Reynolds, *Retromania*, pp. 26-8.

[116] Reynolds, *Retromania*, pp. 26-8.

[117] Reynolds, *Retromania*, pp. 26-8.

[118] Jacques Derrida, *Archive Fever*, p. 84. See also María del Pilar Blanco and Esther Peeren, 'Introduction: Conceptualizing Spectralities', in *The Spectralities Reader: Ghosts and Haunting in Contemporary Cultural Theory*, p. 16.

[119] For an examination of this ambivalence in James's work, see Clare Button, '...the papers out of which I have made a connected story...': Archival Memory and the textual

mediator in the fiction of M.R. James', at https://independent.academia.edu/ClareButton

120 MR James, 'The Tractate Middoth' (1911), in *Casting the Runes and Other Ghost Stories*, ed. by Michael Cox, Oxford: OUP, 1987, 117-134, p. 122.

121 MR James, 'The Tractate Middoth' (1911), p. 134.

122 Fisher, *The Weird and the Eerie*, p. 80.

123 Fisher, *The Weird and the Eerie*, p. 61. These eerie landscapes are the subject of *On Vanishing Land* (2013), an audio essay made by Fisher in collaboration with Justin Barton, in which they explore the coastal settings of James's Suffolk.

124 Adam Scovell, *Folk Horror: Hours Dreadful and Things Strange*, Leighton Buzzard: Auteur, 2017, p. 40.

125 Fisher, *The Weird and the Eerie*, p. 61.

126 See, for example, 'The Treasure of Abbott Thomas' (1904) or 'Mr Humphreys and His Inheritance' (1911).

127 'Many commentators', writes ST Joshi, 'have noted the *hairiness* of the James ghost. [...] hairiness is frequently used as a symbol for barbarity.' See ST Joshi, *The Weird Tale*, Austin, TX: University of Texas Press, 1990, pp. 134-5. While Darryl Jones adds: 'James's ghosts have hair, too much hair, hair where there should be none.' Darryl Jones, 'Introduction', in MR James, *Collected Ghost Stories*, Oxford: OUP, 2011, p. xxvii.

128 Nigel Kneale, 'Introduction', in *Ghost Stories of M.R. James*, ed. by Nigel Kneale, London: Folio Society, 1973, v-xi, p. xi.

129 Nigel Kneale, 'Introduction', in *Ghost Stories of M.R. James*, p. ix.

130 Scovell, *Folk Horror*, p. 146.

131 Scovell, *Folk Horror*, p. 5.

[132] Scovell, *Folk Horror*, p. 10. Scovell writes (p. 52): 'James and the ideals he represents create the topographical backbone for Folk Horror. Their horrific and terrifying ruralism plays heavily on other television work from the period in which they were popularly adapted, to the point where almost all of the Folk Horror in question has aspects of or, at the very least, some minor facets of the man's work under their soil. As will be seen, the haunted objects, the landforms, the unseen horrors, the ghosts, the demons, the spirits and the very essence of the landscape, all play key roles in the most pertinent and most widely regarded examples of British Folk Horror television. James is the man who honed all of these themes into a body of work perfectly ripe for screen adaptations. He is, therefore, the ever-present protector of the crown that guards Folk Horror's shores from attack and calamity.'

[133] Describing James, Michael Cox writes: 'Ever a loyal Anglican and steadfast in the Christian principles of his Victorian childhood, he had little time for the post-war world. He loathed James Joyce, Aldous Huxley, and modern art, and never had any patience with politics'. See MR James, *Casting the Runes and Other Ghost Stories*, Introduction, p. xv.

[134] MR James, from the Introduction to *Ghosts and Marvels*, ed. by VH Collins (Oxford, 1924) and reprinted in 'Appendix: M.R. James on Ghost Stories', in MR James, *Casting the Runes and Other Ghost Stories*, p. 339.

[135] MR James, 'Ghosts – Treat them Gently!', *Evening News* (17 April 1931) in 'Appendix: M.R. James on Ghost Stories', MR James, *Casting the Runes and Other Ghost Stories*, p. 348.

[136] Dylan Trigg, 'The Ghosts of Place', *The White Review*, August 2013.

137 'There is a special charge', Mark Fisher observes, 'to be had from disinterring these works in which "time is out of joint" in our current dehistoricized, end-of-history moment. It was James who established the template that the other writers – consciously or not – would follow.' See Mark Fisher, 'What is Hauntology?', *Film Quarterly*, Vol. 66, 1 (Fall 2012), 16-24, pp. 20-21.

138 Julia Briggs, *Night Visitors: The Rise and Fall of the English Ghost Story*, London: Faber, 1977, p. 14. Writing in 1990, ST Joshi echoes Briggs' complaint: 'The ghost story as such does not allow very much room for expansion or originality; when some writers attempt to do so, they either fail [...] or, in succeeding, produce tales that can no longer be called ghost stories. It is quite possible that James came to realize this and that this is the reason for the very peculiar, self-reflexive nature of his later work.' See ST Joshi, *The Weird Tale*, p. 142.

139 China Miéville, 'M.R. James and the Quantum Vampire. Weird; Hauntological: Versus and/or and and/or or?' *Weird Fiction Review*, 29 November, 2011.

Part II: Experiments with Time

What is time? Who can explain this easily and briefly? Who can comprehend this even in thought so as to articulate the answer in words? Yet what do we speak of, in our familiar everyday conversation, more than of time? We surely know what we mean when we speak of it. We also know what is meant when we hear someone else talking about it. What then is time? Provided that no one asks me, I know. If I want to explain it to an inquirer, I do not know.

Saint Augustine, *Confessions* (AD 397)[1]

Time present and time past
Are both perhaps present in time future
And time future contained in time past.
If all time is eternally present
All time is unredeemable.
What might have been is an abstraction
Remaining a perpetual possibility
Only in a world of speculation.
What might have been and what has been
Point to one end, which is always present.
Footfalls echo in the memory
Down the passage which we did not take
Towards the door we never opened
Into the rose-garden. My words echo

Thus, in your mind.
But to what purpose
Disturbing the dust on a bowl of rose-leaves
I do not know.
TS Eliot, 'Burnt Norton' (1935)[2]

Herefordshire, 1921

On one hot summer afternoon, at the end of June 1921, an elderly businessman and amateur archaeologist named Alfred Watkins (1855-1935) was riding through the countryside near Blackwardine in Herefordshire. Stopping on a high hilltop, he consulted his map before gazing at the view spread out beneath him. It was then that Watkins had his epiphany, a moment of visionary insight which as well as changing his own life was to have an enduring influence upon our future apprehension of the landscape. For in this revelatory instant Watkins was transported through time as the topography of a much older England revealed itself:

> Suddenly, in a flash, he saw something which no one in England had seen for perhaps thousands of years. Watkins saw straight through the surface of the landscape to a layer deposited in some remote prehistoric age. The barrier of time melted and, spread across the country, he saw a web of lines linking the holy places and sites of antiquity. Mounds, old stones, crosses and old crossroads, churches placed on pre-Christian sites, legendary trees, moats and holy wells stood in exact alignments that ran over beacon hills to cairns and mountain peaks. In one moment of transcendental

perception Watkins entered a magic world of prehistoric Britain, a world whose very existence had been forgotten.[3]

Watkins's revelation was as much an experience of dislocation in time as it was in space, a momentary regression to the time of prehistory, in which the landscape of the distant past was revealed within the present, the thoroughfares of an earlier civilisation exposed like veins beneath the skin. Three months later Watkins gave a lecture to the Woolhope Naturalists' Field Club entitled 'Early British Trackways, Moats, Mounds, Camps and Sites' and his archaeological heresy was presented to an unsuspecting public. 'That Lecture', Robert Macfarlane writes, 'would have remarkable results. Its afterlives are with us still. Anyone now interested in British landscape, counter-culture, or both will – at some point – surely find their way back to Watkins.'[4] The theory outlined by Watkins that evening has since been subject to endless scrutiny, but in essence it is a simple one, expressed in a disarmingly straightforward manner:

> My main theme is the alignment across miles of country of a great number of objects, or sites of objects, of prehistoric antiquity. And this not in one or a few instances, but in scores and hundreds. Such alignments are either facts beyond the possibility of accidental coincidence or they are not.[5]

Watkins believed that prehistoric man traversed his world via a system of straight tracks running between conspicuous topographical markers such as hill-tops and tumuli. These tracks, developed for the purpose of trade or navigation, criss-crossed the landscape, running, counter-intuitively, against the natural contours of streams, ridges or valleys in routes which mapped out the shortest distance between these terminal points. The result was a vast network of straight tracks stretching across England and beyond whose traces could still be discerned by those, like Watkins, who knew how to look. Along these alignments, Watkins noticed that place names ending with the suffix 'ley' appeared with remarkable regularity, and thus his theory of ley lines was born.[6]

The following year Watkins published *Early British Trackways* (1922), an expanded version of his Woolhope lecture, and despite the outright hostility of the archaeological establishment, his appealing blend of practicality and enthusiasm struck a chord with his readers. Three years later Watkins published *The Old Straight Track* and, in 1927, the Old Straight Track Club was formed which, until his death in 1935, allowed Watkins to lead his growing band of followers across the English countryside in search of further examples of these prehistoric trackways. Although the intervening millennia had long since erased the network established by these Neolithic wanderers, the countryside still offered ample evidence of their activity which could seemingly be unearthed with little more than a map and a compass. The lasting appeal of Watkins's theory lies in its simplicity, for although these primitive trackways were insubstantial and soon lost, the mark points which they connect have proved far more enduring, their function evolving over the centuries from meeting place and market to burial mound and temple. In this way, features constructed over thousands of years and whose original purpose may long since have been forgotten, retain a local significance through time, embedded in a series of alignments in which time present and time past are overlaid in a kind of topographical palimpsest:

> Imagine a fairy chain stretched from mountain peak to mountain peak, as far as the eye could reach, and paid out until it touched the "high places" of the earth at a number of ridges, banks, and knowls. Then visualize a mound, circular earthwork, or clump of trees, planted on these high points, and in low points in the valley other mounds ringed round with water to be seen from a distance. Then great standing stones brought to mark the way at intervals, and on a bank leading up to a mountain ridge or down to a ford the track cut deep so as to form a guiding notch on the skyline as you come up. In a bwlch or mountain pass the road cut deeply at the highest place straight through the ridge to show as a notch afar off. Here and there, at two ends of the way, a beacon fire used to lay out the track. With ponds dug on the line, or streams banked up into "flashes" to form reflecting points on the beacon track so that it might be checked when at least once a year the beacon was fired on the traditional day. All these works exactly on the sighting line. The wayfarer's instructions are still deeply rooted in the peasant mind to-day, when he tells you—quite wrongly now— "You just keep straight on".[7]

In an illuminating reading of his work, Stephen Daniels draws a parallel between Watkins's vision and that of his contemporary, MR James, whose story 'A View from a Hill' (1925) was published in the same year as *The Old Straight*

Track.[8] At first glance, these two figures, despite their shared love of the English countryside, would appear to have little in common, yet the connection Daniels draws between them is a revealing one which hints at a more occulted view of Watkins's work. James's tale concerns itself, in customary fashion, with the unforeseen and sometimes horrific consequences that may result from the overzealous pursuit of archaeological research. In this instance, however, his story is set not in East Anglia but in Watkins's own Herefordshire, where Fanshawe, on holiday from his academic pursuits, explores the region with an ordnance survey map and a pair of benighted binoculars that allow him to look literally through 'dead men's eyes' into the landscape's past. In its depiction of a less than bucolic English countryside still haunted by the horrors of its past, could James's tale perhaps be interpreted as carrying an oblique warning to those who might seek to follow in Watkins' footsteps?

If this was the case, then such a warning went unheeded. Alongside the enthusiastic response of the public to Watkins's theory, it was soon ascribed a mystical content wholly absent from his stolidly methodological prose. In her novel of 1936, *The Goat-Foot God*, the author, occultist and early ley-hunter, Dion Fortune, describes standing stones and other landmarks of the ley system as 'sighting-marks on the lines of force between the power-centres', an interpretation that was to prove remarkably prescient.[9] For Watkins was later to become the unlikely beneficiary of the counter-cultural movement of the 1960s. Following his death in 1935, Watkins's theories gradually went out of favour, remaining dormant for many years until his fortunes were to revive dramatically with the publication in 1969 of John Michell's *The View Over Atlantis*. Michell's work relied heavily upon Watkins's theory of ley lines, incorporating his work within an amalgam of New Age ideas in which leys were transformed from the trackways of the distant past into a National Grid of telluric force.[10] Yet perhaps this unforeseen transformation from amateur archaeologist to New Age guru would have proven less of a surprise to Watkins than one might suppose. A year before his death he revealed to his son that the epiphany he experienced in 1921 had been preceded by the receipt of an 'unusual gift': 'I have been psychic all my life', he confessed, 'but I have kept it under and never told anyone about it.'[11]

In the decades since Watkins's unexpected return to prominence his theories have been applied increasingly to urban settings and, through works such as Iain Sinclair's celebrated re-mapping of London's topography, *Lud Heat* (1975), his ideas have been co-opted into the practice of psychogeography.[12] Yet just as Watkins's examination of the English landscape may now be viewed as a precursor to contemporary forms of topographical exploration, so too can his theories be seen within the wider context of investigations into the nature of time, both in the 1920s and subsequently, a tradition which culminates in our current engagement with hauntology.

An Experiment with Time: JW Dunne

All but forgotten today, the soldier, aeronautical engineer and philosopher, JW Dunne (1875-1949) rose to prominence in the 1920s as part of a generation of writers, scientists and mystics seeking to explain the nature of time.[13] Two works in particular, both entitled *The Fourth Dimension*, one by CH Hinton (1904) and the other by PD Ouspensky (1909), alongside Einstein's *Relativity* (1905), had helped to popularise the understanding of time as a dimension of space, an argument which fatally undermined the perception of time as a fixed and unquestioned concept.[14] It was against this backdrop of temporal uncertainty that Dunne published *An Experiment with Time* (1927) which proved widely popular with a readership still mourning the losses of the First World War.

With its emphasis upon the survival of the past into the present and beyond, Dunne's *An Experiment with Time* may be seen in some respects as a companion to Watkins's *The Old Straight Track* published two years before, acting as a temporal counterweight to Watkins's predominantly spatial investigation. Certainly, Dunne himself, with his military background and excruciating prose style, seems as unsuited to his subsequent elevation to the role of mystical harbinger as Watkins. Furthermore, Dunne's claims to scientific rigour were similarly invalidated by the 'psychic' confessions of his posthumously published *Intrusions?* (1955) in which he shared his conviction that ever since childhood he had been aware that it was his destiny to deliver an important message to mankind, this message being his own great theory of 'serial time'.[15] One can only presume that JB Priestley, one of the great disseminators of Dunne's ideas, had failed to read this volume when he later claimed that Dunne 'was as far removed from any suggestion of the seer, the sage, the crank and crackpot as it is possible to imagine.'[16]

From the outset of *An Experiment with Time*, Dunne is keen to establish his credentials as a serious scientist: 'this is not a book about "occultism"', he states, 'and not a book about what is called "psycho-analysis".'[17] In fact, what Dunne's book is concerned with is precognition and his belief that future events can be experienced, partially and often non-sequentially, in dreams. Dunne offers several examples of his own precognitive dreams, which, helpfully, in illustrating a book such as his, often appear to be about the nature of time itself. In 1899, he dreams of an argument with a waiter as to the correct time – is it 4.30 in the afternoon or morning? His watch, he dreamt, has stopped at 4.30. He then awakes to discover that his watch has indeed stopped at 4.30, but on checking the time the following morning he finds that his watch must have stopped at the precise moment of his dream. Later in Italy, determined to recreate this 'coincidence' by attempting to focus remotely on what the precise time may be at any given moment, he manages successfully to form a mental image of the exact time: 'I was driven to the conclusion that I possessed some funny faculty of *seeing* – seeing through obstacles, across space, and round corners. But I was wrong.'[18]

In 1901, Dunne dreamt of an expedition arriving in Khartoum, the details of which were confirmed by the *Daily Telegraph* the next day; while the following year his dream of the explosion of the Mount Pelée volcano in Martinique was once again corroborated by the *Daily Telegraph* a short time afterwards. In both instances, what these dreams disclosed were not the historical events themselves but rather the reporting of them subsequently in print, as if he had access to the newspaper in advance of the events it recorded.[19] Two years later, in 1904, his dream was of a factory fire in Paris; this and the previous examples were chosen by Dunne from a group of 20 or so precognitive dreams he was to experience over more than a dozen years prior to the First World War, the accuracy of which allowed him to conclude:

> These dreams were not percepts (impressions) of distant or future events. They were the usual commonplace dreams composed of distorted images of waking experience, built together in the usual half-senseless fashion peculiar to dreams. That is to say, if they had happened on the nights after the corresponding events, they would have exhibited nothing in the smallest degree unusual [...] They were the ordinary, appropriate, expectable dreams; but they were occurring on the wrong nights. [...] No, there was nothing unusual in any of these dreams as dreams. They were merely displaced in Time.[20]

Dunne's dreams were characterised by what he described as 'chronological aberration'.[21] Hazy, half-remembered dreams of events and their subsequent reports in the press that one might expect to experience after having read about them, the single, striking, incongruity being that the dreams were occurring *before* the events they alluded to, indicating to Dunne that his experience of time was out of joint, or more precisely, out of sequence. Explaining the cause of these events and determining whether he alone was subject to them was to prove the beginning of his life's work:

> No one, I imagine, can derive any considerable pleasure from the supposition that he is a freak; and, personally, I would almost sooner have discovered myself to be a 'medium'.

> There might have been a chance of company there. [...] I was suffering, seemingly, from some extraordinary fault in relation to reality, something so uniquely wrong that it compelled me to perceive, at rare intervals, large blocks of otherwise perfectly normal personal experience displaced from their proper positions in Time. [...] Time has always been treated by men of science as if it were a fourth dimension. What had to be shown was the possibility of displacement in that dimension. [...] What I wanted to know was: How it got mixed? For 'mixed' was the right word. Between the dream and the corresponding waking experience came the memory of the dream, while the memory of the waking experience followed them all! [...] Was it possible that these phenomena were not abnormal, but normal? That dreams – dreams in general, all dreams, everybody's dreams – were composed of images of past experience and images of future experience blended together in approximately equal proportions?[22]

Dunne sees time from above, spread out beneath him as one might look down upon the landscape from an aeroplane (or, like Watkins, from a hill). From this perspective, however, the landscape that Dunne observes seems curiously incomplete, a lop-sided view of the universe with the 'future' part unaccountably missing, cut off from the growing 'past' by a travelling 'present moment'.[23] For when awake we are denied an overview of time in its entirety by a self-imposed mental barrier which prevents us seeing beyond the present moment as we move along within it. It is only in dreams that we ascend to a point at which we are able to move both backwards and forwards in time, in an unhindered fashion, 'continually crossing and recrossing that properly non-existent equator which we, waking, ruled quite arbitrarily athwart the whole'.[24] Dunne's perception of time as a fourth dimension with duration in space, draws on Einstein's vision of the universe as a four-dimensional map, the block universe through which the course of an individual's life may be plotted as a timeline. Dunne is aware that such a view of time would once have been regarded as heretical, but by the time at which he was writing the classical theory of time was no longer in place and Dunne regarded it as his role to provide mankind with a replacement.

Dunne's solution is what he calls 'Serial Time', an unwieldy theory which he struggles to articulate clearly. Time flows through a four-dimensional universe but, in order for our conscious mind to measure its own journey along its individual timeline, it requires access to a higher vantage point from which it can ascertain the broader vista of time in its entirety. This vantage point is provided in dreams when our mind, free from our waking experience of a perpetual present, is able to operate on a higher level of consciousness and to glimpse its own future.[25] This further dimension of time explains Dunne's precognitive dreams, and demonstrates that his ability is one which we can all replicate. But there's a catch: 'Serial time requires a *serial observer*', with the consequence that Dunne's theory takes on the defining characteristic of an infinite regression. 'We have seen', Dunne explains, 'that if Time passes or grows or accumulates or expends itself or does anything whatsoever except stand rigid and changeless before a Time-fixed observer, there must be another Time which times that activity of, or along, the first Time, and another Time which times that second Time, and so on in an apparent series to infinity.'[26]

It would appear that we are all serial observers of serial time, although only very few of us ever become aware of this fact, either through the kind of precognitive dreams that Dunne describes, or as a result of the painstaking method he outlines of carefully recording our recollections so as to become aware of our dreams, and when awake, of the tell-tale indicators of future events we experience in our everyday lives. Infinite regress has long been seen, as Dunne acknowledges, as a fallacy exposing the weakness of one's argument, but in this instance he argues it is in fact 'the proper and valid description of mind's relation to its objective universe.'[27] But the idea of multiple selves and multiple streams of time, infinitely regressing is one which is hard to sustain, for like any infinite series, it begs the question of a first cause or observer at the apex of such a regression, the final arbiter of this everlasting process. As an Anglican, Dunne was able to tailor his theory of serial time to that of Christian theology, by introducing God as the ultimate observer. For while we must die, the consciousness whose existence is revealed through our dreams lives on, *An Experiment with Time* and its sequels revealing Dunne's increasingly mystical preoccupation with the existence of an eternal soul:

> Serialism discloses the existence of a reasonable kind of 'soul' – an individual soul which has a definite beginning in absolute Time – a soul whose immortality, being in other dimensions of Time, does not clash with the obvious ending

> of the individual in the physiologist's Time dimension [...] It discloses the existence of a superlative general observer, the fount of all that self-consciousness, intention, and intervention which underlies mere mechanical thinking, who contains within himself a less generalized observer who is the personification of all genealogically related life and who is capable of human-like thinking and prevision of a kind quite beyond our individual capabilities. In the superlative observer we individual observers, and that tree of which we are the branches, live and have our being.[28]

Dunne's often tortuous attempts to elucidate his theory, even with the support of numerous diagrams, simply emphasise the difficulty he faced in translating a theory of time into layman's terms. The fact that his book proved hugely popular and has been frequently reprinted, despite its obvious limitations, only highlights the appeal of a theory that his readers could explore, literally, in their sleep. Dunne produced three further volumes explaining the theory of serial time: *The Serial Universe* (1934); *The New Immortality* (1938) and *Nothing Dies* (1940). In them, as in *An Experiment with Time*, he is most successful in transmitting his ideas when he expresses them through a range of visual metaphors. The most easily recognisable of these is the idea of time as a stream or current, its waters flowing ceaselessly from past to future; but elsewhere he employs a more sophisticated image, that of a piano keyboard. In waking life, the pianist – you or I – plays a note at a time as he moves from left to right, from past to future, but in dreams we are freed from this linear sequence and are free to play the keyboard as we choose, our past and future mingling in a discordant and unpredictable fashion.[29] It is in *The Serial Universe* (1934), however, as Colin Wilson explains, that Dunne employs an image which encapsulates his central idea like no other, that of a painter who paints himself into the foreground of his picture:

> In order to explain this concept, he [Dunne] uses the image of a man painting a picture. The painter looks at the world in front of him and tries to transfer it on to canvas. Having done that, it strikes him that his picture of the world is incomplete, because he has failed to include himself. So he paints a second picture, this time showing himself painting the first picture. But that is incomplete too. For it now strikes him that in order to paint this second picture, he had to 'get outside' himself, and regard himself as a physical object, a part of the world. This means that another 'him' has somehow risen above the first one, a 'Self No.2'. So he paints another picture [...] And so on, ad infinitum.[30]

This pictorial representation of infinite regression is named the Droste effect after a Dutch brand of cocoa, the original tin bearing an image designed by Jan Misset in 1904, in which another tin is held up by another woman bearing the same image, and so on. But the idea of a picture recursively appearing within itself has a long history, and can be seen in works from Giotto to Escher, where it is regarded as an example of *mise en abyme* ('to put in the abyss'), a shorthand for eternity. Dunne's painter was to become a staple image of 1970s artwork, in which time is characterised as an eternal repetition of identical moments, a trap in which both the painter and, it would seem, the observer, may become forever ensnared.[31] Of course, it is precisely this perception of time as one of unending repetition which has since been recognised as intrinsic to hauntology. 'The image of the painter painting a picture expresses a truth about consciousness', Colin Wilson concludes, 'Man *is* capable of infinite regress; it is impossible to catch him.'[32]

An Experiment with Time inspired an eclectic group of writers from TS Eliot and JRR Tolkien, to Agatha Christie, HG Wells and Graham Greene, but Dunne's most ardent supporter was JB Priestley, whose series of 'time plays', which includes both *Time and the Conways* (1937) and *An Inspector Calls* (1945), owes a clear debt to Dunne's theory.[33] In 1963, Priestley used the BBC *Monitor* programme to appeal to the public to submit evidence of their precognitive dreams, resulting in a deluge of testimony detailing dreams, visions and other purported glimpses of the future. Yet Priestley's acceptance of Dunne's ideas was far from uncritical, and in *Man and Time* (1964), his vast overview of temporal theory in which Dunne's ideas are discussed in some detail, he highlights what is perhaps the most intractable problem of Serial Time, the apparent contradiction between free will and a predetermined future:

> The future can be seen, and because it can be seen, it can be changed. But if it can be seen and yet be changed, it is neither solidly there, laid out for us to experience moment after moment, nor is it non-existent, something we are helping to create, moment after moment. If it does not exist, it cannot be seen; if it is solidly set and fixed, then it cannot be changed. What is this future that is sufficiently established to be observed and perhaps experienced, and yet can allow itself to be altered?[34]

Priestley has no answer to the problem he identifies, perhaps because none exists. Colin Wilson, however, writing in 1978, attempts a solution of his own, using the analogy of a car journey to illustrate that while the future may be broadly mapped out for us, the details remain within our power to control, dependent upon the degree of mental attention we are willing to exert:

> Yet although the journey is more-or-less predetermined, all the minor decisions remain free: what I think en route, where I stop for lunch, whether I listen to the car radio or not [...] And what determines my degree of freedom? The answer lies in the word 'alertness' or attention. If I am tired or bored, I drive automatically – that is to say, my robot does the driving [...] and my will goes to sleep. [...] If, on the other hand, I am wide awake, intensely enjoying the scenery, the journey will become far less predictable. I may slow down [...] I may decide to take a side road [...] I am now exercising my freedom of choice.[35]

Dunne's theory of time, Wilson suggests, offers us an overview of the future, but one in which the details remain obscure and unsequential, an array of moments which come to us in dreams but which we may then, like the pianist, artist or driver, choose to orchestrate, depict or navigate as we wish. But along with Priestley and many of his contemporaries, there was another writer who was equally enchanted by Dunne's vision of time, and similarly aware of its shortcomings:

Theologians define eternity as the lucid and simultaneous possession of all instants of time, and declare it a divine attribute. Dunne, surprisingly, presumes that eternity already belongs to us, as corroborated by the dreams we have each night. In them, according to him, the immediate past and the immediate future intermingle. Awake, we pass through successive time at a uniform speed; in dreams we may span a vast zone. To dream is to orchestrate the objects we viewed while awake and to weave from them a story, or a series of stories. [...] Dunne assures us that in death we shall finally learn how to handle eternity. We shall recover all the moments of our lives and combine them as we please. God and our friends and Shakespeare will collaborate with us.

So splendid a thesis, makes any fallacy committed by the author insignificant.[36]

Jorge Luis Borges's essay on Dunne, written in 1940, may be seen as a counterpart to his celebrated story 'Funes the Memorious' (1942) in which the protagonist, having fallen from his horse, finds himself able to remember everything, his life thereafter spent enumerating the endless and overwhelming detail of each passing moment. Borges's tale, like so much of his work, is concerned with the paradoxes of time and memory, and it is surely in response to Dunne's theory that he offers a further metaphor for the endless and unfathomable circularities of time: the library. In a return to a setting made familiar through the stories of MR James, Borges's 'The Library of Babel' (1941) visualises the universe as a library of infinite extent, its endless expanse of identical rooms furnished by bookshelves containing volumes within which every possible alphabetic permutation is recorded. The volumes and their contents follow no order or pattern and the librarians pass their time in search of an index that might explain or give meaning to their lives. Perhaps it is here, in the total library, that we can see Dunne's theory to its full effect, as every moment of time, past, present and future is archived in an endless and randomly distributed series of volumes awaiting classification in our dreams.

It is easy to be dismissive of Dunne's beliefs and to regard them, like those of Alfred Watkins, as little more than the wish-fulfilling fantasises of an inter-war generation disorientated by the upheavals of history. Yet these theories have since worked their way into the margins of mainstream science and culture, occupying the point at which time, memory and the landscape intersect. Challenging our perception of history as linear and sequential, these ideas return recurrently and in unexpectedly modified forms, manifesting themselves through literature, music and film, and establishing a tradition of their own. It was out of experiments with time such as these that hauntology was to evolve.

TC Lethbridge and Residual Haunting

'Dreams are respectable: ghosts are not. Yet there seems to be much in common between the two phenomena. They both belong to a different level of awareness from the one normally used in waking life.'[37] Reading the words of TC Lethbridge (1901-1971) today, a figure who is in many respects a direct successor to JW Dunne, it is difficult to determine which man has since attained the greater degree of obscurity. Dunne's works are widely ignored but *An Experiment with Time* at least remains in print. Lethbridge's works were widely read during his heyday, the countercultural revival of the 1960s and 1970s, but his readership, like Dunne's before him, soon declined. Yet in recent years his work has attracted a renewal of interest, albeit muted, and in 2011 he was the subject of a biography by Terry Welbourn.[38] This modest revival has been, at least in part, the result of his recognition as an important precursor to hauntology, a fact best illustrated by a number of quotations from Lethbridge which now adorn various releases on the Ghost Box label: 'The television picture is a man-made ghost'; 'Are ghosts "television" pictures carried by forces of resonance from a projecting machine in one mind to a receiving machine in another?'[39]

Lethbridge is remembered nowadays, if at all, principally as a parapsychologist, a practitioner of dowsing and prolific author, whose books advocate a spectrum of esoteric practices from precognitive dreaming and telekinesis to psychometry and ufology. But Lethbridge, like Alfred Watkins before him, was firstly an archaeologist whose increasingly unorthodox methodology was similarly disparaged by the academic community. For many years Lethbridge was the Keeper of Anglo-Saxon Antiquities at the Cambridge University Museum of Archaeology and Ethnology and it was here that he developed a lifelong interest in the myths and beliefs of Early Medieval Britain. Increasingly disillusioned with academic life, however, Lethbridge resigned his position in 1957 and moved to Devon where he began work on a series of books, the subject of which he referred to simply as the 'odd.' It was the first of these, *Ghost and Ghoul* (1961), that was to introduce the idea for which he remains best known, that of residual haunting.

Broadly defined as the belief that haunting is in some sense analogous to a recording, the idea of residual haunting suggests that the natural world is embedded with the mental impressions of emotional or traumatic events, some dating back millions of years. These can subsequently be replayed, our brains acting as receivers with which to decode such ghostly transmissions. As we shall see, this was an idea which was to be immortalised in one of the most resonant of all hauntological texts, Nigel Kneale's television play, *The Stone Tape* (1972). In fact, it is largely as a result of Kneale's popularisation of what was to become known as 'Stone Tape Theory', a label often mistakenly attributed to Lethbridge himself, that Lethbridge's ideas have since been absorbed into the 'hauntological timestream'.[40] Lethbridge's attempts to explain the supernatural through recourse to contemporary technology was by no means unique to him, however, nor was his belief that the environment is capable of storing and projecting traces of human emotion wholly without precedent. In his *Ninth Bridgewater Treatise* (1837) the polymath and pioneering computing engineer, Charles Babbage (1791-1871) outlined the possibility that spoken words may leave permanent impressions in the air, aural residues which only later become inaudible. 'The air itself', he wrote, 'is one vast library on whose pages are for ever written all that man has ever said or woman whispered', speculating that at some point in the future man might be able to rewind time to retrieve these lost voices from the past.[41] Later, Edmund Gurney (1847-88) and Eleanor Sidgwick (1845-1936), both members of the Society for Psychical

Research (SPR), introduced the concept of 'place-memory' as an explanation for haunting, proposing that certain locations could act as a type of spiritual conductor, preserving traces of past events which could subsequently be accessed by certain psychically attuned individuals. In 1886, Gurney, along with fellow members of the SPR, Frederic Myers (1843-1901) and Frank Podmore (1856-1910), published *Phantasms of the Living* which explored hundreds of cases in which apparitions of living people had been seen, often at the moment such people had *imagined* themselves being there.[42] Haunting was coming to be seen less as a ghostly manifestation than as an example of mental projection, in which the subject was able to transmit an audible or visual trace through time and space. In 1939, the Welsh philosopher and then president of the SPR, HH Price (1899-1984), proposed that such memory traces were recorded via the medium of a universal 'psychic ether', an intermediary between spiritual and physical reality, composed of images and ideas.[43] But the figure who was perhaps the first to suggest that ghosts might not only be projections but recordings, was the British physicist, Sir Oliver Lodge (1851-1940), who, like so many of his contemporaries, appears to have conducted his scientific career in tandem with his paranormal interests. He wrote in *Man and the Universe* (1908):

> Take, for example, a haunted house [...] wherein some one room is the scene of a ghostly representation of some long past tragedy. On a psychometric hypothesis, the original tragedy has been literally photographed on its material surroundings, nay, even on the ether itself, by reason of the intensity of emotion felt by those who enacted it; and

> thenceforth in certain persons an hallucinatory effect is experienced corresponding to such an impression. It is this theory that is made to account for the feeling one has on entering certain rooms, that there is an alien presence therein, though it is invisible and inaudible to mortal sense.[44]

Just as Lodge, in seeking to explain the supernatural through recourse to scientific speculation, falls back upon the principal technological medium of his day, photography, so too does Lethbridge, writing in 1961, employ the most current means of transmission at his disposal: television. For, if ghosts are simply recordings of past (or future) events, what better way to illustrate this fact than through comparison with a technology which promised, in the 1960s, not only to bring such spectres to life, but to do so in colour?[45] 'The whole production', writes Lethbridge, recalling an early encounter with the supernatural, 'was exactly comparable to a television scene. There was the same curious lack of atmosphere and the same general grey drabness. The figures were just pictures. I do not know whether I saw them with my eyes or whether they appeared in the mind direct. But, in whatever manner they were presented, I feel pretty sure that they were not spirits. They were pictures projected by somebody other than myself and I was nothing more than the receiving set.'[46]

Written during an era since regarded as the golden age of television in the UK, Lethbridge's reliance upon this striking televisual metaphor can at times appear a little obsessive, as if Mike Teavee had escaped from the pages of Roald Dahl's *Charlie and the Chocolate Factory* (1964) and grown up to become a parapsychologist. Increasingly, one feels that Lethbridge's conception of the paranormal has been reduced to one viewed through the frame of a television screen, an endless broadcast which we experience as the viewers:

> The engineers of the B.B.C. do not write the programmes which they send out. They are not the power which sends out the broadcast. They are not even the machines which take the photographs. Yet their minds are necessary before the broadcast can take place. It is probably much the same with the production of ghosts. Some mind thinks up the programme, but he does not necessarily provide the force. His mind may only harness it for the purpose. [....] there is nothing that anyone need be afraid of in the sight of a ghost. The great bulk of these are no more than mental pictures produced by living people. It is even on record that some are deliberately produced. The method of projection is probably the natural equivalent of mechanical television, just as telepathy is the natural equivalent of ordinary broadcasting. The machines used for it are human minds and the power is provided by the force known as resonance, which appears to be akin to electro-magnetism.[47]

Ghost and Ghoul is a curious blend of autobiographical accounts of archaeological excavations, alongside encounters with ghouls, ghosts, telepathy, astral projection, psychometry, precognition, and even an account of the 'little people' that had so exercised the late Victorian imagination. All of which is then explained in a passably scientific manner, and presented in a pleasant anecdotal style with occasional sketches and expository drawings in the manner of Dunne. Lethbridge's overarching thesis is that such things are not out 'there' in the world but are projections of past and future images displaced in time, embedded in the natural world and replayed through those 'sensitives' with the ability to see and hear them. In Lethbridge's schema the transmission of ghostly phenomena is a process that requires at least two people, a projector and a receiver, plus an observer if the event is to be recorded.[48] Such an arrangement rather weakens his televisual analogy in which the passive observer is not required to interact with what they are watching; but Lethbridge seems willing to propose a technological solution for any supernatural scenario. Elsewhere he describes the performance of an exorcism in terms of jamming a radio signal, and phenomena from telekinesis to psychometry and precognition are all explained through recourse to a force called 'resonance', a curiously underdeveloped concept that appears to have much in common with similarly unsubstantiated referrals by the Victorians to a universal ether.[49]

Lethbridge recalls the story of a gypsy who came to his house unannounced one day, offering to read his fortune in return for an old thin coin she claimed he possessed. He had no knowledge of such a coin, but she was insistent and finally grew angry at his repeated denials. Three years later, in his new home 200 miles away, Lethbridge found a coin fitting her description. The solution: the gypsy's receiving 'settings' were askew and so she was out of kilter in both time and space.[50] This tale could easily have been found within the pages of Dunne's *An Experiment with Time*, for what it reveals, aside from Lethbridge's belief in precognition, is the concomitant sense that time is somehow out of joint. 'There is clearly something entirely wrong with our conception of time', he concludes.[51] Like Dunne before him, Lethbridge believed that precognitive dreams demonstrate that the course of our lives has already been recorded at another temporal level. Memories of our existence, both past and future, may be extracted from the mind of another person, in a manner Lethbridge demonstrates through recourse to a familiar technological metaphor:

> To our time scale, the future exists and it exists months and even years ahead. Why this should be the case we do not know. But, if we accept the idea that ghosts are comparable to television, it is not difficult to suggest a comparison between a life to a cinema film. Until the cinema film is put on to the projector, it only exists as a reel of material on a drum. You can, however, take it up and unwind it and examine shots at different points on the film. It looks very much as if pre-cognition and retro- or post-cognition are like that. How much you can alter your cinema is unknown. A man-made film can be cut about and have sections added, or removed, at the wish of the operator.[52]

Lethbridge returned to this idea in later works, suggesting that in sleep we revisit the projection room again and again to examine the film of our lives. But in his attempts to simplify Dunne's account of precognition, Lethbridge came up against the same problem, that of infinite regression, or as he describes it: 'an infinite number of people looking over an infinite number of films at the same time.'[53] Through divination, Lethbridge came to believe that inanimate objects had the ability to store information, contained within a surrounding field whose radius could be measured by the pendulum. In this way, just as the field present in woods, water and mountains could be calculated, so too could ideas and emotions themselves project a measurable response. Ultimately, both death and time itself, so Lethbridge believed, could be interpreted through the pendulum, allowing him to speculate upon the nature of the afterlife. Lethbridge's investigations led him to conclude that such an afterlife existed, albeit in a perpetual present outside of time altogether, a kind of atemporal museum in which all an individual's memories were preserved.[54] Colin Wilson has likened Lethbridge's conception of this second level of consciousness to the BBC Sound Archives; but the idea of an endless library of timeless memories once again recalls Borges' 'Library of Babel' with its shelves spanning eternity.[55]

Lethbridge rightly believed himself to be writing at a time of great change, but his belief that advances in technology would soon bring paranormal investigation within the purview of mainstream science have since been shown to be misplaced. In fact, his optimistic faith in scientific progress and his belief in rational explanations for a panoply of supernatural practices encourage one to regard Lethbridge, not as he appeared to regard himself, as a scourge of Victorian superstition, but rather as something of a Victorian himself. In his recognition of the possibilities afforded by emerging technologies, however, both to capture moments in time as well as to record its progression, Lethbridge was truly a man of his age. His insistence upon the seemingly limitless capacity of film and television to manufacture a 'timeless' reality was very much a product of the 1960s, an era which promised a technological future in which time would be managed and controlled for the benefit of all.[56] As we shall see, it is precisely this belief (or delusion) that technology has the potential to unravel the complexities of time itself that informs Nigel Kneale's *The Stone Tape*, and it is here that Lethbridge's legacy to hauntology may be found, his exploration of the intersection between current technology (soon to be rendered obsolete) and the future it sought (but failed) to create foreshadowing the concerns of later writers such as JG Ballard and Mark Fisher.

Nigel Kneale and the Stone Tape Experiment

In his introduction to *The Uncanny*, Nicholas Royle argues that this is a term characterised by a particular take on 'things more ancient, archaic, immemorial'. Using the example of Stonehenge, Royle quotes from Emerson's recollections of a visit to the stones in the company of Thomas Carlyle:

> Stonehenge, in virtue of the simplicity of its plan, and its good preservation, is as if new and recent; and a thousand years hence, men will thank this age for the accurate history it will yet eliminate. We walked in and out, and took again and again a fresh look at the uncanny stones. The old sphinx put our petty differences of nationality out of sight. To these conscious stones we two pilgrims were alike known and near.[57]

Stonehenge is uncanny, Royle affirms, both new and old, yet seemingly timeless, provoking a sense of fascination and repetition in those who come within its orbit. And the date of Emerson's visit? It took place in July 1848, returning us once again to the moment at which Marx's spectral manifesto was first published.[58] Stonehenge may well be uncanny, but it is also hauntological.

What is it exactly about hauntology and stone circles? Standing stones have a well-established cinematic and televisual history, from Jacques Tourneur's *Night of the Demon* (1957) to Ben Wheatley's *Sightseers* (2012), by way of the 1970s and a plethora of films employing such stones as a narrative device.[59] Could it be, however, that rather than focusing upon the alignment of the stones and the rituals enacted within them, it is in fact the material from which they are constructed that is of the foremost significance? In her brief but thorough demolition of the scientific arguments of Lethbridge and his successors, Sharon A Hill notes that adherents of Stone Tape theory tend to favour particular forms of bedrock or building stone such as quartz or limestone in support of their claims.[60] Needless to say, Hill regards such preferences as equally misguided, but the question remains as to why people believe this particular medium can enable the storage and transmission of human emotion through time. The answer is surely more cultural than scientific. Standing stones have long been seen as repositories of deep time and ancient memory, evidence of rituals whose significance is no longer clearly understood.[61] These artefacts from civilisations long since vanished are temporally incongruous, reminders of a time before recorded history, whose very existence disrupts our sense of human chronology. But what if this past could be unlocked? Theorists such as TC Lethbridge, John Michell and Erich von Däniken suggest that these stones are evidence of our alien ancestry, their function not sacred but technological, their existence pointing not only towards our distant past but also to an as yet unimagined future. It was ideas such as these that the writer Nigel Kneale (1922-2006) popularised in his best known works.

Kneale's work is often regarded as the missing link between the haunting repetitions of MR James and the more technologically alert fictions of JG Ballard, works in which the nightmares of the deep past and anxieties of the near future are brought into a direct and uncomfortable proximity. Like James, Kneale employs artefacts from an undisclosed past to disrupt the present; like Ballard, he is aware of the alienating effects of technological change. But the hallmark of Kneale's work is one he shares with Lethbridge: the search for material answers to questions of the paranormal. Like Lethbridge, Kneale sought such answers in the emerging technologies of his day but he was wary of the often unquestioning faith such technologies aroused in both the scientific community and the political establishment. Such fears are foregrounded in the adventures of his most famous creation, Professor Bernard Quatermass, through which Kneale explores ideas of genetic memory, alien technology and societal breakdown. Throughout his career, Kneale replayed such ideas alongside the hauntological themes of temporal repetition and dislocation. In 'Minuke', for example, from his debut collection, *Tomato Cain and Other Stories* (1949), Kneale introduces the idea of a location which displays a deeply embedded malevolence. In this story a young couple are subjected to horrifying sounds of breathing which emanate from the walls of their new home, as the house destroys itself in its desire to drive its inhabitants away. In a rehearsal of *The Stone Tape*, and the idea that stone can act as a storage material for past trauma, the story implies that the source of these emanations is the Norse gravestones from the burial ground on which the house was first constructed.[62]

The idea of a present haunted by the past was taken in an unexpected new direction in Kneale's television play *The Road* (1963).[63] Set in rural Britain in 1770, *The Road* follows a freethinking Squire as he struggles to explain what appears to be a haunting: each year on Christmas Eve a local copse becomes the site of inexplicable sounds and disembodied screams. The presumption is that the land is afflicted by the ghosts of some terrible past event, but at the conclusion of the play we learn that the true source of these disturbances lies not in the past but in the future. Squire Hassell and his family are experiencing a premonitory echo from 200 years hence, as their haunted copse, now overlaid by a road, is used to transport a terrified population fleeing nuclear attack. Broadcast soon after the Cuban Missile Crisis, at a time when such a future seemed only too plausible, *The Road* demonstrates how the present may be disrupted not only by the persistence of the past but by traces of those futures yet to materialise. In this respect Kneale's play acts as a precursor to hauntology as well as supporting the precognitive temporal models espoused by Dunne and Lethbridge. Within a wider body of work that has since inspired something of a cult following, it is perhaps this play which is most deserving of such an audience. For having been broadcast only once, on 29 September 1963, the videotape of *The Road* was subsequently wiped, in an act of erasure that foreshadows the plot of *The Stone Tape* itself.[64]

In terms of its television, 1972 was a remarkably haunted year, producing not only the anthology *Dead of Night*, but also

Lawrence Gordon Clark's adaptation of MR James's *A Warning to the Curious*. It is *The Stone Tape*, however, Nigel Kneale's hauntological time-capsule, which continues to resonate most powerfully today.[65] *The Stone Tape* begins with the arrival of a firm of electronics specialists at their new research centre, a recently renovated Victorian house reputed to be haunted. Amongst them is the computer programmer, Jill, who, as she arrives, narrowly avoids a collision with two vans, which she perceives momentarily as 'two huge, de-focussed shapes like standing stones in motion, slowly blundering and blending, looming over her.'[66] Shaken but unhurt she joins her colleagues in the house. Their attempts to create a new recording medium are soon disrupted by a ghostly manifestation. This takes place in the computer storage room, whose ancient stone wall, considerably older than the remainder of the house, has recorded the psychic impression of a spectral figure and is able to project this image to those, such as Jill, who are receptive enough to see and hear it. Recognising that such an occurrence may provide precisely the new medium they have been seeking, the head researcher, Peter Brock, redirects their efforts into analysing this encounter. They soon learn that the ghost is that of a maid who died in 1890 and that the site on which the house now stands has a recurrent history of ghostly activity.

Having identified the stone from which the room is built as ragstone, quarried since Roman times and used to construct much of medieval London, Brock realises that he may have located the source material of centuries of haunting, a medium which not only records powerful emotion but which replays it continually thereafter. In their attempts to record the ghost of the maid, however, the team have inadvertently erased her record, wiping the tape and leading Brock to conclude that their experiments have been a failure. It is only Jill who is able to recognise the truth: 'It's the concept of a tape that's wrong. It's more like a great depth [...] she was only in the surface layer, the most recent. [...] There'd be much older impressions underneath. Much deeper. [...] Some deep-level record, much older. So old and ... shapeless.' In erasing the record of the haunting from 1890, much older layers have been exposed, for the room is embedded with the deeper memory of thousands of years of residual haunting, each layer retaining the malignant trace of its traumatic past. At the conclusion of the film, threatened by the presence of 'shapeless things' moving towards her, Jill retreats to the room, but it is too late: 'They are hunting her. Huge forms, terrifying in their very lack of definition, with here and there eye-like dots of red light. [...] Instead of the walls there are standing stones round a moonlit space. And there the shapeless things are circling, closing in [...] Then she falls. It is a long way down.' Alerted by her screams, Brock enters the room to find Jill dead; later he returns to find the walls reverberating with the sound of her calling out his name: 'And there is nothing he can do. Except stand there stunned by the knowledge ... that there is a new voice on the stone tape'.

Just as Kneale was willing to apply a Freudian interpretation to the work of MR James, so too have critics such as Mark Fisher and Adam Scovell since extended this gesture to an analysis of Kneale's work. Fisher interprets the ceaseless repetition of the haunting in *The Stone Tape* as analogous to the traumatic compulsion to repeat observed by Freud in *Beyond the Pleasure Principle* (1920) in which it is symptomatic of those in whom the experience of time has broken down.[67] While Scovell uses Freud's claim in his *Studies On Hysteria* (1895) that 'hysterics suffer mainly from reminiscences' to illustrate his point that, in Kneale's writing, the past haunts in such a literal way 'as to cause mental and even physical collapse in the people of the present.' Indeed, Scovell argues that rather than employing this 'hysterical metaphor' to determine the behaviour of his characters, Kneale expresses it in geographical terms, the room at the heart of *The Stone Tape* itself the living embodiment of an hysterical case existing 'in a state of permanent reminiscence of a past trauma.'[68]

But rather than through Freud, Kneale's play is perhaps best understood as part of the tradition of temporal experimentation exemplified by Dunne and Lethbridge. What the script makes clear, but which the film fails to convey, is the manner in which Kneale's narrative is bookended by the vision of standing stones, which marks Jill's arrival and which she witnesses at the moment of her death. Lost in translation from script to film, these stones act as the true motif of Kneale's work, symbolic of the horrors of deep time and illustrative of the recording medium through which past trauma is transmitted. Furthermore, the unsettling vision Jill experiences on her arrival reveals a precognitive glimpse of her future, a glimpse which horrifies her but which she fails to understand. For, as the theories of Dunne and Lethbridge suggest, her future has already been recorded. It is this which explains the powerful sense the film conveys that Jill is simply fulfilling her allotted role within an historical cycle played out over aeons. Several hauntological themes coalesce in *The Stone Tape*: deep time and the persistence of memory; stone as the psychic repository of trauma; analogue technology and the obsolescence of the future; temporal disjunction and the repetition of the past.

As we come to consider the work of Alan Garner and Susan Cooper, Kneale's work provides a powerful reminder that as much as haunting is a function of time so too are these recurrent events deeply embedded within the landscapes against which they are played out.

Inner Time: Alan Garner

Nowhere is the impact between topography and chronology felt more keenly than in the work of Alan Garner (b. 1934). The recognition that certain landscapes may resonate with the histories of the events they have played host to is a hallmark of hauntology, and within Garner's work such a belief is paramount. As a result, Garner has been allocated a place alongside MR James and Nigel Kneale as the third figure in a triumvirate of writers whose works are characterised by 'landscapes stained by time, where time can only be experienced as broken, as a fatal repetition.'[69] In his explorations of the mythical substratum of Cheshire and Wales, as unearthed in two of his most celebrated novels *The Owl Service* (1967) and *Red Shift* (1973), Garner's vertical descent through time past is governed not by a linear view of history but rather by an idiosyncratic and highly personal alternative that he has termed 'inner time'.

The Owl Service is an example of 'low' fantasy in which, unlike the pure fiction of 'high' fantasy, fantastical elements intrude upon and disrupt the pattern of everyday life. Throughout Garner's work, these elements of the fantastic are drawn from myth, whose repetition through time disrupts the linear flow of history, irrupting into the present with unpredictable, or rather all too predictable, consequences. Set in Dinas Mawddwy in Gwynedd in the late 1960s, *The Owl Service* follows three teenagers, Alison, Roger and Gwyn, as they are drawn into re-enacting the mythic cycle embedded within the landscape of their local valley. Inspired by his reading of *The Mabinogion* while on a family holiday in the Dyfi Valley, Garner chose to rework the myth of Blodeuwedd (Alison), the woman who is magically made out of flowers for her husband, Lleu (Gwyn), the man cursed to never find a wife.

According to the myth, Blodeuwedd conspires with her lover Gronw (Roger) to kill Lleu, but he survives by turning into an eagle and escaping, only to return and take his revenge. Blodeuwedd is transformed into an owl, while Gronw is killed by Lleu with the spear that pierces what becomes known as the Stone of Gronw. Overlaid with contemporary concerns over class, national prejudice and sexual awakening, the valley becomes the backdrop to the latest repetition of an ancient and seemingly unending cycle. The myth is obscurely articulated by the gardener, Huw Halfbacon, a figure who seemingly experiences both linear and mythic time simultaneously, an anachronism captured in his speech through which myth is translated into a perpetual present:

> "There is a man being killed at that place," said Huw: "old time." [...] "He is standing on the bank of the river, see, and the husband is up there on the Bryn with a spear: and he is putting the stone between himself and the spear, and the spear is going right through the stone and him." [...] "Yes, sir, that is how it is happening, old time."[70]

Myth retains its power through repetition, and each generation must rework the story to its tragic (owls) or benign (flowers) conclusion. It is the chance (or predetermined) discovery of an old dinner service in the attic that initiates the latest iteration of the myth as Alison, Gwyn and Roger find their relationships and behaviour irresistibly conforming to the preordained pattern of this mythic cycle. The linear time of their teenage lives and the deep and unending time of the valley itself are gradually superimposed, as past, present and future meet and intermingle: '"Nothing's safe any more. I don't know where I am. 'Yesterday', 'today', 'tomorrow' – they don't mean anything. I feel they're here at the same time: waiting."'[71] Alison senses that linear time is breaking down in the face of a power outside of time, an energy that builds up periodically within the valley and which can only be released by the children playing out their allotted roles: '"Lleu, Blodeuwedd and Gronw Pebyr. They are the three who suffer every time, for in them the power of this valley is contained, and through them the power is loosed."'[72] Huw recognises the origin of this power, but it is Gwyn who describes their role as conductors of this mythic current: '"I think this valley really is a kind of reservoir. [...] I think the power is always there and always will be. It builds up and builds up until it has to be let loose – like filling and emptying a dam. And it works through people. I said to Roger that I thought the plates were batteries and you were the wires."'[73]

Here, Garner's dialogue touches upon the ideas of Lethbridge in which landscape transmits the power while people act as receivers through which the 'recording' of myth is replayed. In *The Owl Service* it is the Stone of Gronw which acts as the transmitter, the focal point of the myth, the inorganic object in which time accumulates until the moment at which it must be discharged. The material, of course, is significant. Just as in *The Stone Tape* in which the room stores the psychic energy of previous incarnations, in Garner's novel it is the geology of the valley itself which fulfils this function: '"Here: in this valley: now. That is how the power is spent. Through us, within us, the three who suffer every time."'[74] In the end, or rather in this instantiation of the myth, the power is discharged safely and it is flowers and not owls which prevail.[75] *The Owl Service* illustrates a theme which resurfaces throughout Garner's work, most notably in *Red Shift* (1973), in which the re-emergence of the past into the present is presented as having the potential both to be enriching and violently destructive.

In outlining what he understands by myth and its relationship to narrative, Garner has acknowledged his debt to Mircea Eliade, whose work I have discussed in my earlier remarks on Vernon Lee. Evidently recognising him as a kindred spirit, Garner employs Eliade's conception of the 'sacred time' of primitive religion, using the example of the Aboriginal Australian religion as one in which time is experienced in ways wholly at odds with our own.[76] Yet in his search for an example of mythic time with which to align his beliefs, Garner was able to look closer to home. In his recollections of the Welsh holiday which was to inspire *The Owl Service* he describes his friendship with the elderly groundsman Dafydd Rees Clocydd, the model for Huw Halfbacon, and a man in whom the mythic past remained very much alive:

> One day, Dafydd said that he had something to show me. He took me to a farm, and into a stone outbuilding. He pointed

up. "See," he said, "my uncle made that. Good, isn't it?" I was looking at a superb example of a seventeenth-century queen-post roof of oak. I do not doubt that his uncle built it. But how many uncles ago?

The experience clarified what I already knew but had not voiced. The mind that has not been formally educated is not trapped in linear time. Memories of named individuals are identified for about three or four generations. Then the way is blocked, usually by a patriarch, beyond whom there is nothing, and to whom accrete tales and exploits of a giant. But I suspect that they are the accretions onto an individual of generations of history; for, beyond linear oral memory, we are in mythic time, where everything is simultaneously present.[77]

In contrast to his earlier recollections of Wales, however, Garner's account of his return to the Dyfi Valley in April 1969 to begin filming the television adaptation of *The Owl Service* is rather more disturbing, forming the backdrop to a curious, if not wildly eccentric, essay entitled 'Inner Time'. First presented as a lecture at the ICA in 1975, it is here that we find Garner's most sustained attempt to explain his understanding of time and myth.[78] 'Inner Time' begins with Garner describing the malaise he began to suffer from whilst preparing the script for the film of *The Owl Service* in the autumn of 1968. Such was the debilitating exhaustion he experienced that, by the time he found himself on location the following April, he was already close to collapse. The process of revisiting and reworking *The Owl Service* in real time on set was so emotionally demanding that, soon after filming was completed, Garner succumbed to a breakdown. 'The crucial point', Garner notes, 'is that an author's characters are all to some degree autobiographical: and the time of a film or a play is Now; dangerous as it ever was. The distance had gone.'[79] Stripped of the protective distance between himself and his characters afforded to the writer, Garner during filming had found himself increasingly divorced from the world around him as he was plunged into the immediacy of his own creation, a perpetual present from which he was unable to break free. When he sought treatment, the source of Garner's illness was diagnosed through a simple question: '"Was *The Owl Service* written in the past tense and the third person or in the present and the first?"'[80] Garner's psychotherapist had ascertained that the nature of Garner's sickness was essentially one of time, as the original text, written in the past tense and without incident, had then been forcibly translated into the present, with unforeseen consequences. The name for such a disturbance, Garner tells us, is an 'engram':

> It is a memory-trace, a permanent impression made by a stimulus or experience. Music and smell are frequent activators of an engram. We reconstitute whole events from a line of Mozart or the scent of a flower. [...] Every event of life is recorded and is available to us directly; or indirectly through dreams, hypnosis or drugs. [...] Most pleasant or unhurtful experiences are put straight into their files, engrams labelled. It is the unpleasant experience that makes the threatening engram.
>
> Here is a typical pattern of an engram attack.
>
> Something happens to us. We are hurt. We do not like

> being hurt. "It" hurts. The event takes place in outer time, which is four-dimensional, and we, the organism, must continue. So, like an oyster, we enclose the pain, but, unlike the oyster, we produce no pearl. [...] We wrap the engram round with emotional energy. But the engram lives on, because the engram is a creature of inner time, and inner time is one-dimensional; or infinite. The view from outer time is not clear. All events seem to be present simultaneously: only our immediate needs give an apparent perspective. We can check the validity of this argument by calling to mind any two intensely remembered experiences. They will be emotionally contemporaneous, even though we know that the calendar separates them by years. [...] The severity of a given engram attack is related to the coexistence in inner time with all associated engrams, and their combined force threatens us. [...] It is obvious that, within a few generations of compounded inner times, the number of engrams available will approach infinity, and, whether we call the result "inherited inner time", "the collective unconscious" or "patterns of general human behaviour", the day-to-day result is the same.[81]

It is tempting to dismiss Garner's account of his 'engram attack', at times bordering on the incoherent, as a particularly colourful example of 1970s psychobabble. Yet behind the curious terminology, Garner's distinction between inner and outer time seems to reveal a crucial insight into the temporal structure that governs his work: on the one hand, 'inner' or 'one-dimensional' time, the realm of myth and the eternal; and on the other the 'outer' time of our everyday experience.

Events in outer time, both striking and innocuous, leave an impression or 'memory-trace' which, according to Garner's schema, are recorded in inner time as engrams, which may then lie dormant until they are reactivated by external stimuli such as music or smell. As a writer, Garner is compelled to reconfigure such engrams in his work, his characters constituent of this inner landscape, but if, as happened during the filming of *The Owl Service*, inner and outer time come into contact, in this case a memory-trace from the 1950s colliding with the 'now' of 1969, then the consequences can be severe:

> Disorientation, leading to symptoms that resemble madness, can be induced when the engram is made present simultaneously in inner and outer time. [...] The inner time co-ordinates were identical, but they had been externalised to a here-and-now of waking nightmare. Inner time rules of simultaneity and one-dimensionalism had been projected on to a four-dimensional space-time. Which was absurd. Or I was. [...] My all-but insanity, provoked by conditions that externalised my thoughts and memories, jumbled, as actors, so that I was seeing a reality that, for me, was close to schizophrenic illusion, was the spontaneous and ungoverned invasion of the outside world by inner time.[82]

Rather than insanity, however, Garner characterises his illness as a journey into Altjira, or the 'Dreamtime', the mythical realm of Aboriginal Australia, an experience beyond time, from which, thanks to his psychiatrist, he was to return restored and newly energised.[83] Freed from the debilitating effects of his engram attack, Garner now found himself able to access the mythic realm of inner time, no longer a source of fear but one of renewal, an ability whose mastery, he concludes, will allow us to harness our evolutionary potential:

> Inner time may not exist as such. It may be a confusion on my part from many sources; but it is an empirical truth for me, from which I am led to believe that Man is evolving, through that inner time as well as through other time frames, towards awareness of a universe that is conscious rather than effete. And to be conscious is to be responsible: to be responsible is to act: to act is to move: for ever. [...] If I have made the engram phenomenon seem hard, it is because evolution is hard, and we must evolve. I believe that we are evolving towards a hyper-consciousness of the individual, and that one of the evolutionary processes is concerned with inner time, a potential we are made aware of by the action of myth. At certain times in life, especially in adolescence, the potential universe is open to our comprehension, and it is not the engram's fault if we decide to be blind to the light and call on darkness.[84]

In characterising this process in terms of light and darkness, as well as in his identification of adolescence as the period in which the struggle between them becomes manifest, Garner reflects the similarly Manichean struggle between good and evil, which, as we shall see, provides the motif of Susan Cooper's sequence of novels, *The Dark is Rising* (1965-77). But before turning to my discussion of Cooper's work, Garner's distinction between inner and outer time is given its definitive dramatisation in his novel, *Red Shift* (1973).

Writing in 2011, in his introduction to a new edition of *Red Shift*, Garner recalls the moment which was to inspire the novel, a moment which encapsulates the temporal schema at the heart of his work, as well as providing us with a powerfully apt condensation of what we now understand by hauntology:

> I was reading the graffiti on the wall of the waiting room of a local railway station. It was the usual stuff, including one record, in chalk, of teenage romance, written in the form of the ubiquitous mantra: "Janet Heathcote + Alan Flask. It is true." Then the sky fell in on me, and with it, *Red Shift*.
>
> Someone had come back later and had written immediately below the mantra, in silver lipstick, without punctuation or a capital letter, the cramped, single line: "not really now not any more."[85]

This line, 'not really now not any more', acts as a mantra within Garner's novel, its repetition within the text and its usage as the novel's concluding line simply emphasising the temporal repetitions, continuities and distortions with which *Red Shift* is concerned. Garner considered the line as an alternative title to the book, a shorthand for his own experience of the complexities of 'inner' time; for in its forceful suggestion of an alternative temporality, this phrase, much like Hamlet's declaration that 'the time is out of joint', points far beyond the confines of Garner's text in anticipating our own similarly uncertain engagement with the present.[86] Indeed, so perfectly does this phrase appear to summarise Garner's temporal outlook (and increasingly our own), that in his discussion of *Red Shift*, Mark Fisher questions whether its discovery in a piece of anonymous graffiti may be attributed to more than mere chance:

> There is something so eerie, so cryptic, so suggestive about that phrase, especially when written as an anonymous graffito. What did the nameless author of this vagabond poetry mean by it, and what did it mean to them? What event – was it a personal crisis, a cultural event, a mystical revelation of some kind? – prompted them to write it? And did anyone else but Garner ever witness the phrase graffitied onto the railway station wall? Or was it only Garner who saw it? Not that I am suggesting he imagined it – but the phrase so perfectly captures the temporal vortices in Garner's work that it seems as if it could have been a special message meant only for him. Perhaps it was, whatever the "intentions" of the graffiti writer happened to be. [...] To say that there was something fated about Garner's encounter with this graffiti is to redouble the phrase's intrinsic, indelible eeriness. For what does the phrase point to if not a fatal temporality? No now, not any more, not really. Does this mean that the present has eroded, disappeared – no now any more? Are we in the time of the always-already, where the future has been written; in which case it is not the future, not really? [...] What *Red Shift* discloses is not, evidently, a linear temporality, in which different historical episodes simply succeed one another. Nor does it present the episodes in a relation of sheer juxtaposition – in which no causal connection at all is asserted amongst the different episodes, and they are offered to us merely as sharing some similarities. Nor do we have the idea [...] of

> a causality operating "backwards" and "forwards" through time, so that past, present and future have influence upon one another. This latter possibility is the closest to what *Red Shift* seems to be doing, but the novel's scrambling of time is so complete that we are not left with any secure sense of "past", "present" and "future" at all: *not really now any more*. Is there, then, no now because the past has consumed the present, reduced it to a series of compulsive repetitions, and what seemed to be new, what seemed to be now, is only the playing out of some out-of-time pattern? This formulation, perhaps, is closest to the cold fatality that seems to (un)ravel in *Red Shift*: Yet if different historical moments are in some sense synchronous, would this not mean, not that there was no now, but that it is *all now*?[87]

The narrative of *Red Shift* is fashioned, like *The Owl Service*, albeit much less overtly, around its own mythic structure, in this case drawing upon the ballad of Tam Lin, the knight who is rescued from captivity at the hands of the fairies by his true love, Janet. But while Garner's earlier novel interweaves the present with its mythic counterpart, *Red Shift* displays a more complex temporal arrangement, a tripartite division between three historical periods: the Roman occupation during the second century; the English Civil War; and the present of the early 1970s, all of which are closely tied to the geography (and geology) local to Garner himself, and in particular the village of Barthomley and the rocky outcrop of Mow Cop. Within these three periods, the book's three major male characters – Tom, Thomas and Macey – begin to experience time as fragmentary and repetitive, as traumatic experiences are relived and past, present and future momentarily dissolve into a single moment of simultaneity. Such episodes are heralded by the fits experienced by Macey and Thomas in which they are thrust out of linear time and afforded a bewildering glimpse of the future. For in a manner reminiscent of Nigel Kneale's *The Road*, time here 'echoes backwards' and it is not the contemporary character, Tom, whose present is troubled by intrusions of the past, but rather his forebears Macey and Thomas who are haunted by premonitions of a twentieth-century they have no means of understanding. During these moments of temporal disturbance, the distance between the characters falls away and they are briefly conjoined in a state of heightened awareness. As one critic has commented, such episodes as these in which time is experienced as distorted or appears to lapse altogether are symptomatic of schizophrenic illnesses such as multiple personality disorder. In terms of Garner's own 'engram attack' they must surely be seen as incidences of the passage into inner time, that deep, emotional zone in which the rules of linear time no longer apply.[88] For as Macey, the second-century character, repeatedly cries out: 'The distance is gone between us!', a recognition that time and history have been abolished, and one which is reiterated by Tom: 'We're bits of other futures. [...] Time runs out on us.'[89] Providing a degree of continuity in the face of these abrupt and involuntary transports from outer to inner time is an object, an ancient votive axe, wielded by Macey, hidden by Thomas and finally unearthed by Tom. More than three thousand years old, the axe provides Tom with a reassuringly tangible symbol of the past with which to offset the disorientating effects of inner time and the emotional upheaval of his faltering relationship with his girlfriend, Jan. Once again, stone is the material through which time is transmitted, from the church at Barthomley to the quarry on Mow Cop, taking on a crucial role within sacred ritual, a substance afforded the power to incite and quell violence, and to absorb the excesses of emotion, grief and pain.

A 'red shift' is an astronomical term which describes the increase in the wavelength of light as an object moves away from us in space. Garner's use of this title alludes to the novel's wider thematic concern with deep space and its concomitant sense of deep time; in this respect it is reflective of the feelings of emotional isolation experienced by the leading characters, an isolation which is only bridged by their sporadic forays into inner time.[90] The fits that trigger their removal from linear time resemble a dreaming state, and perhaps as a result of the precognitive visions they reveal (but which they cannot comprehend) Garner's novel has been viewed by one critic as an endorsement of the theories of JW Dunne.[91] In his depiction of the transformative and healing properties of inner time, however, Garner owes as much to Eliade as he does to Dunne. Like Eliade he is alert to the mythological conception of time as cyclical rather than sequential, in which history may be transcended through access to an eternal present. Indeed, the same critic has also compared Garner to a shaman whose 'ritualistic exorcisms' lend him creative mastery over time.[92] Ultimately, however, Garner's sense of time is peculiar to himself, residing neither in the precognitive visions of Dunne nor the shamanistic rituals described by Eliade. Instead, his temporal worldview may be characterised as an unfolding cycle of repetition, one which we may transcend through recourse to the deep emotional truths of inner time.

The Old Ways: Susan Cooper

As the work of Alan Garner illustrates so strikingly, the early 1970s was a particularly haunted period in English culture, as questions of disrupted time and the recurrence of the past became widely employed in fiction, music, film and television, in demonstration of the timelessness of the British countryside as well as the historical continuities of the urban past. The latter theme was explored most memorably in two books published in 1975: Maureen Duffy's extraordinary London novel, *Capital*, its name evoking the pre-eminence of the city in national life as well as recalling Marx's great unfinished work; and Iain Sinclair's *Lud Heat* which began his vertical descent through the more arcane aspects of London's past, a trajectory which has preoccupied London writing ever since and which marked the rebirth of psychogeography in a newfound and peculiarly English form. Both these books anticipate our own concern with the patterns of the historical past as it re-emerges in the present; but the work that most closely resembles the particular temporal and mythological exploration of inner time in Garner's fiction, is that of his near contemporary, Susan Cooper (b. 1935), whose sequence of five novels, *The Dark is Rising* (1965-77) not only reaffirms Garner's outlook but recalls us once again to the earlier theories of JW Dunne.

Born a few months apart and later both students at Oxford in the 1950s, Alan Garner and Susan Cooper have since been identified, along with Diana Wynne Jones and Penelope Lively, as part of the 'second Golden Age' of children's literature, the generation of writers who rose to prominence in the 1960s and 1970s (the 'first Golden Age' had spanned the years 1850-1920).[93] Of course, such a classification is a problematic one, particularly in as far as Garner's work is concerned, but these two figures clearly share a common outlook, most notably in their depiction of the ways in which time and place intersect and in the similarly prominent role of myth within their narratives. As in Garner's work, the settings for Cooper's fiction are taken from her own background; in *The Dark is Rising* sequence this identification with place is threefold: the Thames Valley of her upbringing; the Cornwall of childhood holidays; and her family home in the village of Aberdyfi in mid-Wales. Her depictions of these three locations are overlaid by a sense of distance and loss which results from the fact that Cooper moved to America in 1963 before any of these novels had been written. As far as her own imaginative or 'inner' landscape is concerned, as an undergraduate Cooper wrote an article entitled 'The Lost Land' in which she articulates with surprising clarity the world her future fiction would encompass:

> As I read more, the magic world became wilder; the creatures from Anderson and Grimm were joined by the Norse gods and the figures of Arthurian legend, Prospero, Ariel, Puck – all inhabited one dream world. The form of this world was very clear. Its predominant features were hills and trees; immense, rounded, lowering hills, misty blue in the distance; and unending forests, dense and dark, cloaking all the plains. There were rivers – lots of rivers – all swift flowing over rocky courses; and the sea was never far away.[94]

This is the landscape of the mythic past, the backdrop for Cooper's exploration of the Matter of Britain, the cycle of medieval myths and legends centred upon the tales of King Arthur from which many of the ideas and characters in *The Dark is Rising* sequence are drawn. Throughout this cycle of novels, the familiar countryside of our everyday experience is revealed to be merely the visible surface behind which a timeless and Manichean struggle is played out. As Robert Macfarlane remarks: 'All the usual pastoral props are in place [...] But this is only a stage set, soon to collapse – for Cooper is concerned not with Olde Englande, but with uncanny England, deep England, eldritch England.'[95]

Over Sea, Under Stone (1965) is a somewhat unremarkable introduction to Cooper's work. Its tale of three children holidaying in Cornwall who become involved in a search for the grail lacks the complexity of its sequel, *The Dark is Rising* (1973), the novel which lends its name to the sequence, and in which the themes of time and myth are treated in a manner at which its predecessor only hints. An explanation for this striking change in tone lies in the intervening years, a period in which Cooper was to write *J.B. Priestley: Portrait of an Author* (1970), a closely researched biography of the playwright, temporal researcher and great proselytiser of the ideas of JW Dunne. It is here, in Cooper's description of the impact of Dunne on Priestley's worldview, that we find the basis for ideas later to be explored within her own work:

> His [Dunne's] lost world, in the form of the haunting, hovering shadow which drifts continually in and out of his work, has been lost not to the powers of darkness but to

> Time, and thus it cannot be rediscovered, cannot be won back in battle: can never be seen or visited again, except in dreams – unless it is brought back by Time itself. To envisage this takes a certain amount of concentration. Suppose – not easy – if nothing which has ever been can ever stop being, then everything which has ever happened is still happening. If there is, in effect, a fifth dimension from which one can observe not only the present moment but also everything which runs before it and behind – then things which seem lost have never really been lost at all. It is partly because Priestley subscribes to this part of J.W. Dunne's Time theories that this shadow-world, though not shown as redeemable by any defeat of evil, does not seem dead and gone, but emerges as a vision combining might-yet-be with might-have-been. If he is haunted by anything, it is not by the intensity of the darkness enveloping the mountains, but by the unending brilliance of the sun lighting the plain.[96]

In characterising Priestley's thinking in terms of light and darkness, Cooper is once again rehearsing ideas and imagery that would be articulated more clearly in her own fiction, in which the forces of good and evil are engaged in an eternal struggle for dominion over time. There is no mourning for lost time in Priestley's temporal schema, nor in Cooper's fiction, because no time is ever truly lost. For as Cooper outlines in her examination of the work of another temporal theorist, PD Ouspensky, whose ideas were dramatised by Priestley in his play *I Have Been Here Before* (1937), time may be visualised as a three-dimensional spiral within which we are destined to live out our lives, a process of endless repetition whose validity is affirmed to us through those occasional moments of insight we call *déjà vu*:

> We live our lives not once, it suggested, but again and again: entering the same dilemmas, making the same mistakes, coming to the same crossroads and always, after much anguished weighing of possibilities, taking the same road as before. We encounter the same delights and the same miseries, every time as fresh as they were before – though sometimes, at some apparently meaningless moment, there may come like an echo of a familiar phrase of music a sudden momentary flash of memory from some point along the spiral we have already travelled, bringing with it the déjà vu sensation that Priestley put into his title, and that almost everybody has experienced at some time: I have been here before. And then the flash is gone, and our lives go on, repeating their pattern over and over again.[97]

In her account of Priestley's life Cooper explores a panoply of ideas such as these, from *déjà vu* and eternal recurrence, to precognitive dreams and alternate dimensions, all of which challenge a straightforward acceptance of linear time. Perhaps the most significant insight Cooper was to take from her study of Priestley, however, was also the most simple: 'the obvious fact that anyone who writes a novel or a play is automatically creating a different time-scale from the one in which he and his readers actually exist.'[98] For, as Garner was to experience so forcefully during the filming of *The Owl Service*, the act of literary creation demands an immersion in a time-scale quite different from that of our everyday experience, an 'inner' realm at odds with that of the 'outer' time we normally inhabit. As Cooper notes, we may gain momentary access to this altered time-scale not only through the creative impulse but also through moments of great emotional intensity or fear during which one may sense time slowing down; it is the conflict between these two seemingly divergent experiences of time that lies at the heart of her work.

The Dark is Rising (1973) begins on Christmas Eve as Will Stanton, a young boy about to celebrate his 11th birthday, finds himself inducted into the ranks of the Old Ones, a circle of temporal warriors whose role is to defend the light against the powers of the dark. Guided by the oldest of this order Merriman (Merlin), Will must come to terms with his newfound magical abilities as he embarks upon a twofold existence, his life with his family on a farm in the Thames Valley now complemented by his role as the last of the Old Ones, in which he must inhabit 'a different time-scale from that of everyone he had ever known or loved.'[99] *The Dark is Rising* follows Will's journey as he seeks out six elemental signs, the possession of which will enable the light finally to overcome the forces of the dark, protecting humanity from the evil which exists in the realm beyond time. For the Old Ones, ancient and immortal, all times coexist, since time is not fixed but fluid and can be shaped accordingly: 'we are not in real time; at least, we are in past time, and even that we seem to be able to stretch as we wish, to make it go fast, or slow.'[100] Doors through time grant access to the past or future, allowing Will to move between linear and mythic time as he wishes, while his transit through the landscape of linear time is aided by the Old Ways, a series of magically protected pathways through which the Old Ones may pass unchallenged;

'trodden by the Old Ones for some three thousand years', it is as if Alfred Watkins and JW Dunne had come together to establish a spectral network of supercharged ley lines in which the conventional laws of time and space no longer apply.[101]

Old Ones and Old Ways are joined by Old Speech, the ancient language of the order, and throughout Cooper's novel the appellation 'old' is applied across a wide spectrum of phenomena, none of which are necessarily old in linear time (Will, one struggles to recall, is only 11) and which in fact exist outside of time altogether. In this respect they are timeless rather than old, the products of a transcendent realm in which good and evil, myth and magic coexist, occasionally intruding into linear time but more often bypassing human history altogether. In this way, the unremarkable Thames Valley of Will's childhood finds its counterpart in the Old England which lies behind it, a timeless landscape populated by an array of figures from English and Celtic mythology, from Wayland Smith to Herne the Hunter. Unsurprisingly, given his abrupt abduction from a seemingly comfortable childhood existence into a supra-historical realm of elemental warfare, Will experiences feelings of nostalgia for the certainties of his former existence: 'An Old One, he suddenly knew, was doomed always to feel this same formless, nameless longing for something out of reach, as an endless part of life.'[102] This yearning for his past, or at least for the security of linear time, is the price Will must pay for his exclusion from human temporality. As the novel progresses, however, and the tension between his 11-year-old self and that of his newer (or rather older) incarnation becomes increasingly hard to sustain, so with growing incongruity do we hear Will's voice become that of someone ever more familiar. Could it be that JW Dunne was himself an Old One?

> 'There's not really any before and after, is there?' he said. 'Everything that matters is outside Time. And comes from there and can go there.' [...] 'I mean the part of all of us, and of all the things we think and believe, that has nothing to do with yesterday or today or tomorrow because it belongs at a different kind of level. Yesterday is still there, on that level. Tomorrow is there too. You can visit either of them. And all Gods are there, and all the things they have ever stood for.' And, he added sadly, 'the opposite, too.'[103]

Published in 1973, it is tempting to read *The Dark is Rising* as a reaction against the period in which it was written, a time in which the England that Cooper describes was thought in some quarters to be in as great a danger as the novel suggests. Faced by the seemingly overwhelming and chaotic powers of the Dark, the Deep England of centuries-old tradition was in need of magical intervention, and if the present could be frozen or the past revisited, then so much the better. For any evocation of England's mythical history runs the risk of holding up the image of an essential and unchanging past with which to combat an uncertain future. As will be discussed in the following chapter, our exploration of hauntology today returns us unerringly to the England of this period, an era fondly recalled (or angrily dismissed) as the final moment before the post-war consensus was fatally undermined.

The third volume of Cooper's sequence, *Greenwitch* (1974), returns the reader to Cornwall to resume the story of the grail quest, before the narrative moves to Wales for the concluding two episodes, *The Grey King* (1975) and *Silver on the Tree* (1977). These are notable principally for their evocation of place rather than for the temporal complexities which characterise the second instalment of the cycle, but even here we are given sporadic reminders of Cooper's ongoing engagement with earlier experiments with time, articulated once more through the voice of the Old Ones: '*For all times coexist* [...] *and the future can sometimes affect the past, even though the past is a road that leads to the future.*'[104] These voices reach their crescendo in *Silver on the Tree* as the dark is finally vanquished, but just as in the closing sequence of the television adaptation of *The Owl Service*, in which one instantiation of a mythical cycle is concluded only for the next to begin, one is left to wonder whether such a cycle can ever truly end, or even if the idea of such an end can, outside of time, hold any real meaning:

> For ever and ever, we say when we are young, or in our prayers. Twice, we say it, Old One, do we not? For ever and ever ... so that a thing may be for ever, a life or a love or a quest, and yet begin again, and be for ever just as before. And any ending that may seem to come is not truly an ending, but an illusion. For Time does not die, Time has neither beginning nor end, and so nothing can end or die that has once had a place in Time.[105]

Myths of the Near Future: JG Ballard

Has any other writer described the nature of time with imagery as vivid as that of JG Ballard (1930-2009)? Has anyone else anticipated, with such unerring accuracy, the future language of hauntology?[106] 'The Voices of Time'; 'The Time-Tombs'; 'The Dead Time'; 'Chronopolis'; 'Memories of the Space Age'; 'Myths of the Near Future': time is the predominant theme in Ballard's fiction, slowed, curtailed, even abolished. His is a world characterised by stasis, entropy and decay. Yet in any assessment of Ballard's numerous remarks on time, both in his fiction and elsewhere, one encounters a problem familiar to those approaching his work, for having already articulated a critical response of his own, Ballard leaves little foothold for any further commentary.[107] The best course of action is to let his own words speak for him:

> The biggest developments of the immediate future will take place, not on the Moon or Mars, but on Earth, and it is inner space, not outer, that needs to be explored. The only truly alien planet is Earth. [...] For example, instead of treating time like a sort of glorified scenic railway, I'd like to see it used for what it is, one of the perspectives of the personality, and the elaboration of concepts such as the time zone, deep time and archaeopsychic time.[108]

These comments first appeared in 'Which Way to Inner Space?' (1962), an early manifesto of sorts, in which Ballard sets out his belief in the future direction of science fiction, arguing that spaceships and alien planets should be discarded in favour of an exploration of the human psyche.[109] Both in his usage of the term 'inner space' as well as in his suggestion that the traditional trajectory of science fiction should be reset, Ballard's remarks echo those of JB Priestley, a figure who is coming to haunt this account, and whose essay 'They Come from Inner Space' (1953) was surely a significant, if unacknowledged, influence upon Ballard's future thought.[110] Certainly, for both writers, it is the psychological dimension of 'inner space' which offers the infinitely more rewarding source of ideas, amongst them the belief that our concept of time is essentially subjective and rooted in the deep time of our evolutionary past. Here, as throughout his work, Ballard draws upon Freudian principles, in this instance reiterating Freud's notion of 'phylogenetic memory', his belief that human societies unconsciously retain reserves of genetic memory which manifest themselves through myth and ritual. In *Moses and Monotheism* (1939), his highly speculative final work, Freud argues that the Israelites preserved the common memory of their forebear, Moses, despite the suppression of the oral and written records of these events, leading him to conclude:

> What may be operative in an individual's psychical life may include not only what he has experienced himself but also things that were innately present in him at his birth, elements with a phylogenetic origin – an archaic heritage. [...] If we assume the survival of these memory-traces in the archaic heritage, we have bridged the gulf between individual and group psychology: we can deal with peoples as we do with an individual neurotic. Granted that at the time we have no stronger evidence for the presence of memory-traces in the archaic heritage than the residual phenomena of the work of analysis which call for a phylogenetic derivation, yet this evidence seems to us strong enough to postulate that such is the fact.[111]

Freud's ideas were employed by Ballard in *The Drowned World* (1962), the opening novel in a trilogy which explores the nature of time.[112] Here, amidst an apocalyptic future in which the planet has been submerged beneath the primeval swamps of the Triassic era, Ballard uses the backdrop of a decaying London to explore the regression of the human race as it willingly reverts to an earlier evolutionary state. Replete with the surrealistic imagery of Dali and Delvaux, Ballard's novel portrays a small band of increasingly disorientated survivors as they begin to respond to the call of their long-forgotten past, a genetic impulse from 'archaeopsychic' time:

> How often recently most of us have had the feeling of déjà vu, of having seen all this before, in fact of remembering these swamps and lagoons all too well. [...] These are the oldest memories on Earth, the time-codes carried in every chromosome and gene. Every step we've taken in our evolution is a milestone inscribed with organic memories [....] Just as psychoanalysis reconstructs the original traumatic situation in order to release the repressed material, so we are now being plunged back into the archaeopsychic past, uncovering the ancient taboos and drives that have been dormant for epochs. The brief span of an individual life is misleading. Each one of us is as old as the entire biological kingdom, and our bloodstreams are tributaries of the great sea of its total memory. The uterine odyssey of the growing foetus recapitulates the entire evolutionary past, and its central nervous system is a coded time scale, each nexus of neurones and each spinal level marking a symbolic station, a unit of neuronic time. [...] If you like, you could call this the

> Psychology of Total Equivalents – let's say 'Neuronics' for short – and dismiss it as a metabiological fantasy. However, I am convinced that as we move back through geophysical time so we re-enter the amnionic corridor and move back through spinal and archaeopsychic time, recollecting in our unconscious minds the landscapes of each epoch, each with a distinct geological terrain, its own unique flora and fauna, as recognisable to anyone else as they would be to a traveller in a Wellsian time machine. Except that this is no scenic railway, but a total reorientation of the personality. [...] The innate releasing mechanisms laid down in your cytoplasm millions of years ago have been awakened, the expanding sun and the rising temperatures are driving you back down the spinal levels into the drowned seas submerged beneath the lowest levels of your unconscious, into an entirely new zone of the neuronic psyche. This is the lumbar transfer, total biopsychic recall. We really remember these swamps and lagoons.[113]

Neuronics? Biopsychic recall? It is unclear how seriously one should take this riff on genetic memory, articulated here by the familiar Ballardian character of the scientist. Ballard's account verges on parody, a disquisition on time and memory presented in the manner of a medical report; but beneath the pseudo-scientific language Ballard's depiction of archaeopsychic time is consistent with his commitment to 'inner space'. This reworking of the Wellsian fable is one which renders a time-machine unnecessary, for the journey back into the overheated recesses of our primeval past takes place within the confines of our DNA. Of course, as Ballard explained subsequently, the memories at work here are by no means wholly genetic. The overgrown vegetation of *The Drowned World* had first taken root in the Shanghai of his childhood, later fusing with recollections of his years in London to create the dreamlike landscape of the novel.[114] Ballard's traumatic childhood experiences in Shanghai cast a long shadow over his fiction, and 50 years after the publication of *The Drowned World* he was to recall the impact of his wartime internment in awakening him to a new perception of time, one in which the illusory progression of our everyday existence is once again eclipsed by the deeper rhythms of the past:

> Time has been a very important strand in my fiction, partly because of the sort of dislocations I knew as a child, when what appeared to be, on the one hand, a very settled and stable childhood in pre-war Shanghai suddenly came to an end [...] I suddenly saw time come to an abrupt stop, and a very different and ugly sort of clock begin to tick. [...] I think that jolted me into realising that the comforting progress of the clock hands around the day, measuring out our lives, was a huge illusion, and along with it was a huge set of illusions about who we are and our relationships with each other. Many of the characters in my short stories and novels have sudden glimpses into what they realise is a sort of larger reality, that there's a deeper past to the human race, when the everyday clock has stopped and there are much larger clocks whose movements are virtually imperceptible but which cover giant periods of time as the human race evolved. So that all of us, in our brains and spinal columns, carry the memories of the human race as it emerged from

its primitive forbears and began to develop consciousness, beginning, for the first time, to dream.[115]

It is through his recognition of time as essentially twofold, the passage of our everyday lives offset by an awareness of a more expansive calibration of time, that Ballard allies himself to the earlier visions of Garner and Cooper. But Ballard's idiosyncratic temporal perception was soon to undergo an evolution of its own, his portrayal of deep time giving way to a growing preoccupation with the decaying remnants of our recent past, a past characterised increasingly by the unfulfilled promise of a future that had failed to arrive. 'We live in quantified non-linear terms', Ballard claimed in 1967, 'we switch on television sets, switch them off half an hour later, speak on the telephone, read magazines, dream and so forth. We don't live our lives in linear terms in the sense that the Victorians did.'[116] As we have seen, the Victorians experienced their own temporal revolution, as their understanding of the past was radically undermined by evolutionary theory; and yet their faith in the future, and the possibilities it afforded, remained intact. By the end of the 1960s, however, a decade, in the West at least, of unprecedented technological and cultural upheaval, it was our perception of the future that had been overhauled.

'Everything happened during the sixties,' Ballard recalled in 1982, 'it was like a huge amusement park going out of control. And I thought, "Well, there's no point in writing about the future – the future's here. The present has annexed the future onto itself."'[117] Nothing encapsulated this sense that the future had now arrived with greater intensity than the Space Race, a period largely coterminous with Ballard's early career as a writer, beginning with the launch of Sputnik One in 1957 and reaching its zenith in the moon landing of 1969. Looking back on this era today, the energy and dynamism of these achievements now seem inseparable from the cultural and political breakthroughs of the era, as if they were all generated by the same means of propulsion. In light of the powerful sense of nostalgia this era continues to exert, it seems peculiarly apt, as Simon Reynolds has suggested, that the word 'retro' should have emerged in the early 1960s, born of precisely the technology which allowed retro rockets to reverse a spaceship's forward propulsion: 'retro as the cultural counterpart to "reverse thrust", with nostalgia and revivalism emerging in the seventies as a reaction against the sixties' full-tilt surge into the "out there".'[118] Ballard recalls the Sputnik launch ushering in a mood of great optimism and the feeling that a golden era was about to begin. He does not remember sharing in this mood, however, and his outlook has since proven correct: the modest lifespan of the Space Age ending, in Ballard's estimate, with the final Skylab mission in 1974, the first splashdown not to be televised.[119] Furthermore, rather than inaugurating a new technological age, Ballard regards the Space Age as bringing to a close a period which has, since the Industrial Revolution, brought us more than 200 years of achievements in 'nuts-and-bolts technology', without fulfilling the dreams of spaceships and interplanetary travel that science fiction had foreseen.[120] The future, true to form, has materialised in ways entirely other to those we might have expected, leaving us the remnants of a Space Age that is no longer regarded as futuristic but as retro, the optimism of the era overtaken not by pessimism, but by something more pernicious: *nostalgia*:

> Ballard's notion that the sixties had annexed the future came true in a way that he didn't envision. In a hideous twist, the sixties became the major generative force behind retro culture. [...] Through its hold on our imagination, its charisma as a period, the decade that constituted the greatest eruption of new-ness in the entire twentieth century turned into its opposite. [...] It's like we can't get past this past. Neophilia turns into necrophilia.[121]

Ironically, for an era so strongly associated with change, the 1960s have since become encased within the aspic of nostalgia. But the same charge cannot be directed against Ballard's work, much of which celebrates a timeless zone in which nostalgia has no meaning, unless it is coherent to suggest that one may experience nostalgia for the deep time of the primordial past.[122] For Ballard's nostalgia is not for the past but for the future, for the lost future of the Space Age, and it is reflected in strikingly hauntological landscapes in which past, present and future coalesce. This is expressed most memorably in three of his stories from the early 1980s: 'News from the Sun' (1981), 'Myths of the Near Future' (1982) and 'Memories of the Space Age' (1982), three studies upon the same two themes of light and time.[123] In each of these three stories the characters have succumbed to a 'space-sickness' or 'time-plague', their perception of time slowing to a standstill as they enter an increasingly prolonged fugue state. Amidst this over-lit landscape of clocks and cars, abandoned runways and drained swimming pools, objects become endlessly multiplied in a frozen panorama of simultaneity; drained of time and bleached by the sun, man appears to be suffering from the psychological after-effects of his doomed attempt to escape from the planet:

> By leaving his planet and setting off into outer space man had committed an evolutionary crime, a breach of the rules governing his tenancy of the universe, and of the laws of time and space. Perhaps the right to travel through space belonged to another order of beings [...] The brute-force ejection of themselves from their planet had been an act of evolutionary piracy, for which they were now being expelled from the world of time.[124]

Freed from the hold of the past and now experiencing time as little more than an endless procession of images, the fate of Ballard's characters may be interpreted either as a transcendent overcoming of time or as a meaningless regression into an ever diminishing present.[125] Alternating between the ecstatic and the sombre, these three stories replay Ballard's familiar obsessions as he muses upon the nature of time and eternity while exploring the possibilities of flight: 'Flight and time [...] they're bound together. The birds have always known that. To get out of time we first need to learn to fly.'[126] As the typically Ballardian figures of Franklin, Mallory and Sheppard play out their series of ritualised manoeuvres amidst the empty landscapes of Florida and Nevada, Ballard's use of language begins to anticipate that of hauntology itself in an uncanny premonition of our own nostalgia for futures past:

> At the same time, I feel a growing nostalgia for the future, a memory of the future I have already experienced but somehow forgotten. In our lives we try to repeat those significant events which have already taken place in the future. As we grow older we feel an increasing nostalgia for our own deaths, through which we have already passed. Equally, we have a growing premonition of our births, which are about to take place. At any moment we may be born for the first time.[127]

In these stories, time-sickness can be seen as a metaphor, its symptoms of memory loss, withdrawal from the world, and the onset of fugue states, reflective of a wider sense of cultural amnesia in which the past loses its grip in the face of a seemingly perpetual present. In 'News from the Sun', it is not only the returning astronauts who are afflicted by this strange temporal malady but anyone who witnessed the space launches, as if it were the cultural impact of the image which was to precipitate the illness. Given that an estimated television audience of some 650 million watched the Apollo moon landing could it be that, according to the logic of Ballard's story, much of the human race has since been afflicted by a time-plague? In 'Myths of the Near Future', 20 years have passed since the first symptoms of the illness emerged, making the story a projection into the near future of the mid-1990s. By now, however, an additional symptom has emerged. The victims identify themselves so strongly with this iconic moment, perhaps the last event to occur in real time, that they become convinced that they were once astronauts themselves:

> Could it be that travelling into outer space, even thinking about and watching it on television, was a forced evolutionary step with unforeseen consequences, the eating of a very special kind of forbidden fruit? Perhaps, for the central nervous system, space was not a linear structure at all, but a model for an advanced condition of time, a metaphor for eternity which they were wrong to try to grasp. [...] This space-sickness – it's really about time, not space, like all the Apollo flights. We think of it as a kind of madness, but in fact it may be part of a contingency plan laid down millions of years ago, a real space programme, a chance to escape into a world beyond time. Thirty years ago we opened a door in the universe.[128]

Written in the early 1980s, but depicting the aftermath of the Space Age from the perspective of a denuded 1990s, Ballard's diagnosis seems as relevant as ever today, prompting the reader to question whether we ourselves may have been infected by the epidemic of time-sickness he describes in his fiction. Interviewed in 1982, Ballard discusses his perception of our loosening grasp of time, arguing that it is symptomatic of a broader sense of societal dislocation in which the cultural artefacts of our own time can no longer be seen as representative of a particular historical moment as they once were:

> Life itself may be a bit overblown these days – one never knows. It's an interesting time, much more fragmented than if one lived in the late forties, which I did. Then, if one thought of newspapers, magazines, television in its early

> days, the cinema – the whole media landscape generally (the world of publishing, the books that came out on topics of the day, political events around the world), they were all part of one whole – sort of graspable in a way. And it may be that that's going to end. Sections of the landscape will have no connection whatsoever with each other, in the way that many of the fine arts, such as pottery, are more specialised. [...] You can't reconstitute an epoch from looking at a Ming vase – it stands outside time. It's hard to say, but probably nobody will ever again be fully engaged with a sort of central experience. Not in the way people from the thirties can speak of: a shared feeling of everyone being involved in great political currents, when you could see change coming and everybody shared in it equally. Also, great changes are taking place in life in general: the way people live, the standards of living, modern travel. Time will in a sense cease to exist; it won't matter whether you're living in 1982 or 1992 or 2002 – that sense of a single world will go.[129]

This identification of a temporal shift seems remarkably prescient today, Ballard's sense that time has become divorced from culture clearly foreshadowing the emergence of hauntology. Ballard has repeatedly articulated his belief that during his lifetime the way in which we experience time has undergone a fundamental transformation, the optimism of his parents' generation, in which the future was expected to deliver an improvement on the present and past, itself a casualty of the profound dislocation of the Second World War and the onset of the Nuclear Age. Despite, or perhaps because of, the unprecedented levels of prosperity they introduced, the post-war years heralded a growing uninterest in both past and future as the attractions of the present took centre stage:

> In the thirties and forties people had an intense interest in the future. They saw the future as a morally superior world to the one in which they lived. [...] Yet some time around the end of the fifties, the future somehow lost its hold. I think it died. [...] People certainly lost interest in the future. They began to fear the future. And partly, I think, the prosperity in the sixties and seventies induced a kind of infantilism. People stopped dealing with a timescale that lay outside their immediate present. They began to have no sense of what had happened yesterday or of what would happen the day after tomorrow. So people became immersed in the fulfilment of their own needs and their own satisfactions. They literally lost interest in the future. By the same token, they also lost interest in the past. [...] So time has dismantled itself.
>
> I can see a time, probably about midway into the next century, when time will virtually cease to exist. The present will annex both the future and the past into itself. All desires will be fulfilled and people will live in a perpetual present.[130]

According to Ballard, the twentieth century has undergone its own recalibration of past and future, as did the nineteenth, and just as the Victorians were faced with a terrifying expansion of the past, so Ballard's era (and our own) has witnessed the consequences of an all-embracing present, one in which images of the past and future have become dissociated from the histories that gave rise to them. The result has been that amidst our newly fragmented apprehension of time, it has become impossible to see beyond the boundary of this pervasive present, and to ascribe a sense of meaning to the collage of images and histories that surround us. And if, as hauntology suggests, we can no longer conceive of any alternative to the present, then how can we hope to experience anything truly new?

> Everything has been condensed into a kind of high-pressure present where it's almost impossible to visualise anything new happening; it's impossible to think in terms of the day after tomorrow. Elements of the past exist but they've all been reduced to kits, outlines on walls, crashed cars, elements in a sort of huge exhibition. [...] We live in an enormously expanded present, which is just packed like a tenement city with images from the past, and to some extent the future, which have been commandeered, ransacked out of the years past and the years to come [...] what [do] all these elements that are no longer linked by time mean: if they are not linked by time, what are they linked by?[131]

Just as Ballard has identified 1945 as a turning point, the atomic bombs of Hiroshima and Nagasaki that effectively ended his own wartime confinement also instigating an unwillingness to look to the future, so too have there since been other such events, through which our sense of time has been similarly disrupted. As we shall see in the following chapter, one such example is the fall of the Berlin Wall in 1989, a moment that briefly gave rise to a belief that history as we knew it had come to an end. It was the approach of the millennium, however, with all the anxieties such milestones inevitably provoke, which prompted Ballard to ask, 'Does the future still have a future?'[132] In the end, of course, that moment passed without the calamitous upheaval that many had predicted or even hoped for. From the perspective of the twenty-first century one now wonders whether Ballard's vision of the near future has come to pass, and our future has been superseded by the more imaginative extrapolations of science fiction:

> Surprisingly, we appear to have turned our backs on the future, and tend to gaze nostalgically upon a re-invented past that most of us never managed to enjoy the first time around. [...] It may be that we have already dreamed our dream of the future, and have woken with a start into a world of motorways, shopping malls and airport concourses which lie around us like the first instalment of a future that has forgotten to materialize. [...] Did the future arrive too soon, some time around the mid-century, the greatest era of modern science fiction? [...] One reason why the Apollo moon-landings failed to touch our imaginations is that science fiction got there first, just as it has anticipated so much of our lives, effectively taking all the fun and surprise out of existence.[133]

Notes

1 Saint Augustine, *Confessions* (AD 397), trans. by Henry Chadwick, Oxford: Oxford University Press, 2008, p. 230.

2 TS Eliot, 'Burnt Norton' (1935) in *Complete Poems & Plays*, London: Faber, 2004, 171-176, p. 171.

3 John Michell, *The New View Over Atlantis*, London: Thames and Hudson, 1983, pp. 22-23.

4 Robert Macfarlane, 'Introduction' in Alfred Watkins, *The Old Straight Track* (1925), London: Head of Zeus, 2014, xii-xxxv, p. xiii.

5 Alfred Watkins, *The Old Straight Track*, Introduction by Alfred Watkins, p. xlii.

6 Michell, p. 24.

7 Watkins, *The Old Straight Track*, pp. 313-4.

8 Stephen Daniels, 'Lines of Sight: Alfred Watkins, Photography and Topography in Early Twentieth-Century Britain' *Tate Papers*, Autumn 2006.

9 John Michell in his introduction to Alfred Watkins, *The Ley Hunter's Manual: A Guide to Early Tracks* (1927), London: Thorsons, 1983, 5-8, p. 6.

10 Robert Macfarlane writes: '[Watkins's] work would spawn countless theories of occult earth mysteries and New Age psycho-naturalism: stories of telluric lines of force that ran invisibly across countries, their routes marked above ground by megaliths and tumuli, and with dowsing and crystal-swinging allowing their routes to be determined. His leys would inspire cults of goat-foot gods and black-dog lines, and would be folded into theories of psychic energies, magnetic fields, Atlanticism, aliens and other forms of extra-terrestrial presence. They would muddy the waters of mainstream archaeology, and extend archaeology's lunatic fringes for decades. Ley lines would even end up in the songs of Jethro Tull, the land art of Hamish Fulton and the novels

of Thomas Pynchon [...] And this wonderful, tangled web of consequence was set spinning by the murmurings of an amateur prehistorian to a small salon of county burghers.' Robert Macfarlane, 'Introduction' in Alfred Watkins, *The Old Straight Track*, pp. xv-xvi.

11 Allen Watkins, *Alfred Watkins of Hereford*, London: Garnstone, 1972, p. 30, and quoted by Daniels in 'Lines of Sight'.

12 For an account of Watkins's role as a precursor to this movement see Merlin Coverley, *Psychogeography*, Harpenden: Oldcastle Books, 2018, pp. 57-61.

13 For an excellent introduction to Dunne and his work, see Francis Spufford's documentary 'I Have Been here Before', BBC Radio 3 (2014) at https://www.bbc.co.uk/programmes/b04h7lr0

14 It was the mathematician and early writer of science fiction, Charles Howard Hinton (1853-1907) who first introduced the idea of a fourth dimension in his article 'What is the Fourth Dimension?' (1880). His work was to influence, amongst many others, HG Wells, Jorge Luis Borges, Susan Cooper, and Alan Moore, who devotes a chapter of *From Hell* (1989-96) to a discussion of his ideas. As far as he is remembered today, it is principally through his creation of the 'tesseract' to help visualise the idea of four-dimensional perception. Hinton's work also prompted the Russian esotericist, PD Ouspensky (1878-1947) to write his *The Fourth Dimension* (1909).

15 Colin Wilson, *Mysteries: An Investigation into the Occult, the Paranormal and the Supernatural*, London: Watkins, 2006, p. 163. See also Victoria Stewart, 'J.W. Dunne and Literary Culture in the 1930s and 1940s', *Literature & History*, Volume 17, (2), Autumn 2008, 62-81, p. 78.

[16] JB Priestley, *Man and Time*, London: Aldus Books, 1964, 244-261, p. 244.

[17] JW Dunne, *An Experiment with Time* (1927), ed. by Russell Targ, Charlottesville, VA: Hampton Roads, 2001, p. 1.

[18] Dunne, *An Experiment with Time*, p. 20.

[19] Dunne, *An Experiment with Time*, pp. 21-3.

[20] Dunne, *An Experiment with Time*, p. 26.

[21] Dunne, *An Experiment with Time*, p. 28.

[22] Dunne, *An Experiment with Time*, pp. 29-31.

[23] Dunne, *An Experiment with Time*, p. 31.

[24] Dunne, *An Experiment with Time*, pp. 31-32.

[25] For a clear summary of serial time, or at least one that is more intelligible than most, see Guy Inchbald, 'The Last Serialist: C.S. Lewis and J.W. Dunne', *Mythlore*, 134, Spring/Summer 2019, pp. 77-88.

[26] Dunne, *An Experiment with Time*, p. 80.

[27] Dunne, *An Experiment with Time*, p. 121.

[28] Dunne, *An Experiment with Time*, p. 120.

[29] See Mark Pilkington, 'Tangling with Time', *The Guardian*, 18 March 2004.

[30] Wilson, *Mysteries,* p. 164.

[31] It is interesting to compare the figure of Dunne's painter with that of the extraordinary concluding image of the TV series *Sapphire and Steel* (1979-82) whose protagonists become similarly entombed within a temporal trap. The creator of the series, PJ Hammond, writes: 'I've always been interested in Time, particularly the ideas of JB Priestley and HG Wells, but I wanted to take a different approach to the subject. So instead of having them go backwards and forwards in Time, it was about Time breaking in'. See Mark Fisher, 'The Slow

Cancellation of the Future', in *Ghosts of My Life*, p.2.

[32] Wilson, *Mysteries*, p. 165.

[33] Alongside these figures, Dunne's theory has also influenced the work of CS Lewis, Jorge Luis Borges, Buckminster Fuller, Robert Heinlein and Vladimir Nabokov. An unexpected addition to this list is that of the French film director Gaspar Noé, whose notorious *Irréversible* (2002) is filmed in reverse chronological order, culminating (or beginning) with Monica Bellucci's character Alex in a park reading Dunne's *An Experiment with Time*. As Nicholson Baker writes: 'Dunne's *Experiment* seems to have become one of the secret wellsprings, or wormholes, of twentieth-century literature.' See Nicholson Baker, 'Night Vision: The Forgotten Theory of Dreams that Inspired Vladimir Nabokov', *The New Republic*, 21 February 2018.

[34] Priestley, *Man and Time*, p. 258.

[35] Wilson, *Mysteries*, pp. 167-8.

[36] Jorge Luis Borges, 'Time and J.W. Dunne' (1940) trans. by Suzanne Jill Levine, in *The Total Library: Non-Fiction 1922-1986*, ed. by Eliot Weinberger, London: Penguin, 1999, pp. 217-219.

[37] TC Lethbridge, *The Essential T.C. Lethbridge*, ed. by Tom Graves and Janet Hoult, London: Routledge & Kegan Paul, 1980, p. 139.

[38] Terry Welbourn, *T.C. Lethbridge: The Man Who Saw the Future*, Alresford: O-Books, 2011.

[39] Reynolds, *Retromania*, p. 339.

[40] Mark Pilkington writes: 'In the mystic haze of late '60s Britain, T.C. Lethbridge's ideas would converge with the ley line theories of Alfred Watkins, giving birth to the

'Earth Mysteries' movement, and feeding the minds of New Wave psychogeographers Iain Sinclair, Peter Ackroyd (*Hawksmoor*), Alan Moore (*From Hell*), and others whose ideas subsequently flowed into the hauntological timestream.' See Mark Pilkington, 'Hauntologists mine the past for music's future', *boingboing*, 12 October 2012 at https://boingboing.net/2012/10/12/hauntologists-mine-the-past-fo.html

41 Charles Babbage, *The Ninth Bridgewater Treatise*, London: John Murray, 1837, quoted by Sharon A Hill in 'The "Stone Tape Theory" of Hauntings: A Geological Perspective', 11 May 2017 at https://sharonahill.com/2017/05/11/the-stone-tape-theory-of-hauntings-a-geological-perspective/

42 Wilson, *Mysteries*, p. 58.

43 HH Price, 'Haunting and the "Psychic Ether" Hypothesis' (1939), in *Philosophical Interactions with Parapsychology: The Major Writings of H.H. Price on Parapsychology and Survival*, ed. by Frank B Dilley, New York: St Martin's Press, 1995, 17-34.

44 Oliver Lodge, *Man and the Universe*, London: Methuen, 1908, quoted in Wilson, *Mysteries*, p. 64.

45 Colour television was first demonstrated publicly in the UK in 1928; it wasn't until 1967, however, that the BBC first began transmitting regular broadcasts in colour.

46 TC Lethbridge, *Ghost and Ghoul*, London: Routledge and Kegan Paul, 1961, p. 9.

47 Lethbridge, *Ghost and Ghoul*, pp. 10-11. Lethbridge concludes: 'They [ghosts] are pictures produced by human minds. They are not spirits of departed persons from another world. [...] To me they appear to be no more and no less than television pictures. The television picture is a man-made ghost.' (p. 150).

[48] Lethbridge, *Ghost and Ghoul*, p. 53.
[49] Lethbridge, *Ghost and Ghoul*, pp. 40 & 150-1.
[50] Lethbridge, *Ghost and Ghoul*, p. 76.
[51] Lethbridge, *Ghost and Ghoul*, p. 151.
[52] Lethbridge, *Ghost and Ghoul*, pp. 151-2.
[53] TC Lethbridge, *The Power of the Pendulum* (1976) London: Arkana, 1984, pp. 40.
[54] Welbourn, p. 280.
[55] Wilson, *Mysteries*, p. 69.
[56] Welbourn, p. 282.
[57] Ralph Waldo Emerson, *The Collected Works, V, English Traits* (1856), London: Harvard University Press, 1994, p. 157, quoted by Nicholas Royle in *The Uncanny*, pp. 8-9.
[58] Royle, *The Uncanny*, p. 9.
[59] Further examples include *The Owl Service* (1969) dir. Peter Plummer; *A Journey to Avebury* (1971) dir. Derek Jarman; *Psychomania* (1973) dir. Don Sharp; *The Wicker Man* (1973) dir. Robin Hardy; *Children of the Stones* (1977) dir. Peter Graham Scott; *Stigma* (1977) dir. Lawrence Gordon Clark, and *Quatermass* (1979) dir. Piers Haggard. This particular strand of 1970s culture was to reach its pinnacle, however, in Hawkwind's 'Atomhenge' tour of 1976, which featured a futuristic stage-set designed as a cross between the Atomium in Brussels and Stonehenge.
[60] Hill, 'The "Stone Tape Theory" of Hauntings: A Geological Perspective'.
[61] Mark Fisher writes: 'Stone circles confront us with a symbolic structure that has entirely rotted away, so that the deep past of humanity is revealed to be in effect an illegible alien civilisation, its rituals and modes of subjectivity unknown to

us.' See Mark Fisher, *The Weird and the Eerie*, pp. 89-90.

[62] Nigel Kneale, 'Minuke', in *Tomato Cain and Other Stories*, London: Collins, 1949, 34-48.

[63] The scripts of both *The Road* and *The Stone Tape*, along with Kneale's prescient exploration of the alienating effects of reality television, *The Year of the Sex Olympics* (1968), can be found in Nigel Kneale, *The Year of the Sex Olympics and Other TV Plays*, London: Ferret Fantasy, 1976.

[64] In a striking illustration of the changing viewing habits of British television audiences at this time, it was the pioneering snooker programme *Pot Black* that is said to have been recorded over much of the material. See Jonathan Rigby, 'The Promised End: Nigel Kneale's Lost Masterpiece – THE ROAD', in *We are the Martians: The Legacy of Nigel Kneale*, ed. by Neil Snowdon, Hornsea: PS Publishing, 2017, 261-270, p. 269. Reflecting on the fate of Kneale's play, Mark Fisher writes: 'There's something awfully poignant about the thought of a ghost story about the future being lost to that very future.' See Mark Fisher, 'No Futurebleed: Kneale's Hauntology', *k-punk*, 18 October 2003, at http://k-punk.org/no-futurebleed-kneales-hauntology/

[65] 'The ideas of Hauntology have no better example in any form', writes Adam Scovell, 'than in Nigel Kneale's 1972 play, *The Stone Tape*.' See Adam Scovell, 'Analogue Ghosts of the 1970s and Hauntology', *Celluloid Wicker Man*, 20 July 2015, at https://celluloidwickerman.com/2015/07/20/analogue-ghosts-of-the-1970s-and-hauntology/

[66] The script of *The Stone Tape* can be accessed at: http://www.horrorlair.com/scripts/StoneTape.htm.

[67] See Mark Fisher, *The Weird and the Eerie*, pp. 87, and 'No

Futurebleed: Kneale's Hauntology', *k-punk*, 18 October 2003.

[68] See Adam Scovell, 'Technological Hysteria in Nigel Kneale's *The Stone Tape* (1972)', *Celluloid Wicker Man*, 4 December 2014, at https://celluloidwickerman.com/2014/12/04/technological-hysteria-in-nigel-kneales-the-stone-tape-1972/

[69] See Mark Fisher, 'What is Hauntology?', *Film Quarterly*, Vol. 66, 1 (Fall 2012), 16-24, p. 22.

[70] Alan Garner, *The Owl Service* (1967), London: Collins, 1998, p. 43.

[71] Garner, *The Owl Service*, p. 93.

[72] Garner, *The Owl Service*, p. 99.

[73] Garner, *The Owl Service*, p. 138.

[74] Garner, *The Owl Service*, p. 188.

[75] While the ending of Garner's novel is ambiguous – Alison's death is averted but it remains unclear whether the mythical cycle has been terminated or merely postponed – the film version closes with an additional sequence, framed by the hole in the Stone of Gronw, in which three small children can be seen playing, suggesting that the cycle ends only to begin once more.

[76] See the essays 'Achilles in Altjira' (1983) and 'The Voice in the Shadow' (1995) in Alan Garner, *The Voice That Thunders: Essays and Lectures*, London: Harvill, 1997, pp. 39-58 & 146-177.

[77] Alan Garner, 'The Beauty Things' (1996) in *The Voice That Thunders*, 193-207, p. 205.

[78] Alan Garner, 'Inner Time' ('Science Fiction at Large', Lecture at ICA, London, 26 February 1975) in *The Voice That Thunders*, 106-125.

[79] Garner, 'Inner Time', p. 112.

[80] Garner, 'Inner Time', p. 112.

[81] Garner, 'Inner Time', pp. 113-5. A term first used in 1904 by Richard Semon, the engram was later appropriated by L Ron Hubbard in his *Dianetics: The Modern Science of Mental Health* (1950) and has since evolved to become a cornerstone of the pseudo-scientific doctrine of Scientology. At the time of writing, Garner was keen to restore the term to its 'original, philosophical definition': 'Textbooks have a name for the disturbance, but it is a term that has been hijacked and abused by popularisation and by misapplication and redefinition at the hands of tendentious factions, with whom I am anxious not to be associated, especially the Church of Scientology and its gormless substitutes for thought.' See 'Inner Time', pp. 112-3.

[82] Garner, 'Inner Time', pp. 115.

[83] Garner, 'Inner Time', pp. 115-6.

[84] Garner, 'Inner Time', pp. 117-123.

[85] Alan Garner, 'Introduction' (2011) in *Red Shift* (1973), New York: NYRB Classics, 2011, vii-xii, p. x.

[86] Mark Fisher writes: 'This immensely suggestive phrase, Garner's version of "the time is out of joint," captures what is at stake in so much of the present discussion of hauntology.' See Mark Fisher, 'What is Hauntology?', *Film Quarterly*, p. 22.

[87] Fisher, *The Weird and the Eerie*, pp. 90-3.

[88] Charles Butler, 'Alan Garner's *Red Shift* and the Shifting Ballad of "Tam Lin"' in *Children's Literature Association Quarterly*, Normal, IL: Illinois State University, Summer 2001, Vol. 26 (2), 74-83, p. 78.

[89] Garner, *Red Shift*, pp. 33 & 61.

[90] Neil Philip, *A Fine Anger: A Critical Introduction to the Work of*

Alan Garner, London: Collins, 1981, p. 91.

91 Philip, p. 101.

92 Philip, p. 102.

93 See Charles Butler, *Four British Fantasists: Place and Culture in the Children's Fantasies of Penélope Lively, Alan Garner, Diana Wynne Jones and Susan Cooper*, Lanham, MD: Scarecrow Press, 2006, p. 1.

94 Susan Cooper, 'The Lost Land', *Cherwell*, quoted by Charlotte Higgins in 'Susan Cooper: a life in writing', *The Guardian*, 21 December 2012.

95 Robert Macfarlane, 'The Eeriest Novel I Know', *The Economist 1843 Magazine*, July/August 2014.

96 Susan Cooper, *J.B. Priestley: Portrait of an Author*, London: Heinemann, 1970, pp. 18-19.

97 Cooper, *J.B. Priestley*, p. 109.

98 Cooper, *J.B. Priestley*, p. 220.

99 Susan Cooper, *The Dark is Rising*, London: Chatto & Windus, 1973, p.138.

100 Cooper, *The Dark is Rising*, p.122.

101 Cooper, *The Dark is Rising*, p.81.

102 Cooper, *The Dark is Rising*, p. 138.

103 Cooper, *The Dark is Rising*, pp. 164-5.

104 Susan Cooper, 'Silver on the Tree' (1977), in *The Dark is Rising Sequence*, London: Puffin, 1984, 591-786, p. 610.

105 Cooper, 'Silver on the Tree', p. 727.

106 One candidate is William Gibson, whose short story 'The Gernsback Continuum' (1981) is now recognised as a pioneering example of hauntological fiction. In this tale of a man haunted by the 'semiotic phantoms' of the 1930s, Gibson evokes the futuristic imagery of pre-war America, unmoored

from its own era only to reappear in the 1980s. Written in the same year as Ballard's 'News from the Sun' (1981), Gibson's story depicts the similarly incongruous remnants of a future that failed to materialise, reinforcing the sense of a culture submerged beneath the accumulated debris of its recent past. See William Gibson, 'The Gernsback Continuum', in *Burning Chrome*, London: Gollancz, 2017, 28-40.

[107] Simon Reynolds writes: 'One of my fantasy projects that I toyed with as a writer was a book on Ballard and Eno. [...] But the project founders immediately owing to the fact that they are so eloquent about what they do and such brilliant writers, that there'd be zero role for any critic or commentator. There'd be very little to mediate or interpret, as they've said it all, so much better.' See 'Magisterial, Precise, Unsettling: Simon Reynolds on the Ballard Connection.' Interview by Simon Sellars, 2 June 2007 at https://www.simonsellars.com/magisterial-precise-unsettling-simon-reynolds-on-jg-ballard

[108] JG Ballard, 'Which Way to Inner Space?', *New Worlds*, 1962, in *A User's Guide to the Millennium: Essays and Reviews*, London: Harper Collins, 1996, 195-198, pp. 197-8.

[109] Mark Fisher has taken issue with Ballard's use of the term 'Inner Space': 'I have always found this to be a profoundly misleading description. Much more than astronauts floating in *empirical* space, it is the "Outer" which Ballard's suburban cosmonauts investigate: what they confront is time and space *themselves*, as preconditions of all perceptions and experiences, and what their explorations open up is an intensive zone beyond – outside – standard perceptual thresholds.' See Mark Fisher, 'Space, time, light, all the essentials – reflections on

J.G. Ballard season (BBC Four)' (2003) in *K-Punk*, 43-45, pp. 44-5.

110 JB Priestley, 'They Come from Inner Space', *New Statesman* (1953) in *Thoughts in the Wilderness*, London: Heinemann, 1957, 20-26. For a brief outline of Priestley's role in Ballard's fiction, see James Pardey, 'Landscapes from a Dream: How the Art of David Pelham Captured the Essence of J.G. Ballard's Early Fiction', *Ballardian*, 14 June 2010, at http://www.ballardian.com/landscapes-from-a-dream

111 Sigmund Freud, 'Moses and Monotheism: Three Essays' (1939) in *The Standard Edition of the Complete Psychological Works, Vol. 23* (1964), trans. by Angela Richards, London: Vintage, 2001, 7-132, pp. 98-100.

112 Ballard writes: 'In *The Drowned World* I dealt with the past, and employ water as the central metaphor. In *The Drought* I deal with the future, taking sand as the central image. In *The Crystal World* I am concerned with the present, the symbol of which is the diamond or the precious stone which – so I believe – possesses a timeless structure.' See JG Ballard, '1968: Uncredited. Munich Round Up – Interview with J.G. Ballard' in *Extreme Metaphors: Selected Interviews with J.G. Ballard, 1967-2008*, ed. by Simon Sellars and Dan O'Hara, London: Fourth Estate, 2012, pp. 10-13.

113 JG Ballard, *The Drowned World* (1962), London: Harper Perennial, 2006, pp. 43-4 & 74.

114 See JG Ballard, 'Time, Memory and Inner Space', *The Woman Journalist*, 1963, in *A User's Guide to the Millennium*, pp. 199-200.

115 JG Ballard, '2000: John Gray. 'Technology is always a facilitator': JG Ballard on *Super-Cannes*' in *Extreme Metaphors*,

pp. 380-1.

[116] JG Ballard, '1967: George MacBeth. The New Science Fiction' in *Extreme Metaphors*, p. 7.

[117] Reynolds, *Retromania*, pp. 410-11.

[118] Reynolds attributes this version of the term's origins to the design historian, Elizabeth Guffey. See Reynolds, p. xxxi.

[119] JG Ballard, '1979: Christopher Evans. The Space Age is Over' in *Extreme Metaphors*, pp. 123-4.

[120] JG Ballard, '1979: Christopher Evans. The Space Age is Over' in *Extreme Metaphors*, pp. 123-4.

[121] Reynolds, pp. 410-11.

[122] Mark Fisher writes: 'Despite what Jameson himself writes on Ballard, one of the important differences between the Ballard text and pastiche as Jameson describes it is the absence of "nostalgia" or the "nostalgia mode" – an insistent presence in other postmodernist science fiction texts, as Jameson shows – in Ballard's work. Indeed, Ballard's commitment to striking textual innovations – as evidenced in the layout of the pages themselves in *The Atrocity Exhibition* – marks him as something of an anomaly in Jameson's terms; in this sense at least, Ballard seems to be continuous with modernism as Jameson understands it.' See Mark Fisher, 'Why I Want to Fuck Ronald Reagan' (2004) in *K-Punk*, 47-51, pp. 49.

[123] JG Ballard, '1984: Peter Rønnov-Jessen. Against Entropy' in *Extreme Metaphors*, p. 207.

[124] JG Ballard, 'News from the Sun' in *The Complete Stories of J.G. Ballard*, New York: W.W. Norton, 2009, pp. 1019-20.

[125] For an account of Ballard's ambiguous treatment of time in these three stories, see Mike Holliday, 'Ballard and the Vicissitudes of Time', *Ballardian*, 3 July 2008 at http://www.

ballardian.com/ballard-and-the-vicissitudes-of-time

[126] JG Ballard, 'Memories of the Space Age' in *The Complete Stories*, p. 1052.

[127] JG Ballard, 'News from the Sun' in *The Complete Stories*, p. 1026.

[128] JG Ballard, 'Myths of the Near Future' in *The Complete Stories*, pp. 1065-6 & 1078.

[129] JG Ballard, '1982: V Vale. Interview with JGB' in *Extreme Metaphors*, pp. 163-4.

[130] JG Ballard, '1988: Rosetta Brooks. Myths of the Near Future' in *Extreme Metaphors*, pp. 243-5.

[131] JG Ballard, '2006: Jonathan Weiss. 'Not entirely a journey without maps': J.G. Ballard on *The Atrocity Exhibition*' in *Extreme Metaphors*, pp. 460-1.

[132] JG Ballard, 'Back to the Heady Future' (1993) in *A User's Guide to the Millennium*, pp. 192-3.

[133] JG Ballard, 'Back to the Heady Future' (1993) in *A User's Guide to the Millennium*, pp. 192-3.

Part III: Ghosts of Futures Past

If, as a science fiction writer, you ask me to make a prediction about the future, I would sum up my fear about the future in one word: boring. *And that's my one fear: that everything has happened; nothing exciting or new or interesting is ever going to happen again. The future is just going to be a vast, conforming suburb of the soul.* JG Ballard (1982)[1]

"The end of history? The beginning of nonsense!" Margaret Thatcher (1989)[2]

Washington, 1989

In February 1989, the deputy director of the State Department's policy planning staff in Washington was invited to the University of Chicago to give a talk on international relations. An expert on Soviet foreign policy, Francis Fukuyama was by no means a household name. In fact, outside of his field of expertise, he was barely known at all. Before his appointment to Washington, Fukuyama had followed a somewhat unusual academic path for a future State department official which included six months in Paris studying under Roland Barthes and Jacques Derrida, an experience he was to look back on with little affection.[3] Having changed direction on his return to the US, studying political science before taking up a role with the RAND Corporation in Santa Monica, Fukuyama gave his lecture in 1989 against the backdrop of the approaching end of the Cold War. The previous year Moscow had announced that it would no longer intervene in the affairs of its Eastern European satellites, and Fukuyama's provocative address triumphantly asserted the final victory of Western liberalism, and with it the end, as understood in terms of ideological struggle, of history itself. The transcript of Fukuyama's talk soon came to the attention of Owen Harries, editor of the Washington-based journal, *The National Interest*, and in the summer of that year it was published as an article entitled 'The End of History?' Founded in 1985 by the 'godfather of neo-conservatism', Irving Kristol, *The National Interest* was an obscure journal with a modest circulation, and yet the notion of 'the end of history' was catchy enough to capture the attention of a mainstream audience. The response was such that a newsdealer on Connecticut Avenue in Washington was soon able to reveal that the summer issue of *The National Interest* was 'outselling everything, even the pornography.'[4] In November the Berlin Wall fell, only adding a further prophetic lustre to Fukuyama's growing reputation. On 26 December 1991, the Soviet Union voted to dismantle itself and the Cold War was over. In 1992, Fukuyama's book *The End of History and the Last Man* was published (the question mark that had appeared in the title of the article was no longer deemed necessary). The rest, as they say (with the possible exception of Fukuyama himself), is history.

Needless to say, the idea that history had reached its terminus and that the final destination was a 1990s style American liberalism was by no means welcomed by all who read Fukuyama's article. The critical backlash was intense and often characterised by a wilful misreading (if read at all) of Fukuyama's position that suggested, absurdly, that he was proclaiming the end of history as commonly understood rather than that of its broader ideological direction, a distinction he emphasises at the beginning of his essay. As we shall see, amidst the blizzard of counter arguments, it was Jacques Derrida's *Specters of Marx* (1993) that offered the most sustained rebuttal of Fukuyama's position, in turn provoking an equally prolonged critical response of its own, with the result that ten years after the publication of his article, Fukuyama had become, in the words of Fredric Jameson, 'the textbook example [....] and the paradigm case of an apocalyptic pronouncement on the death of the past as such, the utter disappearance of that pre-history we still call History: in other words, the definitive exorcism of spectres and spectrality, the beginning of a market universe which is a perpetual present'.[5] Of course, with the advent of a new millennium approaching, Fukuyama was far from alone in proclaiming the end of history. In fact, his prognosis was rather less apocalyptic than many, for *fin de siècle* periods have often been characterised by a sense of our imminent demise; and while history may have appeared to be at an end, the history of such ends, or 'Endism' as it has been termed, continued to flourish.[6] What was different, or perhaps oddly familiar, about Fukuyama's claim, was that in his vision of the end times, only the Western elect were to be saved, while the Marxist alternative, indeed any alternative, was to be discarded:

> In watching the flow of events over the past decade or so, it is hard to avoid the feeling that something very fundamental has happened in world history. [...] The triumph of the

West, of the Western idea, is evident first of all in the total exhaustion of viable alternatives to Western liberalism. [...] What we may be witnessing is not just the end of the Cold War, or the passing of a particular period of postwar history, but the end of history as such: that is, the end point of mankind's ideological evolution and the universalization of Western liberal democracy as the final form of human government. This is not to say that there will no longer be events to fill the pages of Foreign Affairs's yearly summaries of international relations, for the victory of liberalism has occurred primarily in the realm of ideas or consciousness and is as yet incomplete in the real or material world. But there are powerful reasons for believing that it is the ideal that will govern the material world in the long run.[7]

Whether one regards Fukuyama's position as triumphalist, optimistic or simply misguided, his proclamations have an undeniably messianic tone that recalls the similarly Manichean conflict between the forces of Light and Darkness to be found in the fiction of Susan Cooper, in which we witness another (final) battle for the control of history. Fukuyama's reasoning is informed by a dialectical view of history first propounded by Hegel, and later Marx, in which a clash between thesis and antithesis creates a new synthesis of ideas which is in turn challenged and overcome, until the end point of history is finally attained. In this respect Fukuyama uses a Marxist view of history to proclaim its demise; we have reached the end of history, it is simply not the end Marx envisaged. In fact, what Fukuyama is describing is essentially an end not of history but of ideology, and in this respect, once again, his views are by no means new. Instead they return us to a debate conducted in America in the 1950s, most notably by the sociologist Daniel Bell in his book *The End of Ideology* (1960), in which he claimed that 'ideology, which was once a road to action, has come to a dead end'.[8] But if history (or ideology) has truly come to an end, what will our post-historical future have to offer? The answer with which Fukuyama concludes his essay is, given the confident tone with which it began, surprisingly downbeat, for with the ideological struggle of history now past, what is left to sustain us?

> The end of history will be a very sad time. The struggle for recognition, the willingness to risk one's life for a purely abstract goal, the worldwide ideological struggle that called forth daring, courage, imagination, and idealism, will be replaced by economic calculation, the endless solving of technical problems, environmental concerns, and the satisfaction of sophisticated consumer demands. In the post-historical period there will be neither art nor philosophy, just the perpetual caretaking of the museum of human history. I can feel it in myself, and see in others around me, a powerful nostalgia for the time when history existed. Such nostalgia, in fact, will continue to fuel competition and conflict even in the post-historical world for some time to come. Even though I recognize its inevitability, I have the most ambivalent feelings for the civilization that has been created in Europe since 1945, with its North Atlantic and Asian offshoots. Perhaps this very prospect of centuries of boredom at the end of history will serve to get history started once again.[9]

'The perpetual caretaking of the museum of human history'; 'a powerful nostalgia for the time when history existed': thirty years on, Fukuyama's argument is remembered principally as a triumphalist response to the death throes of the Soviet Union, much less so as a forewarning of post-historical boredom fuelling a nostalgia for the conflicts of the past. And yet it is surely here that his vision of the future has proven most prescient; for while the ideological struggles of today appear far from concluded, his prediction of a perpetual present drained of meaning and stripped of momentum seems much less easy to dismiss.

If Fukuyama's article anticipated the end of the Cold War, his subsequent book, *The End of History and the Last Man* (1992), responds to these events, its title expanded in reference to Nietzsche and his similarly triumphant (or demoralising) conception of the future. Nietzsche's 'last men' were the residue of a complacent society unable to face up to the challenge a godless future, who, in contrast to his more celebrated 'overmen', craved a return to the certainties of the past. Fukuyama likens these figures to those in the West who, faced with the end of history, may be tempted to reject the material security of an unexciting present in favour of a return to past conflicts which, while clearly not in their interests, will at least alleviate their boredom.[10] In essence, Fukuyama is acknowledging that an unchanging future of Western liberalism may, despite the apparent benefits of unbroken peace and economic plenty he ascribes to it, come at a cost that is simply too high for some to bear; for can a future free from any conceivable alternative really prove satisfying? This, it seems, is the real legacy of Fukuyama's position, not an end of history, or even ideology, but of social imagination, and with it the ability to conceive of anything beyond the horizon but the final and all-embracing victory of capitalism. In short, while history may have ended a new era has begun, one which Mark Fisher has termed 'capitalist realism':

> What could happen now that actually existing socialism had collapsed, and capitalism could assume full spectrum dominance, its claims to global dominion were thwarted not any longer by the existence of a whole other bloc, but by small islands of resistance such as Cuba and North Korea? The era of what I have called 'capitalist realism' – the widespread belief that there is no alternative to capitalism – has been haunted not by the apparition of the spectre of communism, but by its disappearance.[11]

Fukuyama's thesis may well have attracted widespread derision, but according to Fisher it has since become 'accepted, even assumed, at the level of the cultural unconscious.'[12] This is to say, even as his claims have been publicly dismissed, so has this disavowal been accompanied by the widely held belief that our sense of history has been diminished, leaving us only the consolations of consumerism, the curation of our cultural heritage, and a nostalgic longing for the past. Yet will the future really be as sterile as Fukuyama suggests? And is there really no alternative?

Derrida and l'hantologie

L'hantologie. This is the origin of all the myriad ideas, both cultural and political, that have since accumulated under this heading. Of course, much is lost in translation, not least Derrida's pun on 'hantologie' and 'ontologie'; they are near homonyms in spoken French, but this aural repetition fails to occur in English with the result that the 'sonic dimension' intrinsic to Derrida's concept is often overlooked.[13] The conceptual fusion between haunting and ontology – the philosophical study of being or existence – survives translation, however, although even here one must tread carefully, for the term *hantise*, translated here as 'haunting', also contains 'the common sense of an obsession, a constant fear, a fixed idea, or a nagging memory', elements of which feed into our understanding of hauntology itself.[14]

Readers familiar with Derrida's broader deconstructive strategies, in which the meanings of seemingly secure terms are queried and undermined, will recognise *l'hantologie* as a successor to earlier concepts, most notably another neologism which when spoken aloud is indistinguishable from the word on which it plays: *différence* and *différance*. The latter word, Derrida's creation, contains both the traditional meaning of 'difference' and, in addition, that of 'deferral', suggestive of the way in which the meaning of a word (in Derrida's philosophy) remains elusive and is constantly deferred.[15] If then, *différance*, may be understood as a concept created by Derrida to emphasise the way in which the meaning of a word (and of language itself) cannot be ultimately fixed, forever eluding our attempts to capture its meaning, so too can hauntology be seen in a similar light, in this case its play on ontology questioning what we mean by 'being' and that which is said to exist, and, by inference, our understanding of time. Derrida's teasing, and often infuriating, attempts to probe and weaken our sense of certainty are achieved by aligning a term with its opposite, or rather its absence – meaning and non-meaning; being and non-being – and by demonstrating the fragility of the border between them. In the case of hauntology, nothing is more illustrative of the border between being and non-being, than that which could be said to be characteristic of both: the ghost. Simultaneously present yet absent, dead yet living, corporeal yet intangible, in time yet timeless, the figure of the ghost fits perfectly within Derrida's deconstructive philosophy, its uncanny presence seemingly undermining the nature of every concept it comes into contact with. Derrida employs his spectral metaphor for good reason, not merely as a tool with which to display his peculiarly destructive form of scepticism, but in this instance as a means of challenging the idea that Marxism is dead and that we have arrived at the end of history. For we can never be free of the ghosts of the past, Derrida claims, those traces of our history that refuse to remain dead but which come back, repeatedly, to haunt the present.

The text of Derrida's book originates in an academic conference held at the University of California, Riverside in April 1993, under the heading 'Whither Marxism? Global Crises in International Perspective'. Derrida's lecture was published later that year and in English translation in 1994, and like all its author's works, *Specters of Marx: The State of the Debt, the Work of Mourning and the New International*, poses the reader very considerable challenges. Jacques Derrida (1930-2004) remains perhaps the most divisive of all major philosophers of the last century, to the point that some still maintain him to be no philosopher at all, merely an intellectual charlatan. Not only can his work be painfully, excruciatingly obscure, but, as many suspect, this may well be simply because he delights in making it so. Those who are seeking some sort of hauntological sourcebook will be disappointed by *Specters of Marx*, in which the term hauntology is mentioned only three times, acting as little more than a footnote to Derrida's wider concerns with Marxism. But his use of the spectre as a metaphor is much more widespread, employed throughout his discussion of Marx's ideas, as well as the means with which he illustrates the increasingly ghostly nature of our communications media and the ways in which information technology has begun to disrupt our perception of time and space.

In their introduction to *Specters*, the editors describe the sense of foreboding that many people felt after the fall of the Berlin Wall, 'a haunted sense that international changes of such magnitude were as likely to result, at least initially, and perhaps for a long time to come, in transformations as malign as they are benign.'[16] For in contrast to the self-congratulatory rhetoric of Fukuyama and his supporters, there was a countervailing mood of hesitancy and alarm arising from the belief that history, far from being over, was following its own course in ways impossible to foresee. The sense that, at this moment of historical rupture, time itself had undergone an unsettling transformation is encapsulated in Derrida's epigram to *Specters*: 'The Time is Out of Joint.' In choosing this phrase from *Hamlet*, the ur-text of literary haunting, Derrida reveals his intention to place the ghost at the heart of his investigation into Marx: 'As in *Hamlet*, the Prince of a rotten State, everything begins by the apparition of a specter.'[17] Shakespeare and Marx, *Hamlet* and the *Manifesto*, Hamlet's father and the spectre of communism, these are the two authors, two texts and two ghosts with which Derrida's work is primarily concerned, each exposing the nature of the spectral as essentially that which returns. 'The *revenant* is going to come. It won't be long', Derrida writes, for by its very nature the revenant 'is literally that which comes back.'[18] Of course, the paradox which Derrida is playing upon here is the fact that both Hamlet and Marx are waiting for the ghostly return of what has yet to appear for the first time. What Marx invokes in his *Manifesto* is the spectre of a communism yet to come, a spectre which appears to be haunting Europe even before it has arrived. This paradox suggests to Derrida that we have been premature in celebrating the demise of communism. Its message will continue to haunt us, just as it has always haunted us, even before it came into being.[19] 'Haunting is historical,' Derrida continues, 'but it is not *dated*, it is never docilely given a date in the chain of presents, day after day, according to the instituted order of a calendar.'[20] The ghost, the revenant, the spectre, these exist both inside and outside of time, both of and beyond history, and so to say we are haunted by Marx's ideas, or by history itself, is to suggest that neither can be said truly to have a beginning or end, for 'a ghost never dies, it remains always to come and to come-back.'[21] The ghost, whether it is Hamlet's father, or by analogy, communism itself, may be ephemeral but it is also timeless, and we therefore have little choice but to accommodate it in the present. Any attempt to dismiss the past is doomed to failure, for the past may be over but it is never past: 'they are always *there*, specters, even if they do not exist, even if they are no longer, even if they are not yet.'[22]

How one interprets paradoxes such as these – as playfully

enlightening or irritatingly opaque – will in large part determine one's broader attitude to Derrida's work. Any symptoms of intellectual discomfort may be alleviated if the reader is prepared to submit to his endless circumlocutions and repetitions, allowing oneself to be carried along by the underlying rhythms of his prose, a submission which makes reading him more enjoyable, or at least less tiresome, but which does little, of course, to reveal the *meaning* which, one hopes, must surely lie ahead. Throughout close readings of Shakespeare and Marx, Derrida returns repeatedly to the spectral and the haunted, but it is in answer to his own, seemingly straightforward, question, '*What* is a ghost?' that we reach our first encounter with *hauntology*:

> What is the *effectivity* or the *presence* of a specter, that is, of what seems to remain as ineffective, virtual, insubstantial as a simulacrum? Is there *there*, between the thing itself and its simulacrum, an opposition that holds up? Repetition *and* first time, but also repetition *and* last time, since the singularity of any *first time*, makes of it also a *last time*. Each time it is the event itself, a first time is a last time. Altogether other. Staging for the end of history. Let us call it a *hauntology*. This logic of haunting would not be merely larger and more powerful than an ontology or a thinking of Being [...] It would harbour within itself, but like circumscribed places or particular effects, eschatology and teleology themselves. It would *comprehend* them, but incomprehensibly. How to *comprehend* in fact the discourse of the end or the discourse about the end?[23]

Those seeking clarity here, in what is the textual origin of hauntology, will no doubt be frustrated, if not surprised, by Derrida's comments, as he tends to answer his own questions by posing a cluster of further ones, the cumulative effect of which is the curious sensation of being carried away from, rather than towards, the answer one might have expected, or at least hoped for. Perhaps, if one is in a charitable mood, this may be taken simply as a stylistic confirmation of Derrida's overriding deconstructive thesis, through which all meaning is endlessly deferred. Here, then, hauntology is presented as the 'logic of haunting', a concept broad enough to contain both eschatology (the end of history, end times) and teleology (the goal or purpose of history or ideology) within it, thus granting it the scope to act as a framing mechanism both for Fukuyama's ideas and Derrida's response to them.

Typically, it is only once he has used a term, that Derrida then chooses to use its second appearance as the opportunity to introduce it (as if for the first time), as if he has somehow forgotten or misplaced it. Once again, it is tempting, if only to render it explicable, to judge this reordering of linear exposition as somehow corresponding to Derrida's wider thesis, in this instance in support of his characterisation of the revenant as that which always returns, but every time as if for the first time. In this instance, hauntology (re-)emerges in a different but allied context, as Derrida discusses 'the medium of the media themselves', a similarly ghostly entity:

> this element itself is neither living nor dead, present nor absent: it spectralizes. It does not belong to ontology, to the discourse on the Being of beings, or to the essence of life

> or death. It requires, then, what we call, to save time and space rather than just to make up a word, *hauntology*. We will take this category to be irreducible, and first of all to everything it makes possible: ontology, theology, positive or negative onto-theology.[24]

Gradually the meaning of hauntology appears to be changing, from the 'logic of haunting' to a broader category which subsumes elements within it not merely of eschatology and teleology, but now ontology and theology too. For a term which, if Derrida is to be believed, is little more than a shorthand, created 'to save time and space', *hauntology* appears to have an ever-expanding remit, one which appears to pervade every category. While in its third and final appearance, Derrida once again recontextualises and reintroduces the term, this time aligning it with the more familiar concepts of being and time: 'To haunt does not mean to be present, and it is necessary to introduce haunting into the very construction of a concept. Of every concept, beginning with the concepts of being and time. That is what we would be calling here a hauntology.'[25]

There are no italics this time, for hauntology has become more closely defined. No longer restricted to our media landscape or interpreted only in ontological and theological terms, it has now come to reside within every concept, and its presence can be felt everywhere and in every time. And time is crucial, for of all the ways in which the spectral manifests itself in Derrida's schema, from the economic and the technological to the political, religious and cultural, it is only as a function of time that the concept of hauntology can be fully understood. The ghost is the figure Derrida employs in his deconstruction of time, the paradoxical figure who seemingly returns from the past into the present and yet which properly belongs to neither; a figure, or equally an idea, whose return heralds not only a repetition of the past but also an anticipation of the future. It is this dual-movement which is the hallmark of Derrida's 'logic of haunting', the belief that we may be haunted both by a past that refuses to be laid to rest and the promise of a future which refuses to be extinguished.

Both here and elsewhere, Derrida's interpretation of Marx as an intrinsically spectral presence, one which haunts the future as a Marxism yet to come, has largely gone unchallenged. But is such a reading correct? Writing in 1967, in his introduction to Marx's *Manifesto*, the historian AJP Taylor draws a rather different picture, noting that instead of unleashing a newfound idea upon the world (as by their very nature manifestos seem obliged to claim), Marx and Engels were in fact appropriating the term 'communism' for their own ends; not then the dreaded spectre of communism to come but rather the return of a ghost with a long and well-documented past:

> Why Communist? [...] It meant rigorously the community of goods and therewith the total abolition of private property. It harked back to the legendary state of primitive communism which, according to Engels, had existed before the economic Fall. Communism had been haunting the world as a spectre long before the days of Marx and Engels. It was an accusation levelled against the early Christians and against the Anabaptists of the sixteenth century. Agrarian communism was a dreaded prospect during the French revolution and sent even Jacobins scuttling under

> the protection of Napoleon. The word also evoked the Commune of Paris, which had been the most advanced revolutionary force in 1793. The two words had of course little real association, Commune being merely a French term for municipal government. But the link served to give the bourgeoisie a fright, and thus to satisfy Marx's sense of humour.[26]

Rather like the residual haunting of *The Stone Tape*, in which one ghostly manifestation is erased only to uncover earlier recordings beneath, so AJP Taylor's comments evoke a similar sense of historical repetition, one in which Marx's proclamation of 1848 may no longer be seen as the first, but merely the latest iteration of a temporal cycle in which the spectre of communism is compelled to return from the past to replay its ghostly message.

Alongside his elucidation of the spectral, Derrida's book also contains an uncharacteristically forthright assault on Fukuyama's position, painstakingly listing the numerous deficiencies which liberalism, if truly the final stage of historical development, has thus far failed to address, from unemployment and homelessness to economic and inter-ethnic warfare.[27] But beyond this inventory of the myriad ills afflicting capitalist societies, Derrida argues that the very idea of an end to history is an illusion, for we will never be able to free ourselves from the ghosts of the past and their claims upon us. Of course, while this argument is directed at Fukuyama and his allies, the idea that history will never reach its conclusion or be able to dispel its ghosts – regardless from which end of the political spectrum they might originate – comes at a cost to

Marxism itself, which proclaims an eschatological belief in the final victory of its own ideas. Perhaps then it is unsurprising that Derrida's book was met with a response that ranged from 'scepticism, to ire, to outright contempt.'[28] For having been largely dismissed by the right, many left-leaning members of Derrida's readership were bemused by what they judged, with good reason, to be a highly unorthodox interpretation of Marx's ideas. One audience, however, in which Derrida's work garnered widespread support was that of academia, for whom *Specters* fuelled something of a boom in all things ghostly. Derrida's book prompted the rehabilitation of the ghost, long since the subject of academic disdain, opening the floodgates to an array of spectrally-themed investigations into almost every form of cultural enterprise, and ensuring that as the new millennium approached, hauntology was to become something of a buzzword.

One writer to express his reservations about Derrida's ideas was Mark Fisher, who admits to having found him a frustrating thinker: 'Deconstruction was a kind of pathology of scepticism', he writes, 'which induced hedging, infirmity of purpose and compulsory doubt in its followers. [...] Derrida's circumlocutions seemed like a disintensifying influence.'[29] Despite his misgivings, however, Fisher acknowledges the force of Derrida's hauntological paradox: that we can be haunted by events which have not yet (or may never) come to pass, and that a concept seemingly as insubstantial and as abstract as hauntology can nevertheless have very real effects. Fisher seeks to rescue the term from its ghostly connotations, however, arguing that the spectre is best understood simply as that 'which acts without (physically) existing', a virtual form whose impact in the real world may be illustrated by the abstractions of late-capitalist finance or through the inner workings of the psyche.[30]

In response to Derrida's remarks in *Specters* concerning the proliferation of ghostly new forms of media technology, Fisher claims that the annexation of space by time enabled by such technologies, allowing spatially distant events to become available to an audience instantaneously, means that hauntology, even at the moment of its conception, was already endemic. Derrida did not live to see the culmination of this process, as the global domination of cyberspace saw the archive of the recorded past grow exponentially, and the consumption of 'materialised memory' rise accordingly. But Fisher suggests it is surely no coincidence that it was in the early years of the new millennium, a moment at which cyberspace 'enjoyed unprecedented dominion over the reception, distribution and consumption of culture' that the concept of hauntology should become such a dominant feature of cultural life.[31] In this respect, the hauntology that Derrida introduces in *Specters*, one whose time is yet to come and whose influence, both culturally and politically, is yet fully to be felt, begins to resemble the condition Marx ascribed to communism in 1848; for alongside the spectre of Marx, there is another spectre haunting Derrida's text, that of hauntology itself. In Derrida's hands hauntology comes to exhibit many of the characteristics of the spectral: like the revenant it comes back repeatedly, each time as if for the first; its form mutates, a ghostly virus infecting all it comes into contact with; its domain becomes ever more widespread both spatially and temporally. Indeed, Derrida's term has long since outgrown him, taking on a spectral existence of its own far beyond the confines of his text, coming to haunt the wider culture and, as we shall see, returning unexpectedly and in unforeseen ways.

The Ghosts of Repetition: WG Sebald

> It had grown uncommonly dark and sultry, the clouds painfully laden as though ready to sear the earth with their translucent acid, when I set out on my Summer holidays. Holidays! The word itself, a stifled and tortuous amalgam of "holly", that fiercest and most spiteful of all trees, with its sharp, shiny, pox-green edges ready to strike out and pierce human skin, causing blood, a dark reddish-grey, greyish-red, to drop out, willy-nilly, onto the earth below, staining the soil in perpetuity, and "days", with its dull echo of daze, in which I so often find myself after finishing these sentences, some of them as long and distracted as those sentences handed out with unnerving efficiency by the Guatemalan Lord Chief Justice to the Netherlandish invaders of the Indonesian island of Iwu-Miju in 1473, after the Brecon uprising commemorated in the poem by Swinburne after he had taken a cup of tea – a cup fatally calamitous for two pure white sugar lumps, who can have known little of their destruction but for those few dreadful seconds when they experienced the unsettling feeling, common to all human civilisation, of being dropped into hot, brown liquid with an abrupt flick of the wrist, there to disintegrate into nothingness, never to return – the entire and dreadful word, "holidays", forcing one to attempt to suppress a mounting sense of dizziness in the

face of looming catastrophe. 'Diary: W. G. Sebald', *Private Eye* (1998).[32]

With his melancholy tone and antiquated style, there can be few writers whose prose lends itself so readily to parody as that of WG Sebald (1944-2001). Within a few years of his untimely death in 2001, Sebald's reputation was such that his works had attained an almost sacred status, his blend of oblique historical research, biography and travelogue, or what Sebald himself described simply as 'prose-fiction', widely regarded as representing the pinnacle of literary achievement. Yet, if works such as *The Rings of Saturn* (1995) and *Austerlitz* (2001) have secured Sebald his place within the canon of late twentieth-century writers, the function of these texts, like the character of their barely visible narrator, remains as elusive as ever. And just as Derrida has revealed the ways in which the spectral has come to infiltrate the present, so too Sebald's work is similarly haunted, both by the ghosts of the past as well as by the exiled or marginalised, those figures whose fate renders them equally displaced in time and space.[33]

First published in Germany in 1995, and in English translation in 1998, *The Rings of Saturn* was Sebald's third novel, if it may be called that, and the work which first brought him widespread acclaim. Ostensibly an account of a series of walks through the Suffolk countryside narrated by Sebald, or rather by a narrator who may be said to closely resemble Sebald, *The Rings of Saturn* employs a methodology central to hauntology, that of reading the landscape through the ghostly presence of its past. In light of Derrida's insistence upon the revenant nature of the past as that which returns repeatedly to haunt the present, Sebald's work seems actively to encourage this process, to the point where it may be more accurately described as portraying a present not merely disrupted by the past but overwhelmed by it. For so intensely reimagined is the past that Sebald evokes that at times the narrator appears more to inhabit the past than to recollect it, taking on the characteristics of a ghost himself, haunting the pages of his book.[34] And given the location of the desolate Suffolk coastline and the particular ghosts this landscape evokes, one wonders if this particular narrator – preoccupied, disorientated, solitary – has not stumbled from the pages of a story by MR James, a bewildered antiquarian who finds himself increasingly beset by memories of the past, overwhelmed by a series of images and events which he can no longer piece together.

In fact, amidst the many ghosts that Sebald's walking tour unearths, that of Monty James is left in peace, for Sebald's account largely overlooks the twentieth century in favour of the literary and historical figures of an earlier era, from Sir Thomas Browne and Chateaubriand to Edward FitzGerald and the Victorian entrepreneur Sir Samuel Morton Peto. The links between such figures and the Suffolk landscape against which their stories are told can often seem tenuous, however, and tellingly the most significant literary intervention in Sebald's novel is one by an author with no overt connection to the region whatsoever: Jorge Luis Borges. For those of Sebald's readers who might wonder to what degree his 'prose-fiction' is an approximation of the truth, *The Rings of Saturn* appears to offer an answer, albeit an ambiguous one, in the form of a passing reference to Borges's celebrated tale, 'Tlön, Uqbar, Orbis Tertius' (1940). Here, Borges describes how a work of fiction gradually comes to intrude upon our world, its narrative slowly contaminating reality before superseding it altogether. 'The indisputable advantages of a fictitious past have become apparent', Borges writes, and Sebald's entire body of work appears to conform to this statement.[35] For as *The Rings of Saturn* moves from memory to memory, narrative to narrative, one voice seamlessly giving way to the next, it soon becomes apparent that the borders between memory and reality, fact and fiction, are decidedly porous. Sebald's narrator inhabits the past as if it were his own memory, his view of history one abstracted from time, and one which Borges's tale once again appears to anticipate:

> The denial of time, so the tract on Orbis Tertius tells us, is one of the key tenets of the philosophical schools of Tlön. According to this principle, the future exists only in the shape of our present apprehensions and hopes, and the past merely as memory. In a different view, the world and everything now living in it was created only moments ago, together with its complete but illusory pre-history. [...] We simply do not know how many of its possible mutations the world may already have gone through, or how much time, always assuming that it exists, remains.[36]

As it turns out, those reading Sebald's work are quite right to be wary of the accuracy of his claims, both as to the identity of his narrator as well as to the memories this version of himself recollects, for these are largely imaginative constructs, in which details are absent or invented, approximations of the past they explore.[37] As for the photographs which adorn his texts, they too cannot be taken at face value, as Sebald was later to acknowledge, since many of them have 'an entirely fictitious relationship to their supposed subjects.'[38] If then, the historical accuracy of Sebald's texts is decidedly unreliable, this fact is only compounded by the narrator's awareness of the fallibility of his memory: 'I could no more believe my eyes than now I can trust my memory.'[39] And just as the narrator seems to display an increasingly fragile sense of the passage of time, his memories curiously lacking in chronological depth, so too are the lives of the people he encounters often similarly afflicted, as if the entire landscape and its inhabitants had succumbed to a collective dyschronia, a 'time-sickness' that sees their memories and their place in the past gradually decay.[40] This is most evident in Sebald's account of those late nineteenth-century landowners, both in Suffolk and in Ireland following the civil war, whose way of life was soon to be abruptly curtailed, as their estates fell into decay, their lifestyles became anachronistic re-enactments of their past, and they were left to play out obsessively the lost routines of their youth. Sebald's journey is punctuated by the remains of such estates, now little more than reminders of the transience of time and memory, and it is lives such as these that his novel momentarily recalls to us before returning them to oblivion. These remembered, or misremembered, lives become increasingly difficult to separate, however, and the landscape can be obscured by the sheer weight of a past from which it struggles to emerge, as the narrator trudges morosely onwards, his fragile health threatened by a growing sense of disorientation and unease:

> No matter how often I tell myself that chance happenings of this kind occur far more often than we suspect, since we all move, one after the other, along the same roads mapped out for us by our origins and our hopes, my rational mind is nonetheless unable to lay the ghosts of repetition that haunt me with ever greater frequency. Scarcely am I in company but it seems as if I had already heard the same opinions expressed by the same people somewhere or other, in the same way, with the same words, turns of phrase and gesture. The physical sensation closest to this feeling of repetition, which sometimes lasts for several minutes and can be quite disconcerting, is that of the peculiar numbness brought on by a heavy loss of blood, often resulting in a temporary inability to think, to speak or to move one's limbs, as though, without being aware of it, one had suffered a stroke. Perhaps there is in this as yet unexplained phenomenon of apparent duplication some kind of anticipation of the end, a venture into the void, a sort of disengagement, which, like a gramophone repeatedly playing the same sequence of notes, has less to do with damage to the machine itself than with an irreparable defect in its programme.[41]

These 'ghosts of repetition' lie at the heart of what we understand by hauntology, linking the compulsion to repeat, a crucial element of the Freudian uncanny, with Derrida's characterisation of the repetitions of history as that which comes back repeatedly to haunt the present, each time as if it were the first. For Sebald's narrator, this disconcerting sense of déjà vu is accompanied by physical symptoms, his time-sickness experienced both as a foretaste of death, and in an analogy that foreshadows hauntology's pop-cultural rebirth, as a technical malfunction, the needle stuck in its groove.

As the parody of his prose style above makes clear, Sebald's narrator often appears to exist on the cusp of imminent breakdown, his default mental state generally one of mild disengagement from his surroundings. In a book that presents itself as a travelogue of sorts, this can leave the reader in a confusing position as he struggles to identify not only the authorial voice but to connect it to the landscape through which this disembodied presence happens to be passing. This disorientating sense of dislocation reaches its zenith as the narrator reaches Orfordness, the site of a now abandoned military research facility, where his symptoms of dyschronia become acute. For having taken shelter from a somewhat unexpected sandstorm, the narrator now enters an apocalyptic landscape of future ruin more familiar from the fictions of Nigel Kneale or JG Ballard:

> But the closer I came to these ruins, the more any notion of a mysterious isle of the dead receded, and the more I imagined myself amidst the remains of our own civilisation after its extinction in some future catastrophe. To me too, as for some latter-day stranger ignorant of the nature of our society wandering about among heaps of scrap metal and defunct machinery, the beings who had once lived and worked here were an enigma [...] Where and in what time I truly was that day at Orfordness I cannot say, even now as I write these words. [...] And then, through the growing dazzle of the light in my eyes, I suddenly saw, amidst the

> darkening colours, the sails of the long-vanished windmills turning heavily in the wind.[42]

This is the point in Sebald's text at which traces of the past become visible in the present, images of an earlier landscape which now re-emerge, superimposed over the ruins of the recent past in a visual expression of the narrator's dyschronia. In his chapter summary, this section of Sebald's walk through Orfordness is labelled 'In another country', emphasising the manner in which memories of the past may return unexpectedly to estrange the landscapes of the present.[43] Throughout the novel, this is a theme Sebald returns to repeatedly, most notably while discussing, or rather channelling the spirit of, Chateaubriand (1768-1848), whose *Memoirs from Beyond the Grave* (1848) contain his recollections of living in exile in Suffolk in 1794. Here, once again, the voices of the narrator and his subject swiftly become indistinguishable, the time between them collapsing as they dwell upon the troubling impact of memory upon the writer:

> But the fact is that writing is the only way in which I am able to cope with the memories which overwhelm me so frequently and so unexpectedly. If they remained locked away, they would become heavier and heavier as time went on, so that in the end I would succumb under their mounting weight. Memories lie slumbering within us for months and years, quietly proliferating, until they are woken by some trifle and in some strange way blind us to life. How often this has caused me to feel that my memories, and the labours expended in writing them down are all part of the same

> humiliating and, at bottom, contemptible business! And yet, what would we be without memory? We would not be capable of ordering even the simplest thoughts, the most sensitive heart would lose the ability to show affection, our existence would be a mere never-ending chain of meaningless moments, and there would not be the faintest trace of a past.[44]

First published shortly after his death in 1848, Chateaubriand's suggestion that without memory our existence would be reduced to an unendurable and meaningless present, immediately recalls us to another publication from that same year, Dickens's *The Haunted Man*, which, as we have seen, dramatises precisely this scenario, providing further confirmation, if any were still required, of the powerful hauntological spell this particular year continues to exert. But the fact that Sebald chose to illustrate his discussion of time and memory through recourse to such canonical literary figures as Chateaubriand and Borges, rather than through reference to writers who have perhaps displayed a more overt appreciation of the Suffolk landscape, has not been universally popular. Despite the seemingly ecstatic response of many reviewers to *The Rings of Saturn*, there have nevertheless been dissenting voices.

The most strident of these has been Mark Fisher, who has written at some length on both Sebald's novel and Grant Gee's film-essay *Patience (After Sebald)* (2012), which retraces Sebald's walk. Fisher came to Sebald in the hope that he might bring the landscape to life in much the same way as had earlier writers such as Henry James and MR James, but he found this process of re-enchantment to be sadly lacking in Sebald's work, instead discovering 'a Mittel-brow miserabilism, a stock disdain, in which the human settlements are routinely dismissed as shabby and the inhuman spaces are oppressive. [...] a literary ramble which reads less like a travelogue than a librarian's listless daydream.'[45] Fisher felt that the people and places Sebald had encountered on his walk, rather than drawing him into a closer communion with his environment, instead had the opposite effect, triggering reveries that took him away, both spatially and temporally, from his surroundings and leaving the reader with the sense that he might never have visited Suffolk at all. Furthermore, Fisher expresses a scepticism towards the 'solemn cult' that had quickly formed around Sebald after his death (a process, it might be argued, which is now being replicated around Fisher himself) arguing that it was the result of a misplaced admiration for Sebald's 'rather *easy difficulty*, an anachronistic, antiqued model of "good literature" which acted as if many of the developments in 20th-century experimental fiction and popular culture had never happened.'[46] It was precisely this antiquated style which alienated Fisher, prompting him to declare Sebald guilty of duplicity, in offering a book that 'induces its readers to hallucinate a text that is not there, but which meets their desires – for a kind of modernist travelogue, a novel that would do justice to the Suffolk landscape – better than Sebald's book actually does.'[47] In short, Fisher viewed Sebald's novel as a triumph of style over content, a novel which outwardly conformed to the tastes of those readers in search of 'good literature' but which failed to deliver upon its promise, its depiction of the Suffolk landscape ultimately lacking in authenticity and depth. He was supported in his assessment by the writer, Richard Mabey, who also failed to recognise Sebald's description of the Suffolk coastline, leaving him feeling 'as if a very close friend had been belittled.'[48]

It seems to me, however, that these criticisms of Sebald's work rather miss the point and that any reader of *The Rings of Saturn* would in all likelihood fail to recognise the landscape he describes, even if they had been born in the early years of Victoria's reign or before. For Sebald's novel is less concerned with place than it is with time, a meditation upon the past and the way that history may be misremembered and fictionalised. Only through the most literal interpretation of his work could it ever be regarded as travelogue, for Sebald is the most unreliable of narrators, his vertical descent through Suffolk's past overlaid by his own recollections as well as those of the writers whose works he evokes. Unlike Derrida's revenant which haunts the present in an ever-familiar form, Sebald's recollection of the past is ever changing, as memory decays and history is reshaped to suit the imperatives of those who employ it. No single voice is given pre-eminence here, each story interpolating the next, the past as fictional as the present.

'It's not hard to see why a German writer would want to blank out the middle part of the 20th century', Fisher writes, 'and many of the formal anachronisms of Sebald's writing – its strange sense that this is the 21st century seen through the restrained yet ornate prose of an early 20th century essayist – perhaps arise from this desire, just as the novels themselves are about the various, ultimately failed ruses – conscious and unconscious – that damaged psyches deploy to erase traumas and construct new identities.'[49] Nowhere in Sebald's work is such a ruse more in evidence than in his final novel, *Austerlitz*, published shortly before his death in 2001. Here, as obliquely as ever, Sebald explores the historical lacuna Fisher describes, through the life of Jacques Austerlitz, a character whose attempts to recover his lost past reveal a life that has been lived almost wholly as fiction, his origins, his family, even his name, not as he believed them to be, all rewritten as a consequence of this blank space at the heart of twentieth-century history. And it is here, fittingly, against the backdrop of the Royal Observatory at Greenwich, that Austerlitz delivers a disquisition on the nature of time which makes clear, or at least casts some light upon, the temporal principles governing Sebald's work:

> Time [...] was by far the most artificial of all our inventions. [...] Could we not claim [...] that time itself has been non-concurrent over the centuries and the millennia? It is not so long ago, after all, that it began spreading out over everything. [...] and thus by an unquantifiable dimension which disregards linear regularity, [time] does not progress constantly forward but moves in eddies, is marked by episodes of congestion and irruption, recurs in ever-changing form, and evolves in no one knows what direction? [...] The dead are outside time, the dying and the sick at home or in hospitals, and they are not the only ones, for a certain degree of personal misfortune is enough to cut us off from the past and the future. [...] [Austerlitz hopes] that time will not pass away, has not passed away, that I can turn back and go behind it, and there I shall find everything as it once was, or more precisely I shall find that all moments

of time have coexisted simultaneously, in which case none of what history tells us would be true, past events have not occurred but are waiting to do so at the moment when we think of them, although that, of course, opens up the bleak prospect of ever-lasting misery and never-ending anguish.[50]

As always, the question remains as to what degree fictional characters may be taken to reflect the outlook of their creator, but Austerlitz's comments above and elsewhere in the novel formulate a view of time clearly in opposition to that of linear history, instead proposing an erratic, unpredictable and largely subjective view of time bound up with memory, and one from which the marginalised and unfortunate may be excluded altogether. As so much of his fiction is concerned with precisely those individuals who have been discarded or misremembered by history, this is a view of time which may be taken as something of a hallmark of Sebald's work, a hauntological perception of time in which the past, rather than being superseded by the present, is coexistent with it. In such a schema, Austerlitz's hope that 'all moments of time have coexisted simultaneously', so that past (and future) may be forever accessible for recall, can be seen as a reframing of Dunne's serialism, in which memories are likewise archived for future re-enactment through dreams. For Austerlitz, however, as for the narrator of *The Rings of Saturn*, it is unclear whether it is we who recall the past through memory, or whether it is us who have been recalled by the summons of those we remember:

It does not seem to me, Austerlitz added, that we understand the laws governing the return of the past, but I feel more

> and more as if time did not exist at all, only various spaces interlocking according to the rules of a higher form of stereometry, between which the living and the dead can move back and forth as they like, and the longer I think about it the more it seems to me that we who are still alive are unreal in the eyes of the dead, that only occasionally, in certain lights and atmospheric conditions, do we appear in their field of vision. As far back as I can remember, said Austerlitz, I have always felt as if I had no place in reality, as if I were not there at all. [...]
>
> Such ideas infallibly come to me in places which have more of the past about them than the present. For instance, if I am walking through the city and look into one of those quiet courtyards where nothing has changed for decades, I feel, almost physically, the current of time slowing down in the gravitational field of oblivion. It seems to me then as if all the moments of our life occupy the same space, as if future events already existed and were only waiting for us to find our way to them at last, just as when we have accepted an invitation we duly arrive in a certain house at a given time. And might it not be, continued Austerlitz, that we also have appointments to keep in the past, in what has gone before and is for the most part extinguished, and must go there in search of places and people who have some connection with us on the far side of time, so to speak?[51]

Austerlitz believes himself to be a ghost, denied a history, home or reality, stranded on the wrong side of time, and in search of a past that must remain forever hidden from him. In this belief he is emblematic of the many ghosts which haunt the pages of Sebald's fiction, and which, his novels seem to suggest, haunt our present too. For Sebald, like Derrida before him, is less concerned with the past itself than with the ways in which it continues to manifest itself in the present, haunting the lives of those who have been marginalised by historical currents beyond their control. Such has been his success, however, that Sebald has himself, since his death, attained just the kind of ghostly presence often ascribed to his characters, his fiction now acting as a template for those following in his footsteps and haunting contemporary writing about place in much the same manner as his narrator was once haunted by the spectres of the Suffolk landscape.

The Return of Nostalgia

'I am so bored of nostalgia', complained James Bridle in 2011, 'Of letterpress and braces and elaborate facial hair. I appreciate these things, but I think there's something wrong with a culture that fetishizes them to the extent that we currently do.'[52] Our understanding of nostalgia has evolved somewhat since the term was first introduced by a Swiss student named Johannes Hofer in his medical dissertation in 1688. Defined by Svetlana Boym (1959-2015), author of *The Future of Nostalgia* (2001) as 'a longing for a home that no longer exists or has never existed', the term's Greek, or rather pseudo-Greek, roots – *nostos* or 'return home' and *algia* or 'longing' – belie their seventeenth-century origin, itself suggesting an element of nostalgia bound up within its etymology.[53] Rather than the cultural or historical usages through which the term is commonly understood today, nostalgia was first seen as a curable disease, akin to a 'severe common cold.'[54] It also appeared to be highly contagious, leading to an epidemic of cases, often including those of 'feigned nostalgia', particularly amongst soldiers serving abroad, which could provoke a drastic response:

> In 1733 the Russian army was stricken by nostalgia just as it ventured into Germany, the situation becoming dire enough that the general was compelled to come up with a radical treatment of the nostalgia virus. He threatened that "the first to fall sick will be buried alive." This was a kind of literalization of a metaphor, as life in a foreign country seemed like death. This punishment was reported to be carried out on two or three occasions, which happily cured the Russian army of complaints of nostalgia.[55]

Less radical cures for nostalgia, Boym informs us, included the application of leeches, warm hypnotic emulsions, opium, or perhaps a trip to the Alps, but naturally it was a return to one's homeland that was regarded as the most reliable treatment for this disorder. Gradually, however, nostalgia became less responsive to treatment, and by the end of the eighteenth century doctors were reporting that even the return home was proving less efficacious than before, and once home the patients often died. Soon a disease which had once been regarded as treatable had become incurable. Long having been seen as a longing for place – a homeland, whether real or imagined – nostalgia is also a longing for time, often for the reassuring rhythms of childhood or at least a happier past (or future) to set against the disappointments of the present, 'a better time, or slower time – time out of time, not encumbered by appointment books.'[56] In short, as Boym explains, the inexorable spread of nostalgia and its growing resistance to treatment was not merely the consequence of dislocation in space but a response to our changing conception of time:

> In a broader sense, nostalgia is a rebellion against the modern idea of time, the time of history and progress. The nostalgic desires to turn history into private or collective mythology, to revisit time like space, refusing to surrender to the irreversibility of time that plagues the modern condition. [...] While many nineteenth-century thinkers believed progress and enlightenment would cure nostalgia, they have exacerbated it instead.[57]

As we have seen, the 'time-revolution' heralded by the work of Darwin and others, vastly extended our perception of the past. Our response was to attempt to manage or contain it, with the result that the mid-nineteenth century saw the creation of museums and memorials through which the past could be safely preserved, as nostalgia was institutionalised. By now the virus could not be contained or its symptoms treated, for nostalgia had become endemic, no longer an individual sickness but a societal one, 'the mourning of displacement and temporal irreversibility' an ineradicable part of the modern condition.[58]

Throughout the twentieth century this obsessive curating of the past has continued, a symptomatic yet futile attempt to control time which has only intensified as new technologies become a facilitator for nostalgia, providing instantaneous access to endless new swathes of the past. As a consequence, while the past has been repackaged as heritage, nostalgia has mutated into hitherto unknown forms including *ersatz* nostalgia, 'for the things you never thought you had lost', and anticipatory nostalgia, 'for the present that flees with the speed of a click'; for, as the rhythms of life accelerate, so nostalgia provides us with a defence mechanism with which to mitigate its effects.[59] Yet just as nostalgia has grown exponentially, so have the objects of its longing grown curiously diminished, from motherland and a misremembered patriotism to kitsch and facial hair, as a sentiment which might formerly have manifested itself through broader political and historical currents, now appears largely directed towards consumerism and the pop-cultural artefacts of our recent past. 'The twentieth century began with utopia and ended with nostalgia', Boym concludes, 'optimistic belief in the future became outmoded, while nostalgia, for better or worse, never went out of fashion, remaining uncannily contemporary.'[60]

Amidst this global epidemic, Boym has identified two main strains of the disease, the restorative and reflective: 'Restorative nostalgia stresses *nostos* (home) and attempts a transhistorical reconstruction of the lost home. Reflective nostalgia thrives on *algia* (the longing itself) and delays the homecoming – wistfully, ironically, desperately.'[61] While the former does not regard itself as nostalgia, but rather as truth and tradition, the latter questions the status of such claims and calls them into doubt; while the former, which manifests itself through religious and nationalist revivals, is concerned with a return to origins, the latter is free from an attachment to a single place or time; while the former is expressed through the rhetoric of 'universal values, family, nature, homeland, truth', the latter is about 'taking time out of time and about grasping the fleeing present.'[62] Whereas restorative nostalgia is concerned principally with space and the restoration of a homeland, it also seeks a return to a specific moment in time. Rigid, inflexible and unchanging, it regards itself and its mission with the utmost seriousness. By contrast, reflective nostalgia is fluid, subjective and individualistic, and can be ironic and playful in its focus upon the past. Even as she identifies these traits within nostalgia, however, so the subject of Boym's enquiry is evolving once again, mutating into new and often competing forms:

> The first decade of the twenty-first century is not characterized by the search for newness, but by the proliferation of nostalgias that are often at odds with one another. Nostalgic cyberpunks and nostalgic hippies, nostalgic nationalists and nostalgic cosmopolitans, nostalgic environmentalists and nostalgic metrophiliacs (city lovers) exchange pixel fire in the blogosphere. Nostalgia, like globalization, exists in the plural.[63]

Where then, does hauntology fit within this eclectic mix? Is it merely one of these new forms of nostalgia? And if so, is it genuine or feigned? Hauntology appears to conform to many of the characteristics Boym outlines in her distinction between opposing forms of nostalgia without aligning precisely to either: it is ironic and lacks seriousness (one hopes); it does not seek a return to the past but rather explores the passage and pattern of time; and yet it also responds to specific historical moments: 1848, 1973, 1989 – forks in the road where things might have turned out differently, moments when new futures might have come to pass. While contemporary nostalgia is truly global in its reach, hauntology is in many ways a peculiarly British phenomenon, concerned with quite specific cultural and temporal markers that distinguish it quite clearly from, for example, its manifestation in American culture. And as the broad historical and cultural scope of this book suggests, it seems to me that while nostalgia may be regarded as an element of hauntology, the latter is too multifaceted to be contained within the boundaries of the former. Nostalgia has a history of its own, one which intersects with that of hauntology but which ultimately follows its own trajectory. In its contemporary form, as Boym concedes, nostalgia is still, despite changing fashions and technological advances, structurally much the same as it has always been, albeit rather more widespread. 'The only antidote to the dictatorship of nostalgia might be nostalgic dissidence', she suggests. 'Nostalgia can be a poetic creation, an individual mechanism of survival, a countercultural practice, a poison, or a cure. It is up to us to take responsibility for our nostalgia and not let others "prefabricate" it for us.'[64]

Alongside Boym, another major theoretician of nostalgia, and one with perhaps a greater claim upon our understanding of hauntology, at least in its current incarnation, is Fredric Jameson (b. 1934), who identified nostalgia as one of the defining elements of his celebrated outline of the postmodern. Jameson's understanding of the concept bypasses the idea of an individual illness or psychological state that Boym describes in favour of what he calls the 'nostalgia mode', a formal nostalgia characterised by certain techniques and repetitions through which the past is replayed for our consumption in the present. Using the examples of films such as *Star Wars* (1977) and, in particular, Lawrence Kasdan's now largely forgotten neo-noir *Body Heat* (1981), Jameson describes how in our postmodern culture, in which our sense of linear time has broken down, we now experience the historical past through nostalgia and pastiche, a shorthand of signs and symbols that allows us to recreate a given era or historical moment. According to Jameson, writing in 1991, our knowledge of and interest in the past has waned to such an extent that, complemented by a similarly diminished ability to imagine the future, we now find ourselves stranded, almost by default, in an endless present of our own creation. It is under such conditions that we are forced into the seemingly paradoxical position of experiencing what Jameson describes as a 'nostalgia for the present.'[65] The erasure of historical time has inhibited our ability both to recall the past and to imagine a future different from the present. In short, the present has expanded to annex both past and future, and having turned away from both we now regard the present with precisely the sense of distance and historical perspective through which we once perceived the past:

> Historicity is, in fact, neither a representation of the past nor a representation of the future [...] it can first and foremost be defined as a perception of the present as history: that is, as a relationship to the present which somehow defamiliarizes it and allows us that distance from immediacy which is at length characterized as a historical perspective. [...] the incorporation of habits of "futurology"

into our everyday life, the modification of our perception of things to include their "tendency" and of our reading of time to approximate a scanning of objective probabilities – this new relationship to our own present both includes elements formerly incorporated in the experience of the "future" and blocks or forestalls any global vision of the latter as a radically transformed and different system. [...] Perhaps, however, what is implied is simply an ultimate historicist breakdown in which we can no longer imagine the future at all, under any form – Utopian or catastrophic. Under those circumstances, where a formerly futurological science fiction [...] turns into mere "realism" and an outright representation of the present [...] an experience of our present as past and as history – is slowly excluded.[66]

Reading this passage today, almost 30 years after it was written, the sense of being trapped in an endless present persists, as does Jameson's description of the foreclosure of the future. It is clear that the thinker most indebted to this analysis is surely Mark Fisher, in whose work one finds many of the ideas first explored by Jameson a generation before. Fisher has acknowledged this debt explicitly, discussing the formative role of Jameson's ideas at some length and describing hauntology as a counterpart to his 'nostalgia mode'.[67] What differentiates these ideas, it would appear, is less a question of content than of degree; for Fisher describes a cultural landscape in which the symptoms of nostalgia that Jameson first identified have now become so acute that they are impossible to overlook, or rather so widespread and all-encompassing that they are no longer noticed at all. The nostalgia mode has expanded in recent decades through technological changes that Jameson was unable to predict. What was once merely a tendency has now become ubiquitous and so deeply engrained that its presence is no longer remarked upon. But if nostalgia needs a 'beyond' to contrast itself against, an 'outside' that has resisted its encroachment, in conditions under which there is no longer any 'now' then is nostalgia still possible? Hauntology is often criticised on the grounds that it is little more than a repackaged form of nostalgia, but given the ubiquity of such nostalgia in contemporary culture, Fisher responds by asking, '*nostalgia compared to what?*'[68] In Jameson's schema, a diminished sense of the past and an imaginative block on the future have left us languishing within an endless present. Today, however, this situation has reached its logical conclusion, and the only option left to us, Fisher suggests, is to revisit those moments which once offered us the possibility of a different way forward and whose promise may sustain us: our nostalgia for the present has given way to a nostalgia for lost futures.

Just as the expansion of nostalgia has accelerated in recent decades, enabled by technologies which render the past ever more accessible, so too have new and exotic hybrids emerged, which share in some of its characteristics but which in other respects are entirely new, products of the changing cultural landscape of the twenty-first century. One example is that of *nomadology*, a term coined by Mark Fisher to describe the sense of unease, akin to a form of travel sickness, engendered by such anonymous environments as airports and shopping malls whose sameness seems to deflect even the possibility of nostalgia for a past that is wholly absent. Instead, these spaces, whose endless repetition the world over leaves one feeling as if one could be anywhere, provoke 'the sickness *of* travel [...] a complement to, not the opposite of, the sickness *for* home, nostalgia.'[69] It is another term, however, this time coined by Fisher's friend and collaborator, Simon Reynolds, which most clearly articulates our current obsession with the recent past and which encapsulates many of the ideas more commonly attributed to hauntology.

Retromania

In the final years of the twentieth century, as the new millennium approached, cultural time appeared to falter. Rather than accelerating towards a moment that had once felt impossibly futuristic, cultural production began to look less to the future than to the past, turning back on itself and rejecting the promise of the new. It was in the 2000s, as this process of cultural anachronism first became endemic, that the music journalist Simon Reynolds (b. 1963) coined the term 'dyschronia' to describe this feeling of widespread temporal disjuncture, arguing that while everyday life has sped up, culture has slowed down.[70] In his book *Retromania* (2011), Reynolds explores the reasons behind this cultural deceleration in astonishing detail, principally through the medium of popular music but also via an array of forms from TV and theatre, to fashion, advertising and architecture. Describing this decade of seemingly endless revival as the 'Re' Decade, Reynolds sets out to explain quite why we have become so obsessed by the cultural remnants of our recent past:

> The 2000s felt different. [...] The sensation of moving forward grew fainter as the decade unfurled. Time itself

> seemed to become sluggish, like a river that starts to meander and form oxbow lakes. [...] Instead of being about itself, the 2000s has been about every other previous decade happening again all at once: a simultaneity of pop time that abolishes history while nibbling away at the present's own sense of itself as an era with a distinct identity and feel.
>
> Instead of being the threshold to the future, the first ten years of the twenty-first century turned out to be the 'Re' Decade. The 2000s were dominated by the 're -' prefix: revivals, reissues, remakes, re-enactments. Endless retrospection [...] recycling: bygone genres revived and renovated, vintage sonic material reprocessed and recombined. [...] As the 2000s proceeded, the interval between something happening and its being revisited seemed to shrink insidiously. [...] The rising tide of the historical past is lapping at our ankles.[71]

Reynolds defines the word 'retro' as a 'self-conscious fetish for period stylisation', acknowledging that the term has become more commonly used as a means of referring to almost anything related to the relatively recent past of popular culture.[72] Of course, ours is not the first era to develop an obsession with the past, and Reynolds offers both the Renaissance reverence for the classical world and the Gothic invocation of the medieval as examples of periods in which the past held particular sway over the present. But what distinguishes the current epidemic of retromania from earlier fascinations with the past, is the fact that our obsession is directed not towards antiquity but to the 'fashions, fads, sounds and stars that occurred within living memory.' 'There has never been a society in human history', Reynolds asserts, 'so obsessed with the cultural artefacts of *its own immediate past*.'[73] The truth of this statement appears impossible to verify; but what is surely undeniable is that the impact of retromania has become so overwhelming that our nostalgia for the recent past is now preventing our culture from moving forward, forcing us to endlessly revisit a past which by comparison with today looks ever more innovative and dynamic. 'But what happens when we run out of past?' Reynolds asks, 'Are we heading towards a sort of cultural-ecological catastrophe, when the seam of pop history is exhausted? And out of all the things that happened this past decade, what could possibly fuel tomorrow's nostalgia crazes and retro fads?'[74] The accumulated weight of our recent cultural history is exerting a gravitational pull so powerful that it has reversed the polarity of contemporary culture away from the future towards the past. The escalation of retromania that we are now living through has not occurred by chance, however, being the direct result of technological changes in the ways in which culture is consumed and distributed: 'We've become victims of our ever-increasing capacity to store, organise, instantly access, and share vast amounts of cultural data. Not only has there never before been a society so obsessed with the cultural artefacts of its immediate past, but there has never before been a society that is *able* to access the immediate past so easily and so copiously.'[75]

Just as the Victorians were faced with a staggering shift in historical perspective as the limits of pre-history were immeasurably enlarged, so the internet has changed our lives in a similarly revolutionary fashion, creating a comparable expansion in the volume of our *recorded* past, an increase not in historical depth but in width, as what was previously lost to history is now saved indefinitely to be consumed at our leisure. The reason for our seeming inability to get ahead of the past, Reynolds suggests, is simply that its mass is now so great, that like light trying to escape a black hole, the future is unable to escape its grasp. Reynolds cites YouTube as a prime example of the 'crisis of overdocumentation' created by the growth of digital technology, arguing that these developments have triggered a profound shift in the function of both individual and collective memory in the face of an astronomical expansion in our capacity to store 'memorabilia, documentation, recordings, every kind of archival trace of our existence.'[76] Yet as we struggle to utilise this space, the growth of which continues to outstrip our attempts to fill it, there is little evidence that our ability to process such information or to use it meaningfully has increased. The consequence is that we are now simply overwhelmed by the sheer volume of information, very little of which we shall ever have the time (or desire) to access. In the pre-internet age we were already inundated with more information than any individual could possibly hope to digest, but crucially most of this was stored out of reach in libraries and archives, access to which required a significant expenditure of time and energy. The arrival of the search engine, however, has erased such delays, destroying the distance between an individual and this ever-growing deluge of information, with the result that the past has become newly available to us in ways which previously we might never have imagined:

> Old stuff either directly permeates the present, or lurks just beneath the surface of the current, in the form of on-

> screen windows to other times. We've become so used to this convenient access that it is a struggle to recall that life wasn't always like this; that relatively recently, one lived most of the time in a cultural present tense, with the past confined to specific zones, trapped in particular objects and locations. [...] Our relationship to time and space in this YouTubeWikipediaRapidshareiTunesSpotify era has been utterly transformed. Distance and delay have been eroded to nearly nothing. [...] The result has been a steady encroachment by past production on the window of attention that current production had hitherto dominated. In a sense, the past has always been in competition with the present, culturally speaking. But the terrain has gradually shifted to the past's drastic advantage [...] The crucial point about the journeys through time that YouTube and the Internet in general enable is that people are not really going backwards at all. They are going sideways, moving laterally within an archival plane of space-time.[77]

Technological change has massively increased the availability of the recorded past and with it our potential sources of nostalgia. In the latter half of the twentieth century, as it became increasingly bound up with popular culture, so nostalgia began to be experienced vicariously, triggered by artefacts that expressed a longing for a bygone era. In this sense, retromania is best understood as a response to a culture which has become so dominated by nostalgia that it now consciously recreates the longing it once sought to provoke. But is our nostalgia for an earlier era a purely reflex mechanism or can it reflect a valid judgement on the comparative merits of different historical periods? Do we long for the past simply because it was superior to the present?

> I've often decried nostalgia but I'm also highly susceptible to that emotion. I can remember being five and looking back wistfully to how great things were when I was four. [...] Nostalgia gets a bad rap, but it can be creative, even subversive. The fact is, certain periods in the life of an individual or a culture are more intense, exciting ... simply better than others; the impulse to go back there may be ultimately counterproductive, but it's perfectly understandable. Nostalgia-driven movements can function as ways of getting through doldrum eras, keeping faith until the next 'up' phase.[78]

If then, as Reynolds suggests, retromania is symptomatic of a culture in creative hibernation, consuming its past until such a time as our faith in the future is reignited, then the roots of our current malaise may be traced back to the early 1970s, and the waning of modernism. Drawing upon the work of Andreas Huyssen (b. 1942), a leading figure in the field of 'Memory Studies', Reynolds refers to what Huyssen calls the 'memory boom', the 'culture-wide obsession with commemoration, documentation and preservation' that characterised the last decades of the twentieth century and which manifested itself through a surge in the foundation of museums and archives.[79] Huyssen characterises this period as a movement away from a concern with 'present futures' towards a focus upon 'present pasts', as the forward momentum of the modernist drive towards the future gradually stalled and went into reverse. This was the cultural shift that institutionalised our preoccupation with the past, giving rise to 'the nostalgia industry with its retro fashions and revivals, postmodernism's pastiche and renovation of historical styles, and the spectacular growth of heritage.'[80]

In 2005, Reynolds first began using the term hauntology in correspondence with Mark Fisher, to describe a sense of the present feeding on the past in new and creative ways. The term was initially applied to a group of musicians working on the Ghost Box label, amongst them The Focus Group, Belbury Poly and The Advisory Circle, but it soon came to include a wider community of artists, mostly based in the UK, who were incorporating rediscovered fragments of recent pop-cultural history into their work. 'Consummate scavengers', as Reynolds describes them, 'the hauntologists trawl through charity shops, street markets and jumble sales for delectable morsels of decaying culture-matter.'[81] Hauntology was quickly adopted by the wider cultural and academic community, where, in its new incarnation, it overlapped with many of the ideas which had first animated Derrida's use of the term a decade earlier. As Reynolds acknowledges, there is a significant crossover between Derrida's ideas and those which were being articulated in 2005, most notably a shared belief in the continued relevance of leftist political projects, and in particular the 'lost utopianism' of the post-welfare state era of benevolent state planning and social engineering.[82] Hauntology, both for Derrida and Reynolds, is bound up with memory: 'memory's power (to linger, pop up unbidden, prey on your mind) and memory's fragility (destined to become distorted, to fade, then finally disappear)'.[83] Employing Freud's term for the grieving process, Reynolds suggests that hauntological music feels ghostly precisely because it is a form of 'memory work', a process which if left unfinished is unable to move beyond that which is being mourned. But what is being mourned here and why cannot it be laid to rest? For Derrida, it was Marxism that was being buried prematurely and which would soon come back to haunt us; for Reynolds, what hauntology mourns is less an ideology than an era, a particular period in post-war British history whose promise remained unrealised, and which has haunted the future ever since.

As we shall see, the precise parameters of this 'lost' period remain open to debate although it came to a close before the election of Margaret Thatcher in 1979, if not earlier in that decade. But in mourning an era rather than simply a set of political beliefs, hauntology has now become firmly associated with the broader culture of the post-war years, and in particular the 'long decade' between 1960 and 1973. Much of the cultural production of this period has since entered what Reynolds calls the 'hauntological pantheon', with the result that hauntology has now become associated with, amongst other things, children's supernatural drama, the music of the BBC Radiophonic Workshop and those films claimed retrospectively by the Folk Horror Revival. Such cultural markers have now become a shorthand for hauntology itself, having 'seeped into the memory fabric of an entire generation (roughly, people born between 1955 and 1975).'[84] But if, Reynolds asks, hauntology has now become indissolubly linked with so specific a cultural and historical moment, ought not this necessarily to limit its appeal? Judging from the widespread currency hauntological ideas currently enjoy, this appears not to be the case, yet Reynolds is surely correct to draw attention to this particular demographic, one which, frequently male and British, he typifies as 'the kind of person who remembers watching *Doctor Who* back when it was *worth* watching.'[85] Furthermore, if hauntology is a product of a particular generation and nationality, then ought we to expect each successive generation within that nationality to produce its own version of hauntology? If this is the case then it becomes difficult to see hauntology as anything other than 'a self-conscious, emotionally ambivalent form of nostalgia that sets in play the ghosts of childhood.'[86] Reynolds recognises that hauntology emerged from much the same cultural conditions – 'the scrambling of pop time, the atrophy of any sense of futurity or forward propulsion' – that generated the tide of nostalgia he rails against in *Retromania*. 'But what makes hauntology different', he argues, 'what gives it an edge, is that it contains an ache of longing – for history itself.'[87] Amidst an 'atemporal smorgasbord' of contemporary culture in which we get to pick and choose from an endless menu of cultural artefacts abstracted from the eras that gave rise to them, both past and future have been decontextualised and diminished, hollowed out by a loss of historical depth. It is hauntology, Reynolds suggests, which offers us the means to escape this cultural impasse, reanimating our sense of past and future, and allowing us to reclaim the possibilities they once afforded:

> Playfully parodying heritage culture, hauntology explores two ways to, if not resist, then perhaps bypass the 'no future' represented by mash-ups and retro. The first strategy involves

> the rewriting of history. If the future has gone AWOL on us, those with radical instincts are necessarily forced to go back. Trying to uncover alternate pasts secreted inside the official narrative, remapping history to find paths-not-taken and peculiar but fertile backwaters adjacent to pop's official narrative, they turn the past into a foreign country. The other strategy is to honour and resurrect 'the future inside the past'. In UK hauntology's case, that's the eyes-on-the-horizon optimism of the post-World War II modernists and modernisers.[88]

In his call to revitalise the present through a rereading of the past, Reynolds advocates a reconnection with what he regards as the more optimistic and forward-thinking outlook which characterised post-war culture, with its promise of a more egalitarian future. Such an attempt to restore the spirit of an era whose hope remains unfulfilled is, of course, an example of precisely the 'nostalgia for lost futures' which has since become something of a slogan for hauntology. In his attempts to locate the origin of this phrase, Reynolds offers a number of possible sources, amongst them Isaac Asimov, Jean Baudrillard, David Toop and Brian Eno, a series which, as we have seen, ought also to include JG Ballard. But the progenitor of this term, Reynolds claims, is the Portuguese poet, Fernando Pessoa, author of the posthumously published *The Book of Disquiet* (1982). Reynolds locates the following passage, written in the early decades of the last century, in which Pessoa describes the oppressive ennui that descends upon him during late afternoons:

> a feeling worse than tedium but for which there's no other name. It's a feeling of desolation I'm unable to pinpoint [...] the physical universe is like a corpse that I loved when it was life [...] And yet what nostalgia for the future if I let my ordinary eyes receive the salutation of the declining day! [...] I don't know what I want or don't want [...] I don't know who I am or what I am. Like someone buried under a collapsed wall, I lie under the toppled vacuity of the entire universe.[89]

Ultimately, Reynolds's call to arms is less political than cultural, a statement of his belief that much musical output in the UK has become moribund and inert in the face of the technological reanimation of the past. Mark Fisher has stated his broad agreement with this analysis, with the caveat that while Reynolds characterises retromania as predominantly a response to technological change, Fisher regards such developments as symptomatic of a deeper political malaise, not least our seeming inability to imagine a future beyond the capitalist reality we inhabit.[90] It is through such a call for a wider engagement with the shortcomings of the present that hauntology maintains its radical edge, a summons to political activism which is nowhere voiced more insistently than in the work of Laura Grace Ford.

The Stain of Place: Laura Grace Ford

Originating in the work of a French theorist writing at a moment of historical disjuncture, only later to re-emerge in the UK in a newly accessible and popular form, it is easy to see why hauntology is often confused with its predecessor and intellectual cousin, psychogeography. It is not only in the manner of their gestation and (re-)birth, however, that these two concepts display a striking family resemblance, for they also share more intrinsic similarities, the spatial expeditions central to psychogeography finding a counterpart in the temporal exploration common to hauntology. Of course, the border between these two concepts is rather less distinct than such a summary would suggest, for journeys made horizontally through space often incorporate a vertical descent through time, while the reverse is equally true, and haunting is as much a function of place as it is of time.

Amongst a small but growing list of candidates to have been proposed as hauntology's literary exemplar in recent years, including Iain Sinclair, WG Sebald, Patrick Keiller, Christopher Priest, Alan Garner and David Peace, it is perhaps Laura Grace Ford whose work best fulfils this role. For it is in her work, with its striking interplay of text and image, that the twin preoccupations of psychogeography and hauntology, of space and time, intersect, in an exploration of urban landscapes far removed from the eerie spaces of the English countryside with which hauntology is now more commonly associated.

Between 2005 and 2009, the writer and artist, Laura Grace (formerly Oldfield) Ford (b. 1973) self-published the zine *Savage Messiah* in a series of 11 issues, collected by Verso in a single volume in 2011. Taking its name from HS Ede's 1931 biography of the sculptor, Henri Gaudier-Brzeska, later the subject of Ken Russell's 1972 film adaptation of the same name, *Savage Messiah* records a series of drifts or *dérives* through various London postcodes, in which a collage of photographs, images and text illuminates a blighted landscape, following a trajectory away from the gentrified centre towards the suburban perimeter and beyond. The overriding ethos is a bracingly anti-nostalgic recuperation of the lost social projects of the 1970s and 1980s whose subsequent decay stands as a timely reminder of a spirit of optimism which has long since been subverted. With its drifts and wanderings, its 'scavenger perambulations, and walks of shame and of hope', *Savage Messiah* has been described as an example of 'avant-pulp psychogeography' in which the erased histories of popular dissent from the 1970s to the 1990s are rekindled in the face of a present animated by a similar spirit of unrest.[91] Ford has since dismissed the label of psychogeography, however, a term whose widespread use, or misuse, has resulted in it losing much of the political radicalism with which it was once imbued, in favour of hauntology, with its own more clearly articulated sense of political engagement. Outlining her adoption of the term, Ford acknowledges the value of her conversations with Mark Fisher, who wrote the introductory essay to *Savage Messiah*, in shaping her understanding of hauntology as a tool with which to uncover the possibilities concealed beneath the city streets:

> I think it's about an idea of history, not a linear trajectory but something scored with breaks and ruptures that time can fold and slip and that moments can recur unexpectedly. I think I approach my work as channelling these threads or historical currents that I think of as lying dormant. When I'm writing about these flashpoints of historical intensity, of militancy, I am collapsing decades and saying these ecstatic moments connect, that each instance is a glimpse of another reality very close to this one.[92]

Such moments of intensity, of historical rupture, when suddenly everything seems possible, recur throughout *Savage Messiah*, as Ford describes her forays through London's recent past. In fact, it is precisely the possibility of such moments and the search for those places (and times) which might trigger them that provides the dynamic behind her investigation of the city's decaying fabric. Yet such spaces and the moments of euphoria they once engendered (and may again) are under threat in neoliberal London; these hidden points of access are increasingly overlaid, buried beneath the weight of anonymous regeneration. 'The need to document the transient and ephemeral nature of the city is becoming increasingly urgent', she warns, 'as the process of enclosure and privatisation continues apace.'[93]

Throughout *Savage Messiah*, Ford seems less concerned in recording the period in which her drifts take place than in recalling those times, both past and future, that her environment evokes.[94] Hence in *Savage Messiah* #1 as she wanders through the Isle of Dogs, the present is overlaid by 'Ghosts of miners, printers, travellers, seething hatred of Thatcher. Sultry July night. Wapping Highway. 1986'; while elsewhere she experiences premonitions of London's future decline: 'Post apocalyptic phantoms of stadia, overgrown velodromes, the dome laid to waste under a convolvulus matrix. London 2013.'[95] These are the multiple Londons that Ford brings to light, her own recollections of the city viewed through the prism of the past, in particular the Thatcherite redevelopment of the 1980s, and shot through with a Ballardian vision of future catastrophe: the post-Olympic ruins of 2013. Ballard's iconic imagery of an overgrown London regressing to some primordial past is something of a touchstone here, but his is not the only name invoked by Ford, as she rosters an entire lineage of urban protest, from De Quincey, Rimbaud and Baudelaire, to Guy Debord and the Situationists, by way of Bataille and Benjamin, Agamben and Mike Davis. These voices are interspersed throughout the text alongside street-level accounts of raves and riots, brawls and skirmishes, sex, drugs and a prevailing mood of barely suppressed rage.

As we move through the sequence of zines, so specific dates begin to flicker by with increasingly regularity: 1981, 2001, 1976, 1988, 1992, 1985. Freed from the constraints of chronological order, intensity of experience becomes the only yardstick. Images of decaying 1960s estates are offset by sporadic glimpses of bindweed and convolvulus as once again we fast-forward to an overgrown 2013 and future ruins merge with those of the recent past. Out of this nexus of names, dates, and places, a pattern begins to emerge: a district, an estate, a moment of uprising or potential change, lost to the past but haunting the present, all dictated by the direction of the drift and the epiphanies it provokes:

> That nexus of dissolution. My loss. Of self. Absenting myself from the life I ended up with. [...] Ghosts of places we imagine, pushed into myth and drunken brags. Always yearning for the time that just eluded us. [...] My fate, never to be content with the present, to walk perpetually through that elegant wilderness. [...] I am immersed in a holographic world [...] 1973, 1974, 1981, 1990, 2013. Always a return. A mirror touch. A different way out.[96]

Ford's London is a spectral city, a holographic representation of a future in which redevelopments such as the Paddington Basin – 'It feels abandoned, a showpiece of a future that never happened' – are contrasted with what remains of the *terra incognita* below, the 'shadowscapes' beneath the Westway, those 'dank corridors defying panopticon mapping.'[97] 'The past holds tight the kernels of repetition and destruction', Ford writes, for these are the twin forces through which time is controlled in the contemporary city, as redevelopment seeks to erase the past and all the promise it once contained, while the familiar hollow mantras are trumpeted by those in power. But Ford's work offers a mantra of its own, a counter-magic which conjures up the spirit of a past that refuses to be laid to rest: 'Spectral traces, embedded in the dirt. [...] Trapped in the present I conjure these scenes.'[98] Scenes which reveal the traces of earlier histories, in which a manufactured future, symbolised by the 2012 Olympics yet to come, is momentarily eclipsed by a glimpse of the city which lies beneath:

> There are moments, caught between sequences, the paused video, the double exposed photograph, when a fragment of truth can be glimpsed, a hidden meaning exposed. It is there in those threshold spaces where the codes of the city form constellations above the din of the street. In the bomb craters, construction sites and abandoned terraces, voices are channelled, forgotten histories exposed and trampled desires flare up in an uncanny rupturing [...] This is one of the enchanted places that slipped out of sight, only to emerge and reconfigure elsewhere.
> 1973/1981/1990/1994/1999/2001/2011/2013[99]

As we arrive at *Savage Messiah* #8, so the sound of these ghostly voices becomes ever more persistent, the series of dates repeated with greater urgency, tapping out a semaphore encoding some hidden meaning, its chronology unstable and repeatedly reconfigured, until finally we reach the question latent within everything that has come before:

> 1973-1974, 1980-81, 1990, 1994, 1999, 2001, 2008/9/10 2013.
> There is a myth that our future has been taken, that no other future is possible. Do you passively accept that?[100]

This is a question central both to *Savage Messiah* and to hauntology itself, and one whose answer lies in the series of dates which proceed it: 1973 – 2013. These are the parameters of Ford's temporal exploration: at one end the recession which marked the beginning of the end of the post-war consensus, ushering in the neoliberal project, the effects of which Ford's journeys lay bare; at the other, the future calamity that awaits if such a project remains unchecked, the future ruins of the spectacular society; in between, moments of political instability and crisis, flashpoints in which alternative futures can briefly be glimpsed, different paths taken, potential opportunities to effect change whose promise still lives on. It is these moments of social and economic upheaval which Ford returns to repeatedly throughout her work, temporal fissures awaiting the moment of their re-enactment. The chronology is fluid, mutable, dates repeated and rearranged in line with the breakdown of historical time in the hauntological present, a fractured time in which events have become unmoored from the contexts which gave rise to them. In *Savage Messiah* #10, an issue devoted entirely to a projection of a post-apocalyptic London (Is it easier to imagine the end of London than to think of an alternative to capitalism?), the temporal deck is shuffled once again: '1973, 1990-93, 1998 and 2001-2 2008 1973 returning 2012 2013'.[101] Here, Ford anticipates the future timeline of hauntology itself, as that revenant year, 1973, returns once again to disrupt our sense of linear time, the present arcing back to reconnect with the early 1970s and the hope it once offered, in the face of a future that provides us with only more of the same.

In *Savage Messiah* #11 Ford brings her sequence to an end with 'a special issue tracing the paths from East End to the New Towns, from the riot cities of 1981 to the future insurrections of 2010-2013.'[102] In what she describes as 'a willing into being, a vision of the future', Ford moves beyond London's frayed perimeter to Dagenham, Hatfield and beyond, in search of the insurrectionary spirit of 1981, a year in which Ford herself was only a child, but one whose message of resistance and revolt colours her entire project, a rehearsal for those conflicts yet to come:

> 1981, Britain lit up with uprisings, riots, a feverish grab at something beyond everyday existence. Time out of joint. The summer of 1981 seized by a warped temporality, an attenuated present.
>
> Because suddenly in the blazing heat, out of the scorched landscapes came a sense of urgency. 1995, 2003, 2010, and 2013. [...] There's no change heralding the next epoch, it's just us as the swarming underclass, the surplus people

> animated round fires lighting up the tawdry streets. It's coming. The next epoch. To some it's too late. [...] There are certain historical moments where constellations of social upheaval flare up and illuminate Britain's cities July 1981. 2011 2012 2013 ...[103]

Of course, from today's perspective we can see that the revolutionary futures that her work wills into being have yet to come to pass. The London Olympics of 2012 came and went, erasing large swathes of the city in its wake, but as yet its monuments are not the overgrown ruins she so powerfully imagines. Rather than marking the end of this temporal cycle, as she may have hoped, 2013 has been subsumed within an ever-growing history of lost futures, another moment of unrealised potential. But *Savage Messiah* remains rather more than merely a work of misdirected speculation, providing an example of hauntology at its most politically engaged, alongside a biography of its author: 'This decaying fabric, this unknowable terrain has become my biography, the euphoria then the anguish, layers of memories colliding, splintering and reconfiguring.'[104]

In his introduction to *Savage Messiah*, written in 2011, Mark Fisher notes that in neoliberal London, as in so many other cities, 'the struggle over space is also a struggle over time and who controls it. Resist neoliberal modernisation and (so we are told) you consign yourself to the past.'[105] Ford's work confronts such abuses of history, resisting the attempt to forge an image of the future at odds with reality, a spectacle of regeneration built on advertising and propaganda that masks an everyday experience of struggle and deprivation. The target here is Blair's 'Cool Britannia' rebranding of the city, against which Ford 'deploys anachronism as a weapon', the makeshift feel of *Savage Messiah*, with its use of scissors and glue in place of digital reproduction, recalling the samizdat publications of an earlier era, with their less glossy, more temporary aesthetic.[106] As Fisher acknowledges, Ford's drifts through the city remain, superficially at least, a clear example of psychogeography in action. Such a reading is supported by Greil Marcus in his preface to the 2019 edition of *Savage Messiah*, in which he describes Ford's work as 'the most convincing follow-through there is on the project of poetic urban-renewal inaugurated by the situationists [...] where an all-night drift down the streets might so scramble time that 1848 would exert a stronger spiritual gravity than 1954.'[107] By invoking the spirit of 1848, however, Marcus's comments recall us once again to the spectral origins of hauntology, resulting in a face-off between Fisher's introduction and Marcus's preface, as Ford is reclaimed from the ranks of the psychogeographers:

> Rather than subsuming *Savage Messiah* under the increasingly played-out discourses of psychogeography, I believe it is better understood as an example of a cultural coalescence that started to become visible (and audible) at the moment when Ford began to produce the zine: hauntology. [...] The specters here were not so much ghosts from an actual past; they were instead the traces of futures that had never arrived but which once seemed inevitable. [...] Haunting is about a staining of place with particularly intense moments of time [...] Ford is alive to the poetry of dates. 1979, 1981, 2013: these years recur throughout *Savage Messiah*,

> moments of transition and threshold, moments when a whole alternative time-track opens. 2013 has a post-apocalyptic quality [...] But 2013 could also be Year Zero: the reversal of 1979, the time when all the cheated hopes and missed chances are finally realised. *Savage Messiah* invites us to see the contours of another world in the gaps and cracks of an occupied London.[108]

If, as Fisher suggests, haunting is about a 'staining of place with particularly intense moments of time', then Ford's London is truly a spectral city and *Savage Messiah* an exemplary hauntological text; for nowhere is the fabric of the city imbued with a greater intensity than in these pages. Ford's work succeeds in restoring a sense of time and place to a landscape threatened with erasure, and in doing so she illustrates the ways in which hauntology can resist the ongoing attempts of those who seek to misrepresent or overwrite the past and the futures it once promised.

The Foreclosure of the Future: Mark Fisher and Capitalist Realism

> The failure of the future haunts capitalism: after 1989, capitalism's victory has not consisted in it confidently claiming the future, but in denying that the future is possible. All we can expect, we have been led to believe, is more of the same – but on higher resolution screens with faster connections. Hauntology, I think, expresses dissatisfaction with this foreclosure of the future. Mark Fisher (2010)[109]

Almost three decades have now elapsed since Derrida first introduced the concept of hauntology to the world; it is no longer his name, however, but that of Mark Fisher (1968-2017) with which this term is more commonly associated. Perhaps this is because hauntology was never more than tangential to Derrida's broader deconstructionist aims; perhaps it is simply because Fisher was the first (alongside Simon Reynolds) to develop the term in a popular and accessible manner. In either case, while Derrida remains father to the term, it is Fisher who has become its patron-saint and elucidator in chief. An academic and cultural theorist, Mark Fisher is best known for his influential blog, k-punk, which he began writing in 2003. The 'k', which instinctively recalls the work of one of Fisher's most revered writers, Franz Kafka, is in fact derived from κυβερ, Greek for 'cyber', and is invoked, so Simon Hammond tells us, 'in a capacious sense – not only as genre but a wider social and cultural tendency, facilitated by new technologies.'[110] Fisher's first book, *Capitalist Realism*, was published in 2009 and was followed by his most overt engagement with hauntology, *Ghosts of My Life* (2014), a collection of writings, many of which had first appeared on his blog. *The Weird and the Eerie* was released in 2016 and the collected edition of his writings, *K-Punk*, in 2019. Since his untimely death in 2017, Fisher's work has continued to find a wider audience, with the result that hauntology, having debuted in the 1990s and been both resurrected and written off in the 2000s, is now enjoying another, more prolonged period in the cultural spotlight.

The return of hauntology in a newly repurposed format in the mid-noughties – what Fisher later described as its 'second (un)life' – was initially restricted to the 'ghostly' sound of a small group of artists, whose music appeared to lament the failure of the future.[111] But whereas critics such as Simon Reynolds and others have interpreted this failure primarily at the level of culture, diagnosing a nostalgia for the recent past facilitated and accelerated by technological change, Fisher regarded these developments as symptomatic of a wider failure of imagination, a loss of faith in the future which stemmed from an inability to conceive of any other society than our own:

> What haunts the digital cul-de-sacs of the twenty-first century is not so much the past as all the lost futures that the twentieth century taught us to anticipate. The futures that have been lost were more than a matter of musical style. More broadly, and more troublingly, the disappearance of the future meant the deterioration of a whole mode of social imagination: the capacity to conceive of a world radically different from the one in which we currently live.[112]

Fisher regards the roots of our current impasse as being much deeper than their cultural manifestation might suggest, pointing towards a more widespread societal malaise. In short, the imaginative deficit that hauntology brings into focus is not simply cultural in origin but political. The most sustained expression of this belief is found in *Capitalist Realism* (2009) in which Fisher's primary thesis is neatly encapsulated in the title of his opening chapter: 'It's easier to imagine the end of the world than the end of capitalism'.[113] This slogan captures precisely what Fisher means by capitalist realism: 'the widespread sense that not only is capitalism the only viable political and economic system, but also that it is now impossible even to *imagine* a coherent alternative to it.'[114] Fisher illustrates this point through a bravura reading of Alfonso Cuarón's now largely forgotten film *Children of Men* (2006; based on the novel by PD James, 1992) whose portrayal of a dystopian future of mass sterility provides Fisher with a striking metaphor for what he sees as a similar 'absence of the new in contemporary society, culturally moribund and unable to see beyond the conditions of the present catastrophe.'[115] Cuarón's film is an extrapolation of what Fisher perceives to be the crisis of contemporary capitalism: 'But what of the catastrophe itself?', Fisher asks. 'It is evident that the theme of sterility must be read metaphorically, as the displacement of another kind of anxiety. I want to argue that this anxiety cries out to be read in cultural terms, and the question the film poses is: how long can a culture persist without the new? What happens if the young are no longer capable of producing surprises?'[116] The answer Fisher envisages is a future free from innovation and change, one that 'harbours only reiteration and re-permutation', a future that looks rather like the present and the recent past, one in which there are no 'shocks of the new' to come.[117]

If this reading of the future itself feels rather too familiar, as if we have been here before, then it is because we have, as Fisher freely acknowledges, for what he calls capitalist realism 'can be subsumed under the rubric of postmodernism as theorised by Jameson'.[118] It was Fredric Jameson who first identified the growth of pastiche and repetition as heralding the rise of postmodernism in the 1980s; but thankfully we are to be spared a future modelled on that particular decade, for the time being at least. For, while capitalist realism is not an intrinsically new phenomenon, it marks an acceleration and intensification of what has gone before:

> I would want to argue that some of the processes which Jameson described and analysed have now become so aggravated and chronic that they have gone through a change in kind. [...] What we are dealing with now, however, is a deeper, far more pervasive, sense of exhaustion, of cultural and political sterility. [...] For most people under twenty in Europe and North America, the lack of alternatives to capitalism is no longer even an issue. Capitalism seamlessly occupies the horizons of the thinkable.[119]

Writing elsewhere, Fisher has described hauntology as 'postmodernity's doppelganger', arguing that hauntology is a counterpart to Jameson's nostalgia mode, and it is certainly true that his thought owes more to Jameson than to perhaps any other thinker.[120] On this basis, it is tempting to rework the title of Fisher's book to read *Capitalist Realism, or, the Logic of Late Postmodernism*, in reference to Jameson's most celebrated work. Fisher appears to stand in relation to postmodernity much as Jameson did to its predecessor, modernism, and thus while Jameson was able to describe the emergence of postmodernity and with it the growth of nostalgia, Fisher bore witness to an era in which this process has reached its terminal stage. And as Fisher was aware, it only makes sense to talk about nostalgia for the past so long as a foothold remains from which nostalgia can take hold, for once it has become so widespread that it is no longer remarked upon, then nostalgia ceases to operate as before and becomes effectively impossible: 'You have to ask: nostalgia compared to what?'[121]

Capitalist realism, in Fisher's schema, is less a particular set of characteristics common to late-capitalism, than a 'pervasive *atmosphere*, conditioning not only the production of culture but also the regulation of work and education, and acting as a kind of invisible barrier constraining thought and action.'[122] As such, its insidious effects can be felt throughout contemporary society, impacting upon our mental health and manifesting themselves most visibly through the inexorable spread of bureaucracy into every aspect of our lives. Fisher employs a dizzying array of canonical and pop-cultural references in support of his argument, from Kurt Cobain to Ursula Le Guin, Spinoza to Tarkovsky, the Jason Bourne films to the TV parenting programme *Supernanny*, but there are two prevailing spirits whose names are invoked throughout: Jameson and Kafka. The former highlights the conditions out of which capitalist realism first emerged; the latter supplies the all-pervasive sense of blind, anonymous, bureaucracy which Fisher sees as the principal characteristic of working life under capitalist realism. 'The supreme genius of Kafka', Fisher writes, 'was to have explored the *negative atheology* proper to Capital: the centre is missing, but we cannot stop searching for it or positing it. It is not that there is nothing there – it is that what *is* there is not capable of exercising responsibility.'[123] Unable to locate the perimeter to capitalism's seemingly endless domain, we look to our political leaders for guidance, only to find that they are as blindly in thrall to its invisible workings as the rest of us. Yet, if capitalist realism is truly as all-embracing as Fisher suggests, how can one hope to challenge its hegemony?

Fisher ends his book with a note of cautious optimism, arguing that it is precisely capitalist realism's apparent full-spectrum dominance that may in fact be its weakness. In a world in which we can no longer imagine any alternative, the slightest sense that capitalist realism is no longer (and never has been) quite as real as we have been led to believe, may prove fatal:

> The long, dark night of the end of history has to be grasped as an enormous opportunity. The very oppressive pervasiveness of capitalist realism means that even glimmers of alternative political and economic possibilities can have a disproportionately great effect. The tiniest event can tear a hole in the grey curtain or reaction which has marked the horizons of possibility under capitalist realism. From a situation in which nothing can happen, suddenly anything is possible again.[124]

Fisher's book was first published in 2009 in the aftermath of the financial crisis, and it would then have appeared to many that an alternative to capitalist realism was about to make its presence felt. Yet the reaction of governments globally was to protect the capitalist system at all costs. As a result, rather than marking the death knell of neoliberal economics the crash simply ushered in a hitherto unimagined era of economic austerity. But, as hauntology repeatedly emphasises, the glimmers of alternative possibilities that Fisher describes above may be salvaged from the recent past, and in particular those moments whose future potential remains unrealised.

If *Capitalist Realism* was Fisher's major engagement with the politics of the early twenty-first century, then his clearest expression of the function of hauntology within the society that such conditions have created can be found in the introductory essay to his collection, *Ghosts of My Life* (2014). Taking its name from an expression used by the Italian critic Franco 'Bifo' Berardi in his *After the Future* (2011), 'The Slow Cancellation of The Future' now reads as a kind of hauntological manifesto, one in which Fisher's cultural and political preoccupations meet and overlap.[125] Fisher's essay explores what he describes as the 'deflation of expectations' that have characterised both cultural and political life in the UK in recent decades, a feeling of 'belatedness, of living after the gold rush' which is as 'omnipresent as it is disavowed.'[126] The paradox of the recent past is that while our sense of temporality may have been eroded, as linear time gives way to a strange kind of simultaneity, so has our lived past in fact been one of massive change both culturally and technologically. From Thatcherism to globalism via mass computerisation and a revolution in communications technology, the last 40 years have seen unheralded political and societal transformation, and yet rather than experiencing a sense of time accelerating, the opposite seems to be true. Rather than feeling that we are living through a period of endless transformation, our overriding sense is one of stasis or 'stuckness'. 'There ought to be something astonishing about this,' Fisher argues, 'it is the fact that there is no such response that simply confirms how widespread, how normalised anachronism has become in contemporary culture, so ubiquitous, in fact, as to have rendered it completely invisible.'[127] We can no longer clearly articulate a sense of the present or the future with the result that we are seemingly growing oblivious to both.

'Why hauntology?' Fisher asks, 'What has the concept of hauntology to do with all this?'[128] The remainder of Fisher's essay is largely an attempt to answer these questions, both to define hauntology (in as far as such a thing is possible) and to illustrate the ways in which it might offer us a way out of our current predicament.

> Is hauntology, then, some attempt to revive the supernatural, or is it just a figure of speech? The way out of this unhelpful opposition is to think of hauntology as the agency of the virtual, with the spectre understood not as anything supernatural, but as that which acts without (physically) existing. [...] we can provisionally distinguish two directions in hauntology. The first refers to that which is (in actuality is) no longer, but which remains effective as a virtuality (the traumatic 'compulsion to repeat', a fatal pattern). The second sense of hauntology refers to that which (in actuality) has not yet happened, but which is already effective in the virtual (an attractor, an anticipation shaping current behaviour). The 'spectre of communism' that Marx and Engels had warned of in the first lines of the Communist Manifesto was just this kind of ghost: a virtuality whose threatened coming was already playing a part in undermining the present state of things. [...] The era of what I have called 'capitalist realism' – the widespread belief that there is no alternative to capitalism – has been haunted not by the apparition of the spectre of communism, but by its disappearance.[129]

Fisher's formulation of hauntology consists of two component parts, two opposing historical currents: the 'no longer' and the 'not yet'. The former haunts the present from the past, returning repeatedly, a revenant without physical form but one which continues to make its presence felt. The latter haunts the present from the future, through the unfulfilled promise of that which never came to pass but which may yet do so. The former returns to us, the latter awaits us, but in both instances their impact is felt now, in the present, either as repetition or anticipation, shaping our hopes (or fears) and guiding our actions. In either case, however, what haunts us need not be an object, event or individual, nor even a moment or an era, but rather we may be haunted by the promise contained within an entire way of life:

> What's at stake in 21st century hauntology is not the disappearance of a particular object. What has vanished is a tendency, a virtual trajectory. One name for this tendency is popular modernism [...] What is being longed for in hauntology is not a particular period, but the resumption of the processes of democratisation and pluralism [...] What should haunt us is not the no longer of actually existing social democracy, but the not yet of the futures that popular modernism trained us to expect, but which never materialised. These spectres – the spectres of lost futures – reproach the formal nostalgia of the capitalist realist world.[130]

In the face of the seemingly perpetual crisis of late-capitalism, hauntology directs us back to the moment at which neoliberalism first took hold, to the lost, or rather prematurely truncated, movement that Fisher describes as 'popular modernism'. Broadly speaking, the period between the Festival of Britain in 1951 and its abeyance in the early years of the Thatcher government, popular modernism reaffirms a faith in the social institutions of the post-war years and the optimistic and forward-looking spirit they represented. But more than this, popular modernism is for Fisher as much about a particular ethos as it is about institutions, a 'cultural ecology' loosely shaped by public service broadcasting, postpunk, brutalist architecture, Penguin paperbacks and the BBC Radiophonic Workshop.[131] This was the ethos into which Fisher was born in 1968 and which was subsequently to shape his thinking, both culturally and politically, a trajectory that was interrupted by neoliberalism and whose demise has haunted his and later generations ever since.

Fisher concludes his essay with the acknowledgement that hauntology, far from being fixed and immutable, exists in many different forms, some benign, some less so.[132] Such an admission is a necessary reminder that the ghosts of the past may materialise in many different forms. The difference between hauntology in Britain and America, for example, the latter iteration more focussed upon the 1980s than its British counterpart, illustrates a divergence in cultural forms. Politically, however, hauntology remains uniformly wedded to the political left. Indeed, if there is a blind spot, both in Derrida and Fisher's articulation of hauntology, it is a seeming lack of awareness that the ghosts, spectres and revenants of an earlier age may invoke a quite different politics to that espoused by those on the left and one not necessarily of our choosing. This is a significant oversight, for it seems to me that rather than the spectres of Marx or even those of popular modernism, the prevailing spirit of the last 30 years in the UK is one which has been conjured from an altogether different point on the political spectrum: that of Thatcherism. In recent decades both right and ostensibly left wing governments have invoked, or at least acknowledged, Thatcher's legacy in support of their agenda; and in this respect the most farsighted literary response to her seeming immortality is surely that of Iain Sinclair's *Downriver* (1991) in which Thatcher, removed from power shortly before the book's publication, is recast as the Widow, a monstrous figure from the ranks of the undead.[133] One might perhaps be forgiven for thinking, reading the work of Fisher and others, that while the ghosts of the right are laid to rest forever, never to return, it is only the spectres of the left that remain to haunt our culture and our politics. It seems to me, however, that it is in fact the ghosts of the right who have returned unbidden to haunt us, less publicly perhaps but with no less an effect.[134]

The particular trajectory that hauntology follows, and which this book describes, is one which originates in 1848 before progressing via a series of jump-cuts towards the present day. At first merely a precursor to, or premonition of, later events, including that of its own birth in the 1990s, hauntology maps the deceleration of cultural time in the early twenty-first century as it begins to plot a new course back towards the recent past. This new trajectory rejoins the time stream at a particular moment, a brief period of time to which hauntology returns repeatedly, perhaps obsessively: the closing years of the long decade of the late 1960s and early 1970s. At the end of his life, Mark Fisher was engaged in a new project, one which sought to excavate the lost potential of these few years, a reappraisal of the past that might offer us a route out of our present crisis. Tragically, just as this period never reached its zenith, so too was Fisher's own trajectory curtailed, and what he began under the heading of 'Acid Communism' remains only in the form of an unfinished introduction.

If it is the spectre of Marx which has hitherto been hauntology's resident spirit, then Fisher begins 'Acid Communism' by invoking another spectre, one whose promise remains similarly unfulfilled:

> The closer the real possibility of liberating the individual from the constraints once justified by scarcity and immaturity, the greater the need for maintaining and streamlining these constraints lest the established order of dominion dissolve. Civilisation has to protect itself against the spectre of a world which could be free.[135]

These comments, written by Herbert Marcuse in 1955, are employed here by Fisher to convey the spirit of optimism that momentarily came to the fore in the late 1960s, as the utopianism of the countercultural movement was bolstered by the growth of socialist and social democratic governments in the UK and around the world. This was a moment in which an entire nexus of radical ideas briefly converged to offer us a glimpse of a different kind of future, one in which the spectres of capitalist exploitation and totalitarianism might finally be laid to rest. In the end, of course, such a future failed to materialise, but Marcuse's 'spirit of a world which could be free' lives on as the 'not yet' of a future whose potential remains unfulfilled. In this respect, hauntology may be characterised by the continued challenge posed to the present by these two spectres: Marx and Marcuse, the former invoked by Derrida, the latter by Fisher, in summoning up the spirit of two moments in history when radical change appeared not only possible but imminent.

The outline for this, his final book, is built upon Fisher's assertion that over the last 40 years the prevailing orthodoxy of neoliberalism has sought to exorcise the spectre of Marcuse's 'world which could be free', its removal paving the way for the rise of capitalist realism. 'Neoliberalism', Fisher explains, 'is best understood as a project aimed at destroying – to the point of making them unthinkable – the experiments in democratic socialism and libertarian communism that were efflorescing at the end of the Sixties and the beginning of the Seventies.'[136] Fisher identifies the violent fall of the Allende government in Chile in 1973 as the founding event of capitalist realism, a historical juncture at which one possible future was discarded in favour of another, the consequences of which we have been living through ever since. Such a profound change of direction has meant that these few years have since come to feel impossibly remote from our own, 'like a deep past so exotic and distant that we cannot imagine living in it, and a moment more vivid than now – a time when people really lived, when things really happened.'[137] So radical is the impulse that still emanates from this period, however, that our historical understanding of the era has since been 'continually re-narrated', as its democratic and egalitarian ethos grows ever more dangerously at odds with that of neoliberalism. But what if the counterculture was not the end of this era, a degeneration of 1960s idealism, as has since been commonly supposed, but rather a 'stumbling beginning' to a decade whose potential has been airbrushed from history? 'What if the success of neoliberalism was not an indication of the inevitability of capitalism', Fisher asks, 'but a testament to the scale of the threat posed by the spectre of a society that could be free?'[138] If this is so, then it is not the 1960s whose spirit we should be harnessing but the 1970s, for it is here, behind the retrospective 'monstering' this period has since received, that we may still glimpse the possibilities inherent to the period at the moment of their erasure. Revisiting this period today, however, no longer requires us to perform an act of recollection so much as one of 'unforgetting', a counter-exorcism of the spectre of a world which could be free:

> *Acid Communism* is the name I have given to this spectre. The concept of acid communism is a provocation and a promise. It is a joke of sorts, but one with very serious purpose. It points to something that, at one point, seemed inevitable, but which now appears impossible: the convergence of class consciousness, socialist-feminist consciousness-raising and psychedelic consciousness, the fusion of new social movements with a communist project, an unprecedented aestheticisation of everyday life.
>
> Acid communism both refers to actual historical developments and to a virtual confluence that has not yet come together in actuality. Potentials exert influence without being actualised. Actual social formations are shaped by the potential formations whose actualisation they seek to impede. The impress of "a world which could be free" can be detected in the very structures of a capitalist realist world which makes freedom impossible.[139]

Viewed from the third decade of the twenty-first century, almost 50 years on from yet another example of a revolution that failed to happen, it can prove increasingly wearisome to mine the seam of such nearly-moments in search of the traces of what might have been. Of course, such exhaustion might itself be viewed as symptomatic of the 'consciousness-deflation' characteristic of neoliberalism, merely another strategy with which to avert our gaze from the message buried beneath the carefully curated surface of the recent past. This, at least, is the message with which Fisher concludes his own preliminary investigation of this period, exhorting us to reverse the process by which confidence is converted into dejection. 'We must regain the optimism of that Seventies moment', he concludes.[140]

According to the critic, Tom Whyman, Fisher's 'Acid Communism' may be regarded as an 'experiment in applied hauntology', a twofold strategy which on the one hand attempts to uncover the reasons behind our current impasse, and on the other unearths 'the resources the left can draw upon if it wants to defeat neoliberalism'.[141] Such a manoeuvre, Whyman claims, marks hauntology's final transformation from 'critical academic tool to a category of political aesthetics, and lastly into the key that might unlock the future', an evolution from merely interpreting the world to changing it that Marx himself would surely have applauded.[142] Of course, the paradox here is that if we want to change the present we must do so by returning to the past, first to understand what went wrong and then to re-implement the message that we failed to act upon first time around. Politically, at least, the idea of a return to the 1970s remains a hard sell, although as capitalism staggers from one crisis to the next, a decade that has long been perceived (from a neoliberal viewpoint) as a byword for political and economic disaster, now looks considerably more appealing. On the level of culture, however, Fisher's exhortation now hardly seems necessary, at least not for those of us of a certain age or temperament, who have already embarked upon an inward exodus back to this era. 'The 70s exert a particular fascination now that we are locked into the new world', wrote Fisher in 2005, 'The 70s is the time before the switch, a time at once kinder and harsher than now. [...] Try to imagine England in 1979 [...] Pre-VCR, pre-PC, pre-C4. Telephones far from ubiquitous [...] The postwar consensus disintegrating on black and white TV.'[143] As we continue to pull away from the 1970s temporally so we appear to be moving ever closer culturally, and while the feat of imagination Fisher proposed then may well have appeared a challenging one, it now seems increasingly less so.

Back to the 1970s: The Folk Horror Revival

Following a strictly linear chronology, one might expect this final chapter, which focusses largely upon events which took place almost half a century ago, to appear elsewhere in this book, perhaps alongside the earlier discussion of the work of Alan Garner and Susan Cooper. Yet just as the folk horror revival repeats and reworks the cultural and political forms of a bygone era, so too is it very much a phenomenon of the second decade of the twenty-first century, one which perfectly encapsulates the way in which cultural time has folded back on itself, as it follows a return trajectory back to the 1970s. While the newly rediscovered version of that decade may closely resemble the original, however, it is one that has been reshaped by the forces of nostalgia and historical revision into something rather different. For as Mark Fisher has reminded us, 'The actual post-psychedelic, quasi-Eastern Bloc seediness of the 70s is unretrievable; kitsch wallpaper and bell bottoms are transformed instantly into Style quotations the moment the camera falls upon them. [...] Hearing T-Rex now doesn't remind you of 73, it reminds you of nostalgia programmes about 1973.'[144] The mitigating effects of nostalgia, which screen us from the reality of the past by filtering our recollections through the cultural and political lens of the present, have coloured our perception of the 1970s perhaps more than any other decade in post-war British history. This is the time and the place from which folk horror first emerged and towards which it is now returning.

Discussions of folk horror frequently begin (and often conclude) with yet another effort to define this subject, movement, or tendency – even here there is little unanimity – for perhaps the only characteristic of folk horror that seems widely agreed upon is that it is highly resistant to all such attempts at classification. The term itself is, or has become, a misleading one, for having outgrown its confinement within the horror genre that gave birth to it, it has since embraced an eclectic range of cultural offshoots, many of which now bear only a tenuous relationship to its original form. Andy Paciorek, who convened the Folk Horror Facebook group in 2014, 'to celebrate and create new forms of folk horror', answers his question, 'What is Folk Horror?' with the acknowledgement that 'one may as well attempt to build a box the exact shape of mist; for like the mist, Folk Horror is atmospheric and sinuous.

It can creep from and into different territories yet leave no universal defining mark of its exact form.'[145] Folk horror, he tells us, has been around since at least the 1920s, but it didn't appear in its current guise until 2003 when Piers Haggard, in an interview with MJ Simpson for *Fangoria* magazine, used the term to describe the evolution of his film *The Blood on Satan's Claw* (1970):

> I went to a few horror films and figured out what seemed to be essential. But I was determined to make it as it needed to be made. I didn't want to breach the genre but I didn't want to follow it under any sort of enslavement. I guess I was trying to make the thing seriously, as if it was real. Also, to me the countryside was terribly important. I grew up on a farm and it's natural for me to use the countryside as symbols or as imagery. As this was a story about people subject to superstitions about living in the woods, the dark poetry of that appealed to me. I was trying to make a folk-horror film, I suppose.[146]

The term was later popularised by Jonathan Rigby and Mark Gatiss in their BBC4 television series *A History of Horror* (2010), in which they extrapolated from Haggard's remark to include a trilogy of films which 'shared a common obsession with the British landscape, its folklore and superstitions'.[147]

These three films, Michael Reeves's *Witchfinder General* (1968), Haggard's *The Blood on Satan's Claw* (1970) and Robin Hardy's *The Wicker Man* (1973), have since been canonised as the 'unholy trinity' of folk horror, spanning the five-year period from the peak of the countercultural movement in the UK to its effective demise. But this triptych of skewed morality, atavistic pagan ritual and human sacrifice, all set against the backdrop of a sinister but sun-drenched rural landscape is not the end of this sequence but its beginning, for rippling outward from this moment in time and place, the folk horror revival has since identified an ever-growing list of candidates for inclusion within its ranks. According to whose account you prefer, these three films either establish the basis of the genre (or sub-genre), with the odd precursor in films such as Jacques Tourneur's adaptation of MR James's 'Casting the Runes', *Night of the Demon* (1957), or, as Andy Paciorek suggests, folk horror ought properly to be placed within a much broader historical and internationalist tradition. 'It all began in Denmark in the year of 1922', Paciorek writes, starting with Benjamin Christensen's fictionalised documentary of the occult, *Häxan* (1922), before he traces the development of folk horror through a panoply of films from Mario Bava's *Black Sunday* (Italy; 1960) and Kaneto Shindo's *Onibaba* (Japan; 1964), to Walter Grauman's *Crowhaven Farm* (USA; 1970) and Peter Weir's *Picnic at Hanging Rock* (Australia; 1975).[148] Of course, extending the range of folk horror's antecedents so dramatically runs the risk of rather diluting the impact of what is already a somewhat nebulous concept. Instead, it seems to me, folk horror is at its most coherent when it remains conjoined to the specific period and geographical setting from which it draws its power: the predominantly rural landscapes of Britain in the late 1960s and early 1970s, a link that is only further emphasised by the fact that, although the origins of folk horror remain cinematic, many of the most memorable examples of the genre are to be found in the television of this period.

From Lawrence Gordon Clark's adaptations of MR James for the BBC *Ghost Stories for Christmas*, such as *A Warning to the Curious* (1972), *Lost Hearts* (1973) and *The Ash Tree* (1975), to episodes of the BBC *Play for Today* such as John Bowen's *Robin Redbreast* (1970), David Rudkin's extraordinary *Penda's Fen* (1974) and John Mackenzie's adaptation of Alan Garner's *Red Shift* (1978); from the ITV adaptation of Garner's *The Owl Service* (1969), to *Children of the Stones* (1977) and the works of Nigel Kneale: *The Stone Tape* (1972), *Murrain* (1975) and *Beasts* (1976).[149] It is in these and other programmes of their day that we encounter the weakened or distorted sense of temporality characteristic of hauntology alongside those traits more common to folk horror, such as the revival of the mythic or folkloric past and a portrayal of landscapes imbued with violence, both real and imagined. Perhaps the most chilling, however, and certainly the most unlikely revival of television from this period is that of the Public Information Film, examples of which include *Lonely Water* (1973) and *Apaches* (1977). With their graphic demonstrations of the dire fate which lurks within seemingly the most innocuous of surroundings, those exposed to such films as children will have struggled to forget them.

In what is to date the only systematic attempt to understand the elements intrinsic to folk horror, Adam Scovell argues that it is no longer possible to capture such a disparate body of work within the confines of a single overarching definition. Instead, he suggests, folk horror ought to be regarded as 'a way of opening up discussions on subtly interconnected work and how we now interact with such work. If anything its genealogy is less important than its stark ability to draw links between oddities and idiosyncrasies, especially within post-war British culture.'[150] Such links form the basis of what Scovell calls the 'folk horror chain', a 'set of narrative traits that have causational and interlinking consequences.'[151] This chain consists of four interlinked themes or characteristics common to folk horror: firstly, landscape, 'where elements within its topography have adverse effects on the social and moral identity of its inhabitants'; secondly, the isolation such landscapes engender, 'whether it be just a handful of individuals or a small-scale community'; thirdly, the 'skewed belief systems and morality' and 'the halting of social progress' encountered in such communities; and finally, what Scovell labels 'happening/summoning' or the belief 'that these ideas will manifest through the most violent and supernatural of methods.'[152] These are the themes which can be observed in the films and television programmes listed above, although Scovell regards such traits as characteristic not only of folk horror but as equally representative of the decade that gave rise to them, the true nature of which has been revealed to us by hauntology:

> Whether or not it was genuinely as paranoid as it is now perceived, the culture surrounding the 1970s in Britain has in itself become a form of Folk Horror through the mechanisms of Hauntology, whereby the traumas seen and unseen within the period are now repeating through our constant rediscovery of such culture [...] Hauntology presents Britain in the 1970s as a place of skewed morality, of isolated Brutalist zones, of the 'Urban Wyrd' and of paranoid, dystopian delusions surrounding the treatment of women and children. In other words, Hauntology shows

the decade in its true guise; not just the place where Folk Horror was produced most abundantly but itself the most terrifying form of Folk Horror conceivable.[153]

In Scovell's depiction of folk horror, this is a movement whose key characteristics are mirrored in the reality of the period that produced them. But if this is true of the 1970s, what of its revival in recent years through which such themes are replayed? Scovell identifies a further function of folk horror in its ability to 'reflect on past political moments that provide a temporal link between the era of the counter-culture and the present day (showing both the differences and the horrific likenesses between the periods).'[154] If its origin, or at least its heyday, is indissolubly linked to the rise and fall of the British counterculture, the revival of folk horror has manifested itself rather more obliquely and its parameters remain much less easy to ascertain.

Perhaps the most explicit acknowledgement of the folk horror tradition in recent years is to be found in the films of Ben Wheatley, whose *Kill List* (2011) offers a reworking of the ritualistic violence of *The Wicker Man* set against the socio-economic backdrop of austerity Britain. Unlike its predecessor, however, in Wheatley's film occult ritual is no longer symbolic of a countercultural opposition to society's norms, but is instead portrayed as a reactionary force, the means through which the political and economic elites exert their control over society.[155] It is Wheatley's film *A Field in England* (2013), however, which is more representative of the return to the land with which folk horror is commonly associated. In this instance, as its title suggests, the action remains firmly enclosed within the borders of a single field and is played out against the backdrop of the English Civil War, a return to an earlier period of radical unrest which also provided the setting for *Witchfinder General*. Elsewhere, films such as Robert Eggers' *The Witch* (2015) and Ari Aster's *Midsommar* (2019) demonstrate the continuing relevance of folk horror motifs.

But the revival of folk horror has been expressed through a multiplicity of forms from film and photography, to music, literature and art; and just as the rebirth of hauntology was facilitated by new media technologies so too has the folk horror revival similarly flourished through its online presence. It is here that the process of temporal re-enactment reaches its most sinister and surreal pitch in Richard Littler's *Scarfolk*, his horrifyingly familiar depiction of a town in North West England forever trapped within the 1970s, a place where 'hauntology is a compulsory subject at school.'[156] Painstakingly reassembled through the visual aesthetic of the public information poster, *Scarfolk* brings to life many of the most recognisable tropes of cultural life in the UK during this period, albeit in a relentlessly satirical fashion. On this revised map of the UK, Scarfolk is joined by the town of Belbury. Named after the fictional village invented by CS Lewis in his novel *That Hideous Strength* (1945), Belbury was appropriated by Jim Jupp and Julian House to reflect the quaint but uncanny ethos of village life that informs their label, Ghost Box. The label's blog is presented through the format of the Belbury Parish Magazine, while the village is also reflected in the name of Jupp's musical alter ego, Belbury Poly. One further location worthy of note here is that of Chris Lambert's Black Meadow, a similarly eerie invention purported to be found in the North

York Moors, and described as 'a place of disappearances, strange traditions and bizarre phenomena, ancient magicks, Meadow hags, horsemen and Bramble children.'[157]

In his recent outline of the history of folk horror, Ben Myers prefaces his account with a striking statistic: between 1801 and the present day, the proportion of the population of England and Wales living in towns and cities increased from 17 to 81.5 per cent.[158] It is this mass movement from a predominantly agricultural past to a post-industrial present, Myers suggests, which provides the impulse behind folk horror, one which has rendered the countryside an 'increasingly alien territory'. Urbanites are 'unnerved by the space, the silence', he writes, 'they fear their countryside, their own past.'[159] It was the back-to-the-land movement of the 1960s which first informed folk horror's characteristic mood of ambivalence towards the countryside, viewed on the one hand as welcoming and revitalising, and on the other as sinister and unyielding, a sentiment that has returned in recent years at a time in which the countryside appears threatened as never before. 'For some of us', Myers concludes, 'the idea of our island becoming little more than a series of interlinked retail parks with its countryside reduced to a brisk, cordoned-off procession around some Neolithic standing stones is a far more horrific prospect than the fantastical powers of an unearthed relic, ancient rituals or rustling in the hedgerow. And, let's face it, it's more likely too.'[160] Myers's comments find a counterpart in those of Robert Macfarlane, who has also explored our changing perception of the countryside and the cultural forms through which such attitudes are expressed. Writing in 2015, Macfarlane identified a striking sense of unease, manifested through a body of work which 'explores the English landscape in terms of its anomalies rather than its continuities, that is sceptical of comfortable notions of "dwelling" and "belonging", and of the packagings of the past as "heritage", and that locates itself within a spectred rather than a sceptred isle.'[161] Macfarlane harnesses an array of examples from across the spectrum of what he calls 'landscape culture', in support of his assertion that the cultural resurgence we are experiencing is 'an attempt to account for the turbulence of England in the era of late capitalism':

> The supernatural and paranormal have always been means of figuring powers that cannot otherwise find visible expression. Contemporary anxieties and dissents are here being reassembled and re-presented as spectres, shadows or monsters [...] We are, certainly, very far from "nature writing", whatever that once was, and into a mutated cultural terrain that includes the weird and the punk as well as the attentive and the devotional. Among the shared landmarks of this terrain are ruins, fields, pits, fringes, relics, buried objects, hilltops, falcons, demons and deep pasts. In much of this work, suppressed forces pulse and flicker beneath the ground and within the air (capital, oil, energy, violence, state power, surveillance), waiting to erupt or to condense. [...] What are those pressing concerns, though, and what are the sources of this unsettlement?[162]

In answering these questions, Macfarlane locates several factors behind the revival of the eerie, from the environmental despoliation of the countryside to the role of the political left in exposing the spectral effects of capitalism. But it is the rise of surveillance culture to which he gives particular emphasis, the visible manifestation of which may be seen in 'the military and security infrastructure that occupies much of England's land and air space, from Salisbury Plain to Otterburn to Foulness.' Explaining the attraction that this 'dispersed geography of conflict and surveillance' has held for writers such as Alan Garner, Mark Fisher and WG Sebald, Macfarlane notes that a sense of being watched is a crucial element of the eerie: 'It isn't hard to see why contemporary eerie culture should be drawn to such evidence of record and detection. If the eerie is [...] about the experience of being watched by a presence that you cannot perceive, then this, certainly, is another cause for its present relevance. For the state has never before been as able to detect and follow the movements of its subjects.'[163] Macfarlane's essay offers a convincing account of the reasons behind the recent re-emergence of the eerie in our depiction of the English countryside, but what remains less clear is why the concerns he outlines are so often expressed through a revival of cultural forms so specific to the 1970s. What is it about the 1970s that still speaks to us so insistently?

In his refreshingly revisionist account of the period, *When the Lights Went Out: What Really Happened to Britain in the Seventies* (2009), the historian Andy Beckett challenges our relentlessly downbeat assessment of this decade, asking why it is that we remain so nostalgic for an era that we have been talking down ever since. 'I have been hearing what was wrong with Britain and British politics in the seventies all my adult life', Beckett writes, 'No other political theme has been as unrelenting. The seventies were grim. The seventies were the hangover from the sixties. The seventies were violent. The seventies were a dead end. Above all: we don't want to go back to the seventies.' And yet almost as soon as that decade was over, Beckett notes, we embarked upon a cultural revival that has since culminated in the 1970s outstripping the 1960s as 'the British nostalgia market's favourite.'[164] Beckett demonstrates that while Britain underwent a period of profound change in the 1970s, it was by no means the unmitigated disaster that is popularly supposed; indeed on certain social and economic indices it stands up well in comparison to the years which were to follow.[165] But what is most striking in Beckett's account is his description of how a decade that had once seemed a distant memory, and which we were widely encouraged to treat as such, has in recent years begun to feel much closer to our own:

> Largely unnoticed at first, another oil crisis began to develop. Inflation and unemployment began to rise. The Labour government began to struggle. The Conservatives began to revive. Sterling and the FTSE index began to slide. Trade unionists concerned about their living standards began, regardless of the government's difficulties, to go on strike. [...] Collapsing banks were even nationalised.[166]

Reading these comments today one might be forgiven for thinking they were a summary of the 1970s economic misfortunes. In fact, they appear in Beckett's account of the years between 2005 and 2008, a time which he recalls as one in which the 1970s began to come back into focus, as 'certain forgotten seventies phrases – "stagflation", "oil shock", "government pay policy", "government bail-out" – began to be taken out of their display cases.'[167] Of course, alongside such forgotten phrases, another term made its return during this period, for these were hauntology's comeback years, a cultural concept with an unerring focus upon the 1970s returning at the very moment at which that decade's political and economic difficulties had become visible in our own. 'A very seventies unease has seeped back into how we see the world', Beckett affirmed in 2009, 'Economic crises, floods, food shortages, terrorism, the destruction of the environment: these spectres, so looming in the seventies, did not go away during the eighties and nineties; yet they faded – they were quite easy to forget about. Now they have returned [...] it is possible to wonder how many of Britain's seventies problems were ever really solved.'[168]

It was this sense of unease which manifested itself in the return of hauntology in 2005, and which later gave rise to the revival of folk horror, itself a cultural expression of hauntology, and one in which the socio-economic upheavals of the day are reflected. For just as Britain was a place of social unrest in the 1970s, so too has it been again in recent years, from the financial crash of 2008 and the period of austerity which followed in its wake, to fears over immigration and the class and racial tensions exacerbated by Brexit. Today, it seems unclear whether we have returned to the 1970s or if the spectres of that decade have returned to us, never having been laid to rest as many had hoped or believed, but rather lying dormant through the intervening years before returning to haunt us once again. Re-emerging at a moment of imminent threat, hauntology is the early warning signal that alerts us to the perils of the present by transporting us to a similar moment of crisis in our recent past, reminding us of how things might have been, and may yet be.

Notes

[1] JG Ballard, '1982: V Vale. Interview with JGB', in *Extreme Metaphors*, 146-169, p. 148.

[2] This response to Fukuyama's thesis is one which is commonly attributed to Thatcher. See, for example, Jason Burke, 'History Man', *The Guardian*, 27 July 2004.

[3] 'I was turned off by their nihilistic idea of what literature was all about,' Fukuyama recalls. 'It had nothing to do with the world. I developed such an aversion to that whole over-intellectual approach that I turned to nuclear weapons instead.' See James Atlas, 'What is Fukuyama Saying? And to Whom is He Saying It?' *The New York Times Magazine*, 22 October 1989.

[4] Atlas, 'What is Fukuyama Saying?'.

[5] Fredric Jameson, 'Marx's Purloined Letter' in *Ghostly Demarcations: A Symposium on Jacques Derrida's Specters of Marx*, ed. by Michael Sprinker, London: Verso, 1999, 26-67, p. 63.

[6] Stuart Sim, *Derrida and the End of History*, Cambridge: Icon Books, 1999, pp. 12-13.

[7] Francis Fukuyama, 'The End of History?', *The National Interest*, 16 (Summer 1989), 3-18, p. 3.

[8] Daniel Bell, *The End of Ideology: On the Exhaustion of Political Ideas in the Fifties* (1960), quoted by Sim, p.18.

[9] Fukuyama, 'The End of History?', p. 16.

[10] Mark Fisher sees a fictional counterpart to Nietzsche's 'last men' in the later work of JG Ballard. In novels such as

Millennium People (2003) and *Kingdom Come* (2006) Ballard's affluent middle-class protagonists appear acutely afflicted by Fukuyama's post-historical malaise, to the extent that they pursue societal breakdown as an antidote to the stifling boredom engendered by lives of empty consumerism. See Mark Fisher, 'What are the Politics of Boredom? (Ballard 2003 remix)' in *K-Punk*, pp. 57-61.

[11] Fisher, *Ghosts of My Life*, p. 19.

[12] Mark Fisher, *Capitalist Realism: Is There No Alternative?*, Winchester: Zero Books, 2009, pp. 6-7.

[13] Mark Fisher, 'Home is Where the Haunt is. *The Shining's* Hauntology' in *Ghosts of My Life*, p. 120.

[14] Jacques Derrida, *Specters of Marx*, trans. by Peggy Kamuf, London: Routledge, 2006, p. 224, n. 2.

[15] Sim, p. 33.

[16] Bernd Magnus & Stephen Cullenberg, 'Editor's Introduction' (1994) in *Specters of Marx*, p. vii.

[17] Rather than inspiring the title of his book, as one might have expected, Derrida reveals that it was shortly *after* choosing 'Specters' as his title that he reread Marx's *Manifesto*: 'I knew very well there was a ghost waiting there, and from the opening, from the raising of the curtain. Now, of course, I have just discovered, in truth I have just remembered what must have been haunting my memory: the first *noun* of the *Manifesto*, and this time in the singular, is 'specter'.' See Derrida, *Specters*, p. 2.

[18] Derrida, *Specters*, pp. 2 & 224, n. 1.

[19] Sim, p. 42.

[20] Derrida, *Specters*, p. 3.

[21] Derrida, *Specters*, p. 99.

[22] Derrida, *Specters*, p. 176.
[23] Derrida, *Specters*, p. 10.
[24] Derrida, *Specters*, p. 63.
[25] Derrida, *Specters*, p. 202.
[26] AJP Taylor, 'Introduction' in Karl Marx and Friedrich Engels, *The Communist Manifesto*, Harmondsworth: Penguin, 1967, 7-47, pp. 27-8.
[27] Derrida, *Specters*, pp. 100-103.
[28] Michael Sprinkler, 'Introduction', in *Ghostly Demarcations*, p. 2.
[29] Fisher, 'The Slow Cancellation of the Future', in *Ghosts of My Life*, pp. 16-17.
[30] Fisher, 'The Slow Cancellation of the Future', in *Ghosts of My Life*, pp. 18-19.
[31] Fisher, 'The Slow Cancellation of the Future', in *Ghosts of My Life*, p. 20.
[32] [Craig Brown], 'Diary: W. G. Sebald', *Private Eye*, 958, 4 September 1998, p. 25.
[33] See John Wylie, 'The Spectral Geographies of W.G. Sebald', *Cultural Geographies*, 2007, Vol. 4, No. 2, 171-188, pp. 175-8.
[34] In his review of Sebald's *Austerlitz*, Andy Beckett writes: 'Often, reading Sebald does not feel like reading about the past, as much as seeing the world through the eyes of someone from the past. The sepia language and the ease of reference to Victorian bodies of knowledge can make you wonder, sometimes, whether the author is actually some sort of ghost.' Andy Beckett, 'Long and Winding River: Andy Beckett on W.G. Sebald's Austerlitz, a meandering journey through time, place and genre', *The Guardian*, 29 September 2001.
[35] Jorge Luis Borges, 'Tlön, Uqbar, Orbis Tertius' (1940),

quoted by WG Sebald in *The Rings of Saturn*, trans. by Michael Hulse, London: Harvill, 1998, pp. 70-71.

[36] Borges, 'Tlön, Uqbar, Orbis Tertius', quoted by Sebald in *The Rings of Saturn*, pp. 153-4.

[37] For an account of Sebald's fictional reworkings of the past, both in *The Rings of Saturn* and in his earlier novel, *The Emigrants* (1996), see Edward Parnell, *Ghostland: In Search of a Haunted Country*, London: Collins, 2019, pp. 253-265.

[38] In his introduction to Sebald's *Austerlitz*, James Wood reveals that Sebald once confided to him that about 30 per cent of the photographs in *The Emigrants* (1992) were fictitious. See James Wood, 'Introduction' (2011) in WG Sebald, *Austerlitz*, trans. by Anthea Bell, London: 2001, p. xxi.

[39] Sebald, *The Rings of Saturn*, p. 212.

[40] For a reading of Sebald's novel that foregrounds this sense of decaying memory see Adam Scovell, 'Memory and Disintegration in the Work of W.G. Sebald and The Caretaker', *Celluloid Wicker Man*, 15 June 2017, at https://celluloidwickerman.com/2017/07/03/memory-and-disintegration-in-the-work-of-w-g-sebald-and-the-caretaker/

[41] Sebald, *The Rings of Saturn*, pp. 187-8.

[42] Sebald, *The Rings of Saturn*, p. 237.

[43] It is another novel in which the narrator recalls his memories of the East Anglian countryside, LP Hartley's *The Go Between* (1953), whose celebrated opening line – 'The past is a foreign country; they do things differently there' – surely provides the source for Sebald's summary of the Orfordness section of his novel.

[44] Sebald, *The Rings of Saturn*, p. 255.

[45] Mark Fisher, 'Postmodern Antiques: *Patience (After Sebald)*',

Sight & Sound, April 2011, in *Ghosts of My Life*, pp. 202-207, pp. 202-3.

46 Fisher, 'Postmodern Antiques: *Patience (After Sebald)*', p. 203.

47 Fisher, 'Postmodern Antiques: *Patience (After Sebald)*', p. 205.

48 Fisher, 'Postmodern Antiques: *Patience (After Sebald)*', p. 206.

49 Fisher, 'Postmodern Antiques: *Patience (After Sebald)*', p. 203.

50 Sebald, *Austerlitz*, trans. by Anthea Bell, London: Hamish Hamilton, 2001, pp. 141-4.

51 Sebald, *Austerlitz*, pp. 261 & 359-60.

52 James Bridle, 'Hauntological Futures', 20 March 2011, at https://booktwo.org/notebook/hauntological-futures/

53 Svetlana Boym, *The Future of Nostalgia*, New York: Basic Books, 2001, p. 3.

54 Svetlana Boym, 'Nostalgia and its Discontents', *The Hedgehog Review*, Vol. 9 (2), 22 June 2007, p. 2.

55 Boym, *The Future of Nostalgia*, p.5.

56 Boym, 'Nostalgia and its Discontents', p. 2.

57 Boym, 'Nostalgia and its Discontents', pp. 2-3.

58 Boym, 'Nostalgia and its Discontents', p. 3.

59 Boym, 'Nostalgia and its Discontents', p. 4.

60 Boym, 'Nostalgia and its Discontents', p. 3.

61 Boym, 'Nostalgia and its Discontents', p. 7.

62 Boym, 'Nostalgia and its Discontents', p. 7.

63 Boym, 'Nostalgia and its Discontents', p. 10.

64 Boym, 'Nostalgia and its Discontents', p. 11.

65 See Fredric Jameson, *Postmodernism: or, the Cultural Logic of Late Capitalism*, London: Verso, 1992, pp. 279-296.

66 Jameson, p. 293-4.

67 Fisher, 'The Slow Cancellation of the Future' in *Ghosts of My Life*, pp. 8-13.

[68] Fisher, 'The Slow Cancellation of the Future' in *Ghosts of My Life*, p. 25.

[69] Mark Fisher, 'Nomadalgia: The Junior Boys' *So This is Goodbye*' (2006) in *Ghosts of My Life*, p. 197.

[70] 'The future didn't disappear overnight', Fisher writes, 'If the late 1970s and early 80s were the moment when the current crisis of cultural temporality could first be felt, it was only during the first decade of the 21st century that what Simon Reynolds calls "dyschronia" has become endemic. This dyschronia, this temporal disjuncture, ought to feel uncanny, yet the predominance of what Reynolds calls "retromania" means that it has lost any *unheimlich* charge: anachronism is now taken for granted.' See Fisher, 'The Slow Cancellation of the Future' in *Ghosts of My Life*, pp. 14-16.

[71] Reynolds, *Retromania*, pp. x-xii.

[72] Reynolds, *Retromania*, p. xii.

[73] Reynolds, *Retromania*, p. xiii.

[74] Reynolds, *Retromania*, p. xiv.

[75] Reynolds, *Retromania*, p. xxi.

[76] Reynolds, *Retromania*, p. 56.

[77] Reynolds, *Retromania*, pp. 56-68.

[78] Reynolds, *Retromania*, p. 239.

[79] Reynolds, *Retromania*, pp. 22-3. See also Andreas Huyssen, 'Present Pasts: Media, Politics, Amnesia', in *Public Culture*, Vol. 12 (1), Winter, 2000.

[80] Reynolds, *Retromania*, p. 23.

[81] Reynolds, *Retromania*, p. 328.

[82] Reynolds, *Retromania*, p. 330.

[83] Reynolds, *Retromania*, p. 335.

[84] Reynolds, *Retromania*, p. 341.

85 Reynolds, *Retromania*, p. 343.

86 Reynolds, *Retromania*, p. 343.

87 Reynolds, *Retromania*, p. 355.

88 Reynolds, *Retromania*, p. 361.

89 Reynolds, *Retromania*, pp. 368-9.

90 Mark Fisher, 'Hauntology, Nostalgia and Lost Futures', Interviewed by Valerio Mannucci and Valerio Mattioli for *Nero* (2014) in *K-Punk*, p. 689.

91 Sukhdev Sandhu, 'Avant-Pulp Psychogeography', *American Book Review*, January/February 2013, Vol. 34, No. 2, pp. 6-7.

92 Laura Oldfield Ford, 'Ghosts of the City: The Savage Art of Laura Oldfield Ford, *Good Trouble*, 9 March 2017, at https://www.goodtroublemag.com/home/ithrs76u4di0qgfo9gzj7tv4reb18r

93 Mark Fisher, 'Introduction: Always Yearning for the Time That Just Eluded Us' (2011), in Laura Grace Ford, *Savage Messiah*, London: Verso, 2019, ix-xviii, p. ix.

94 In his preface to the 2019 edition of *Savage Messiah*, Greil Marcus writes: 'The past is a shadow, an angel, a demon: most of what Ford recounts seems to be taking place in the'70s or the'80s or the '90s, with the first decade of the twenty-first century a kind of slag-heap of time – of boredom, enervation, despair, and hate – that people are trying to burrow out from under'. See Greil Marcus in Laura Grace Ford, *Savage Messiah*, Preface, p. vi.

95 Laura Grace Ford, *Savage Messiah* #1 in *Savage Messiah*, London: Verso, 2019.

96 Ford, *Savage Messiah* #2 in *Savage Messiah*.

97 Ford, *Savage Messiah* #3 in *Savage Messiah*.

98 Ford, *Savage Messiah* #4 in *Savage Messiah*.

[99] Ford, *Savage Messiah* #7 in *Savage Messiah*.

[100] Ford, *Savage Messiah* #8 in *Savage Messiah*.

[101] Ford, *Savage Messiah* #10 in *Savage Messiah*.

[102] Ford, *Savage Messiah* #11 in *Savage Messiah*.

[103] Ford, *Savage Messiah* #11 in *Savage Messiah*.

[104] Fisher, 'Introduction' in Ford, *Savage Messiah*, p. ix.

[105] Fisher, 'Introduction' in Ford, *Savage Messiah*, p. x.

[106] Fisher, 'Introduction' in Ford, *Savage Messiah*, p. xiv.

[107] Greil Marcus in Ford, *Savage Messiah*, Preface, p. v.

[108] Fisher, 'Introduction' in Ford, *Savage Messiah*, p. xviii.

[109] Mark Fisher, 'They Can be Different in the Future Too: Interviewed by Rowan Wilson for *Ready Steady Book* (2010)' in *K-Punk*, p. 634.

[110] Simon Hammond, 'K-Punk at Large', *New Left Review*, 118, July-August 2019, 37-66, p. 47.

[111] Fisher, 'What is Hauntology?', p. 16.

[112] Fisher, 'What is Hauntology?', p. 16.

[113] This is a remark which has previously been attributed both to Fredric Jameson and Slavoj Žižek. See Fredric Jameson, *The Seeds of Time*, New York: Columbia University Press, 1994, p. xii, and Slavoj Žižek, *Mapping Ideology*, London; Verso, 1994, p. 1. Patrick Keiller also uses the phrase in *Robinson in Space* (2010) as Fisher notes in his discussion of the film. See Mark Fisher, 'Tremors of an Imperceptible Future: Patrick Keiller's *Robinson in Ruins*', *Sight & Sound*, November 2010, in *Ghosts of My Life*, 225-232, p. 227.

[114] Fisher, *Capitalist Realism*, p. 2.

[115] Fisher, *Capitalist Realism*, p. 2.

[116] Fisher, *Capitalist Realism*, p. 3.

[117] Fisher, *Capitalist Realism*, p. 3.

[118] Fisher, *Capitalist Realism*, p. 7.

[119] Fisher, *Capitalist Realism*, pp. 7-8.

[120] Mark Fisher, '"You have always been the caretaker": the spectral spaces of the overlook hotel' (2007) in *K-Punk*, p. 172.

[121] See 'Capitalist Realism: Mark Fisher interviewed by Joe Kennedy', *3:AM Magazine*, 28 July 2010 at https://www.3ammagazine.com/3am/capitalist-realism/

[122] Fisher, *Capitalist Realism*, p. 16.

[123] Fisher, *Capitalist Realism*, p. 65.

[124] Fisher, *Capitalist Realism*, pp. 80-1.

[125] Berardi writes: 'Born with punk, the slow cancellation of the future got underway in the 1970s and 1980s'. See Franco Berardi, *After the Future*, Edinburgh: AK Press, 2011, p. 18.

[126] Fisher, 'The Slow Cancellation of the Future' in *Ghosts of My Life*, p. 8.

[127] Fisher, 'The Slow Cancellation of the Future' in *Ghosts of My Life*, p. 10.

[128] Fisher, 'The Slow Cancellation of the Future' in *Ghosts of My Life*, p. 16.

[129] Fisher, 'The Slow Cancellation of the Future' in *Ghosts of My Life*, pp. 18-9.

[130] Fisher, 'The Slow Cancellation of the Future' in *Ghosts of My Life*, pp. 22-7.

[131] Fisher, 'The Slow Cancellation of the Future' in *Ghosts of My Life*, p. 22.

[132] Fisher writes: 'By now, it should already be very clear that there are different senses of the word hauntology at play in *Ghosts of My Life*. There is the specific sense in which it has

been applied to music culture, and a more general sense, where it refers to persistences, repetitions, prefigurations. There are also more or less benign versions of hauntology.' See Fisher, 'The Slow Cancellation of the Future', p. 28.

133 In an interview with John Pilgrim, Sinclair explains his characterisation of Thatcher in the following terms: 'She was a kind of fictional construct accidentally dragged out of suburbia with, luckily, a very wealthy sharp husband who could put up the money for this, and there she is and then all the worst things that are in British society kind of focus on her. I don't think it's that she's a sort of a Hitlerian demagogue with a vision that manages to persuade the country, it's more that she swallows it and then plays it back and I used it as a mask, of sort of being a witch, not in a benevolent way'. See 'A Magic out of London: Iain Sinclair at the British Museum' in *Otherworldly: Folk Horror Revival at the British Museum*, ed. by Andy Paciorek, Durham: Wyrd Harvest Press, 2017, p. 139.

134 For a rare example of an engagement with hauntology from the political right, see Christopher Pankhurst, 'Albion's Hidden Numina: *Folk Horror Revival*', 21 December 2015, at https://www.counter-currents.com/2015/12/folk-horror-revival/

135 Herbert Marcuse, *Eros and Civilisation: A Philosophical Enquiry into Freud*, London: Routledge, 1987, p. 93, quoted by Mark Fisher in 'Acid Communism (unfinished introduction)', *K-Punk*, 753-770, p. 753.

136 Fisher, 'Acid Communism (unfinished introduction)', p. 754.

137 Fisher, 'Acid Communism (unfinished introduction)', p. 755.

138 Fisher, 'Acid Communism (unfinished introduction)', p. 757.

139 Fisher, 'Acid Communism (unfinished introduction)', pp.

757-8.

[140] Fisher, 'Acid Communism (unfinished introduction)', p. 770.

[141] Tom Whyman, 'The Ghosts of Our Lives', *New Statesman*, 31 July 2019.

[142] Whyman writes: 'To understand why our politics have become so bad, we must confront the spectres of what caused things to turn out this way. To devise an approach to the present, we must find our way back to the possibilities inherent in the world at the lost moment, when it looked like there might be a chance for things to turn out for the better. That is both the relevance and the promise of hauntology.'

[143] Mark Fisher, 'No Longer the Pleasures: Joy Division' (2005) in *Ghosts of My Life*, p. 50.

[144] Mark Fisher, 'The Past is an Alien Planet: The First and Last Episodes of *Life on Mars*' (2006) in *Ghosts of My Life*, p. 76.

[145] Andy Paciorek, 'Folk Horror: From the Forests, Fields and Furrows: An Introduction', in *Folk Horror Revival: Field Studies* (Second Edition), ed. by Andy Paciorek, Durham: Wyrd Harvest, 2018, p. 12.

[146] Andy Paciorek & Darren Charles, 'Welcome Fools: An Introduction to Folk Horror' in *Otherworldly: Folk Horror Revival at the British Museum*, p. 21.

[147] Adam Scovell, *Folk Horror: Hours Dreadful and Things Strange*, Leighton Buzzard: Auteur, 2017, p. 10.

[148] See Andy Paciorek & Darren Charles, 'Welcome Fools: An Introduction to Folk Horror' in *Otherworldly: Folk Horror Revival at the British Museum*, pp. 23-28.

[149] For a helpful overview of the principal examples of folk horror in film and television, see Adam Scovell, 'Where to Begin with Folk Horror', *BFI*, 26 July 2018 at https://www.bfi.

org.uk/news-opinion/news-bfi/features/where-begin-folk-horror

150 Scovell, *Folk Horror*, pp. 5-6.

151 Scovell, *Folk Horror*, pp. 14-15.

152 Scovell, *Folk Horror*, pp. 15-18.

153 Scovell, *Folk Horror*, pp. 124 & 162.

154 Scovell, *Folk Horror*, p. 174.

155 See Aaron Jolly, 'Kill Lists: The Occult, paganism and sacrifice in cinema as an analogy for political upheaval in the 1970s and the 2010s' in *Folk Horror Revival: Field Studies* (Second Edition), pp. 291-304.

156 See Richard Littler's *Scarfolk Council* blog at https://scarfolk.blogspot.com/ as well as his *Discovering Scarfolk*, London: Ebury Press, 2014 and *The Scarfolk Annual*, London: Collins, 2019.

157 See Chris Lambert, 'The Black Meadow at The British Museum' in *Otherworldly: Folk Horror Revival at the British Museum*, pp. 10-17, and his blog, *Tales from The Black Meadow* at: http://blackmeadowtales.blogspot.com/

158 Ben Myers, 'Folk Horror, a history: from The Wicker Man to the League of Gentlemen', *New Statesman*, 26 July 2017.

159 Myers, 'Folk Horror, a history: from The Wicker Man to the League of Gentlemen'.

160 Myers, 'Folk Horror, a history: from The Wicker Man to the League of Gentlemen'.

161 Robert Macfarlane, 'The eeriness of the English countryside', *The Guardian*, 10 April 2015.

162 Macfarlane, 'The eeriness of the English countryside'.

163 Macfarlane, 'The eeriness of the English countryside'.

164 Andy Beckett, *When the Lights Went Out: What Really Happened*

to Britain in the Seventies, London: Faber, 2009, pp. 2-3.

[165] Not only was unemployment in the 1970s historically low by modern standards, but in 2004 the New Economics Foundation devised an index of economic, social, and environmental well-being called the Measure of Domestic Progress (MDP) which calculated that the best year in Britain since 1950 was 1976 (the year of the IMF crisis). See Beckett, p. 4.

[166] Beckett, pp. 520-1.

[167] Beckett, p. 521.

[168] Beckett, pp. 521-2.

Select Bibliography

Baker, Nicholson, 'Night Vision: The Forgotten Theory of Dreams that Inspired Vladimir Nabokov', *The New Republic*, 21 February 2018

Ball, Philip, *Invisible: The Dangerous Allure of the Unseen*, London: The Bodley Head, 2014

Ballard, JG, *A User's Guide to the Millennium: Essays and Reviews*, London: Harper Collins, 1996

– *The Drowned World*, London: Harper Perennial, 2006

– *The Complete Stories of J.G. Ballard*, New York: W.W. Norton, 2009

– *Extreme Metaphors: Selected Interviews with J.G. Ballard*, ed. by Simon Sellars and Dan O'Hara, London: Fourth Estate, 2012

Beckett, Andy, *When the Lights Went Out: What Really Happened to Britain in the Seventies*, London: Faber, 2010

Borges, Jorge Luis, 'Time and J.W. Dunne', trans. by Suzanne Jill Levine, in *The Total Library: Non-Fiction 1922-1986*, ed. by Eliot Weinberger, London: Penguin, 1999, 217-219

– *Fictions*, trans. by Andrew Hurley, London: Penguin, 2000

Boym, Svetlana, *The Future of Nostalgia*, New York: Basic Books, 2001

– 'Nostalgia and its Discontents', *The Hedgehog Review: Critical Reflections on Contemporary Culture*, Vol. 9 (2) 22

June 2007

Bridle, James, 'Hauntological Futures', *booktwo.org*, 20 March 2011 at https://booktwo.org/notebook/hauntological-futures/

Briggs, Julia, *Night Visitors: The Rise and Fall of the English Ghost Story*, London: Faber, 1977

Buse, Peter & Andrew Stott, eds. *Ghosts: Deconstruction, Psychoanalysis, History*, London: Macmillan, 1999

Butler, Charles, *Four British Fantasists: Place and Culture in the Children's Fantasies of Penelope Lively, Alan Garner, Diana Wynne Jones and Susan Cooper*, Lanham, MD: Scarecrow Press, 2006

Colquhoun, Matt, *Egress: On Mourning, Melancholy and Mark Fisher*, London: Repeater Books, 2020

Cooper, Susan, *J.B. Priestley: Portrait of an Author*, London: Heinemann, 1970

– *The Dark is Rising Sequence*, London: Puffin, 1984

Coverley, Merlin, *Psychogeography*, Harpenden: Oldcastle Books, 2018

Daniels, Stephen, 'Lines of Sight: Alfred Watkins, Photography and Topography in Early Twentieth-Century Britain' *Tate Papers*, Autumn 2006, at https://www.tate.org.uk/research/publications/tate-papers/06/lines-of-sight-alfred-watkins-photography-and-topography-in-early-twentieth-century-britain

Davies, Owen, *The Haunted: A Social History of Ghosts*, Basingstoke: Palgrave Macmillan, 2007

Del Pilar Blanco, Maria & Esther Peeren eds., *The Spectralities Reader: Ghosts and Haunting in Contemporary Cultural Theory*, London: Bloomsbury, 2013

Derrida, Jacques, *Specters of Marx: The State of the Debt, the Work of Mourning and the New International*, trans. by Peggy Kamuf, London: Routledge, 1994

– *Archive Fever: A Freudian Impression*, trans. by Eric Prenowitz, Chicago, IL: University of Chicago Press, 1996

Dickens, Charles, *The Christmas Books*, ed. by Ruth Glancy, Oxford: Oxford University Press, 1988

Dunne, JW, *An Experiment with Time*, ed. by Russell Targ, Charlottesville, VA: Hampton Roads, 2001

Eliade, Mircea, *The Sacred and the Profane: The Nature of Religion*, trans. by Willard R Trask, New York: Harcourt Brace, 1959

Fischer, Bob, 'The Haunted Generation', *Fortean Times*, (354) June 2017, 30-37

Fisher, Mark, *Capitalist Realism: Is There No Alternative?*, Winchester: Zero Books, 2009

– 'What is Hauntology?', Film Quarterly, Vol. 66, 1 (Fall 2012), 16-24

– *Ghosts of My Life: Writings on Depression, Hauntology and Lost Futures*, Winchester: Zero Books, 2014

– *The Weird and the Eerie*, London: Repeater Books, 2016

– *K-Punk: The Collected and Unpublished Writings of Mark Fisher (2004-2016)*, ed. by Darren Ambrose, London: Repeater Books, 2018

Fisher, Mark & Justin Barton, *On Vanishing Land*, audio-essay, produced and curated by The Otolith Collective and The Showroom, 2013

Fletcher, John, 'Marx the Uncanny? Ghosts and their Relation to the Mode of Production', *Radical Philosophy*, 75 January/February 1996, 31-37

Ford, Laura Grace [formerly Laura Oldfield Ford], *Savage Messiah*, London: Verso, 2019

Freud, Sigmund, *The Uncanny*, trans. by David McLintock, ed. by Hugh Haughton, London: Penguin, 2003

Fukuyama, Francis, 'The End of History?', *The National Interest*, 16 (Summer 1989), 3-18

Gallix, Andrew, 'Hauntology: A not-so-new critical manifestation. The new vogue in literary theory is shot through with earlier ideas.' *The Guardian*, 17 June 2011

Garner, Alan, *The Voice That Thunders: Essays and Lectures*, London: Harvill, 1997

– *The Owl Service*, London: Collins, 1998

– *Red Shift*, New York: NYRB Classics, 2011

Gibson, William, 'The Gernsback Continuum' in *Burning Chrome*, London: Gollancz, 2017, 28-40

Hammond, Simon, 'K-Punk at Large', *New Left Review*, 118, July-August 2019, 37-66

Hill, Sharon A, 'The "Stone Tape Theory" of Hauntings: A Geological Perspective', 11 May 2017 at https://sharonahill.com/2017/05/11/the-stone-tape-theory-of-hauntings-a-geological-perspective/

James, MR, *Ghost Stories of M.R. James*, ed. by Nigel Kneale, London: Folio Society, 1973

– *Collected Ghost Stories*, ed. by Darryl Jones, Oxford: Oxford University Press, 2011

Jameson, Fredric, *Postmodernism: or, the Cultural Logic of Late Capitalism*, London: Verso, 1992

Joshi, ST, *The Weird Tale*, Austin, TX: University of Texas Press, 1990

Kneale, Nigel, *Tomato Cain and Other Stories*, London: Collins, 1949

– *The Year of the Sex Olympics and other TV Plays*, London: Ferret Fantasy, 1976

Lee, Vernon, *Supernatural Tales*, ed. by I. Cooper Willis, London: Peter Owen, 2004

– *Hauntings and Other Fantastic Tales*, ed. by Catherine Maxwell and Patricia Pulham, Ontario: Broadview Editions, 2006

Lethbridge, TC, *Ghost and Ghoul*, London: Routledge, 1961

– *The Essential T.C. Lethbridge*, ed. by Tom Graves and Janet Hoult, London: Routledge & Kegan Paul, 1980

Littler, Richard, *Discovering Scarfolk*, London: Ebury Press, 2014

Lovecraft, HP, 'Supernatural Horror in Literature' in *At the Mountains of Madness*, ed. by China Miéville, New York: The Modern Library, 2005, 105-173

Luckhurst, Roger, ed., *Late Victorian Gothic Tales*, Oxford: OUP, 2005

Macfarlane, Robert, 'The eeriness of the English countryside', *The Guardian*, 10 April 2015

Machen, Arthur, *The White People and Other Weird Tales*, ed. by ST Joshi, London: Penguin, 2011

– *The Great God Pan and Other Horror Stories*, ed. by Aaron Worth, Oxford: OUP, 2018

Machin, James, ed., *Faunus: The Decorative Imagination of Arthur Machen*, London: Strange Attractor, 2019

Marx, Karl & Friedrich Engels, *The Communist Manifesto*, ed. by AJP Taylor, Harmondsworth: Penguin, 1967

Masschelein, Anneleen, *The Unconcept: The Freudian Uncanny in Late-Twentieth-Century Theory*, Albany, NY: State University of New York Press, 2011

Miéville, China, 'M.R. James and the Quantum Vampire. Weird; Hauntological: Versus and/or and and/or or?' *Weird Fiction Review*, 29 November 2011 at http://weirdfictionreview.com/2011/11/m-r-james-and-the-quantum-vampire-by-china-mieville/

Michell, John, *The New View Over Atlantis*, London: Thames and Hudson, 1983

Paciorek, Andy, ed., *Otherworldly: Folk Horror Revival at the British Museum*, Durham: Wyrd Harvest Press, 2017

– *Folk Horror Revival: Field Studies (Second Edition)*, Durham: Wyrd Harvest Press, 2018

Parnell, Edward, *Ghostland: In Search of a Haunted Country*, London: Collins, 2019

Philip, Neil, *A Fine Anger: A Critical Introduction to the Work of Alan Garner*, London: Collins, 1981

Pilkington, Mark, 'Hauntologists mine the past for music's future', *boingboing*, 12 October 2012 at https://boingboing.net/2012/10/12/hauntologists-mine-the-past-fo.html

Priestley, JB, *Man and Time*, London: Aldus Books, 1964

Prince, Stephen, *A Year in the Country: Wandering through Spectral Fields, Journeys in Otherly Pastoralism, the Further Reaches of Folk and the Parallel Worlds of Hauntology*, A Year in the Country, 2018

Reynolds, Simon, *Retromania: Pop Culture's Addiction to its Own Past*, London: Faber, 2012

Royle, Nicholas, *The Uncanny*, Manchester University Press, 2003

Scovell, Adam, *Folk Horror: Hours Dreadful and Things Strange*, Leighton Buzzard: Auteur, 2017

Sebald, WG, *The Rings of Saturn*, trans. by Michael Hulse, London: Harvill, 1998

– *Austerlitz*, trans. by Anthea Bell, London: 2001

Shaw, Katy, *Hauntology: The Presence of the Past in Twenty-First Century English Literature*, London: Palgrave Macmillan, 2018

Sim, Stuart, *Derrida and the End of History*, Cambridge: Icon Books, 1999

Smith, Andrew, *The Ghost Story, 1840-1920: A Cultural History*, Manchester University Press, 2010

Snowden, Neil, ed., *We are the Martians: The Legacy of Nigel Kneale*, Hornsea: PS Publishing, 2017

Sprinker, Michael, ed., *Ghostly Demarcations: A Symposium on Jacques Derrida's Specters of Marx*, London: Verso, 2008

Spufford, Francis, *I Have Been Here Before*, BBC Radio 3, prod. Mark Burman, 14 September 2014, at https://www.bbc.co.uk/programmes/b04h7lr0

Steinmeyer, Jim, *Hiding the Elephant: How Magicians Invented the Impossible*, London: Arrow Books, 2005

Trigg, Dylan, 'The Ghosts of Place', *The White Review*, August 2013, at http://www.thewhitereview.org/feature/the-ghosts-of-place/

Turner, Jenny, 'Not No Longer but Not Yet', *London Review of Books*, Vol. 41, (9), 9 May 2019, 3-8

Watkins, Alfred, *The Ley Hunter's Manual: A Guide to Early Tracks*, London: Thorsons, 1983

– *The Old Straight Track*, ed. by Robert Macfarlane, London: Head of Zeus, 2014

Welbourn, Terry, *T.C Lethbridge: The Man Who Saw the Future*, Alresford: O-Books, 2011

Whyman, Tom, 'The Ghosts of our Lives', *New Statesman*, 31 July 2019

Wilson, Colin, *Mysteries: An Investigation into the Occult, the Paranormal and the Supernatural*, London: Watkins, 2006

Young, Rob, *Electric Eden: Unearthing Britain's Visionary Music*, London: Faber, 2011

Film & Television

Night of the Demon (1957) dir. Jacques Tourneur
Quatermass II (1957) dir. Val Guest
Quatermass and the Pit (1967) dir. Roy Ward Baker
Whistle and I'll Come to You (1968) dir. Jonathan Miller
Witchfinder General (1968) dir. Michael Reeves
The Owl Service (1969) dir. Peter Plummer
Robin Redbreast (1970) dir. James MacTaggart
A Journey to Avebury (1971) dir. Derek Jarman
The Blood on Satan's Claw (1971) dir. Piers Haggard
The Stalls of Barchester (1971) dir. Lawrence Gordon Clark
Dead of Night (1972) prod. Innes Lloyd
The Stone Tape (1972) dir. Peter Sasdy
A Warning to the Curious (1972) dir. Lawrence Gordon Clark
Lonely Water (Public Information Film; 1973) dir. Jeff Grant
Lost Hearts (1973) dir. Lawrence Gordon Clark
Psychomania (1973) dir. Don Sharp
The Wicker Man (1973) dir. Robin Hardy
Penda's Fen (1974) dir. Alan Clarke
The Treasure of Abbot Thomas (1974) dir. Lawrence Gordon Clark
The Ash Tree (1975) dir. Lawrence Gordon Clark
The Changes (1975) dir. John Prowse
Murrain (1975) dir. John Cooper
Beasts (1976) prod. Nicholas Palmer
The Signalman (1976) dir. Lawrence Gordon Clark

Apaches (Public Information Film; 1977) dir. John Mackenzie
Children of the Stones (1977) dir. Peter Graham Scott
Stigma (1977) dir. Lawrence Gordon Clark
Red Shift (1978) dir. John Mackenzie
Casting the Runes (1979) dir. Lawrence Gordon Clark
Quatermass (1979) dir. Piers Haggard
Sapphire & Steel (1979-82) prod. Shaun O'Riordan
Ghost Dance (1983) dir. Ken McMullen
A View from a Hill (2005) dir. Luke Watson
A History of Horror (2010) dir. Rachel Jardine
Kill List (2011) dir. Ben Wheatley
Patience (After Sebald) (2012) dir. Grant Gee
Sightseers (2012) dir. Ben Wheatley
A Field in England (2013) dir. Ben Wheatley
The Tractate Middoth (2013) dir. Mark Gatiss
The Witch (2015) dir. Robert Eggers
Midsommar (2019) dir. Ari Aster

Websites

A Year in the Country (Stephen Prince)
https://ayearinthecountry.co.uk/
Ballardian (Simon Sellars)
http://www.ballardian.com/
Celluloid Wicker Man (Adam Scovell)
https://celluloidwickerman.com/
Dirty Work (Rob Mowbray)
http://rob-dirtywork.blogspot.com/
Folk Horror Revival (Andy Paciorek)
https://folkhorrorrevival.com/
Ghost Box
https://ghostbox.co.uk/
K-Punk (Mark Fisher)
http://k-punk.abstractdynamics.org/
Laura Grace Ford
lauragraceford.blogspot.com/
Retromania (Simon Reynolds)
http://retromaniabysimonreynolds.blogspot.com/
Reynolds Retro (Simon Reynolds)
http://reynoldsretro.blogspot.com/
Rouge's Foam (Adam Harper)
http://rougesfoam.blogspot.com/
Scarfolk Council (Richard Littler)
https://scarfolk.blogspot.com/

WEBSITES

Tales from the Black Meadow (Chris Lambert)
http://blackmeadowtales.blogspot.com/
The Haunted Generation (Bob Fischer)
https://hauntedgeneration.co.uk/
The Hauntological Society
https://thehauntologicalsociety.tumblr.com/

Index